Preserving Disorder

Preserving Disorder

SELECTED ESSAYS 1968–88

David Widgery

PLUTO PRESS
London Winchester, Mass

First published 1989 by Pluto Press
345 Archway Road, London N6 5AA
and 8 Winchester Place
Winchester MA 01890, USA

Typesetting: Ponting–Green Publishing Services, London

British Library Cataloguing in Publication Data

Widgery, David
Preserving Disorder – (Essays on society and culture)
1. British culture
I. Title II. Series
941.085'8

ISBN 0–7453–0347–1
ISBN 0–7453–0348–X pb

Printed and bound in the United Kingdom by
Billing & Sons Limited, Worcester

To Peter ... and all Sedgwickians

Contents

Part II Vicissitudes

'Our job is not preventing disorder.
Our job is preserving disorder.'
Mayor Daley – Chicago 1968

Introduction
On Not Looking Back

A traveller who left London twenty years ago and returned unprepared wouldn't believe their eyes. A city where imagination was trying to find its way to power is now dominated by the mushy platitudes of advertising executives, estate agents and stuffed-shirt Tories. A society which had started to listen to the case for economic democracy is now deafened by the clatter of the global stockmarkets to stark poverty on its front-doorstep. Instead of the questioning wit and beauty of 1968, no one dares look beyond the capitalist horizon, freedom is redefined as the market and the most stylish accessory is a fat bank balance. What the Parisian workers sarcastically called *metro-boulo-dodo* (travel, work, sleep) has triumphed once again, except that the train has crashed and there are no jobs. The nearest I get nowadays to an acid trip is taking the children to the Foamy Pink car wash.

Looking back on the 1960s from the winter of Thatcher-without-end, it's easy to mock it as one long Dada poem ('Total Revolt! General Strike!! Personal=Political') or narrow it down to student high jinks. But what people thereby forget is that the revolts which started in the universities of North America and Europe rapidly spread across national and class boundaries. If the movement had stayed cribbed and confined to the university campus, it would have mattered little. But it spread through the whole education system and trickled back to the soil of the workers' organisations. Indeed, the students' tactics had often been borrowed from an older, insurgent phase of the workers' movement, the 'sit-in' pioneered by American car workers in the great 1930s' unionisation drives, and 'direct action' techniques used extensively by British soldiers and sailors at the end of the First World War and by the suffrage movement. Just as the UK art-school rhythm-and-blues bands reawoke a North American audience to the black originals, so the students of 1968 began to bring back to the workers' movement its own insurgent traditions. For the most important fact about the student movement in Britain was that it fed into a rising arc of working-class militancy. Indeed, all three unruly spectres which had brought down the old Liberal Party – syndicalism, feminism and republicanism – were once again on the loose. Not only did the miners' strike of 1972 and 1974 finally bring down the Heath government, but the London dockers sprang the Pentonville Five from prison, building workers held their first ever national all-out stoppage, and hospital workers, only nominally organised, took uninhibited action, not just to improve their abysmal wages but to challenge the consultants' use of NHS premises for private practice.

The step from student radicalism or cultural activism into the world of trade union politics was both logical and possible; significant revolutionary socialist organisation was on the cards for the first time for fifty years. In making that transition we were bound to collide with the existing Marxist movements of the time, in my case the International Socialists, a fertile mix of worker-intellectuals from the labour movement and intellectual-intellectuals from the post-Trotskyist Left, who promptly sent me out with a megaphone to organise rent strikes on North London council estates. The ideas which propelled us towards such groups were ill-digested.

There was a general re-discovery of the Russian Revolution and of the various oppositional tendencies in the Soviet 1920s and a tendency to chuck lumps of Trotsky and the young Marx in with some Reich, Bevan and anglicised Situationism and call it 'revolutionary Marxism'. James's highly Hegelianised Marx, Cliff's somewhat anarchistic Lenin and Chris Pallis's popularisation of Cardin were all influential, and Isaac Deutscher, whose biography of Trotsky was so important, spoke memorably at the LSE Old Theatre, a living link with the Polish Left Opposition. Orthodox Trotskyists had orthodox answers and simply quarrelled about labels, anarchists didn't need much in the way of theory, feminism was conceived but unborn, and Third Worldism epidemic. We in the International Socialists imagined ourselves rather sophisticated with our repertoire of Serge, Luxemburg and Lukacs, but others privy to a higher truth simply held up their paperbacks of R.D. Laing's *Politics of Experience* and *Bird of Paradise* across the LSE refectory in the all-conquering fashion of the Red Guards raising aloft the *Thoughts of Mao*. At its best it seemed like a gathering of post-electronic Renaissance people, passionately serious but intoxicated by LSD as well as alcohol and exponents of social theory instead of sword fighting. At its worst it managed to be simultaneously vacuous and interminable. And the youthquake aspect, as some of the essays that follow pointed out at the time, was almost always implausible and dishonest.

Although a product of the student movement, my own political attitudes were further complicated by my involvement in the underground press. And still further confused by a somewhat romantic over-identification with the early days of Women's and Gay Liberation. So I spent a lot of time reconciling my loyalties to inherently unpredictable things like R and B and sexual freedom with an equally passionate membership of a small Marxist grouping in the process of transforming itself from an ideological forum to a force in the workers' movement.

In truth I was never a terribly orthodox International Socialist. I had after all joined the group on the basis that it was the only socialist organisation in Britain to publish a decent obituary of André Breton. And my true hero in the group was neither Tony Cliff with his hurdy gurdy oratory and organisational prowess, nor Nigel Harris with his lucid expositions of international economics, but Peter Sedgwick. Peter is best known as a historian of Bolshevism and the anti-Stalinist Left, although his most important work, *Psychopolitics*, deals with theories of mental illness. But he seemed, like a political time traveller, to have been present at all the great crises and collisions of the twentieth century, now back to advise us. Almost uniquely among the many Marxist intellectuals of the 1956 vintage, he didn't just write about the Left but made it, shaped it and served it as an active member of, first, the 'Socialist Review' group, then the International Socialists, and until the mid-1970s the SWP. He did the donkey work of socialist tendency: meetings, lobbies, internal documents and early morning paper sales through considerable ill-health with unfailing good humour, alongside fellow socialists in the West Riding (his beloved Yorklings) until his tragic and still unexplained death in 1983.

Sedgwick's politics were of Bolshevism at its most libertarian and Marxism at its most warmhearted and witty. He also dressed like a Basque beatnik, wrote footnotes on his own footnotes, collected tins of mulligatawny and was founding editor of *Red Wank: Journal of Rank and File Masturbation*, whose second (and unpublished) issue was to feature 'Great autoerotic revolutionary acts' and 'Coming out as a worker: problems in a TU Branch'. Once, when dubbed 'a Cliffite lapdog' during an intra-Trotskyist debate on Soviet industrial policy in Minneapolis, he snuffled round the platform on all fours and mimed pissing on his opponents' socks before returning to the podium to continue his elegant analysis of the New Economic Policy. To me, Peter had a lot more to do with the autodidactic subversion of 1960s Marxism than Mao, Che Guevara or even our great leader Tariq Ali.

It was certainly being, and remaining, a member of an organised Marxist grouping, as well as my professional work as a doctor, which put me, and kept me, in direct contact with the realities of working-class life. And that probably saved me from all sorts of subsequent silliness and sell-outs. Without 1968 and the SWP I would, no doubt, in the conventional manner of the educationally upwardly mobile, be ensconced in the Department of Community Medicine of a cathedral town with my children down for public school and a sub to the SDP. Instead I got involved in the socialist Left, in medical trade unionism and am still plugging away as a GP in the council flats of East London. And despite the manifest lack of success in the larger tasks we have set ourselves, I persist in regarding the commitment I acquired in 1968 as the most fruitful and rewarding of my adult life. It is one from which I have probably gained more than I have been able to give. It directed the anarchistic impulses and angry prose which are the proper response of 20-year-olds to established authority into more disciplined work in a socialist collective where I have met some of the most educated and delightful people I am likely to encounter. And it has altered 1960s precocity into something more comprehending: a modern Marxism whose grid has latitudes for New Variety and the blues as well as Lenin and Sylvia Pankhurst, but whose equator still remains working-class consciousness and how it can be transformed by socialists into a material force. I'm glad I heard Hendrix live but gladder to have marched with the dockers to the gates of Pentonville Prison. It was wonderful to see the Vietcong flag raised on the Berkeley campus and to attend the first Women's Liberation Conference at Oxford, but it felt even better when the staff and workers at Bethnal Green Hospital voted to occupy against its threatened closure. Above all, it has taught me that the cardinal revolutionary virtue is patience. And that to remain political at all requires involvement in a collective milieu which has broken from bourgeois ideas and which, although consistent in principles, is prepared to be flexible and adventurous in practice.

The second half of this collection reflects on the vicissitudes of a new era, in which I am probably less despondent than someone interested purely in parliamentary party politics. But I have never felt any attraction for the Labour Party, that rectangle of ineffectuality whose 'activity', apart from elections that is, seems to consist mainly of arguing with itself. Nor am I, immunised by a long membership of the SWP, prone to the depression which seems near-terminal among so many socialist intellectuals now becalmed in sophisticated nihilism. Certainly things have got worse, much worse than we imagined possible. The change, in fact, was already apparent in the mid-1970s when Labour was still in office, when life suddenly got less innocent and the good danger of the 1960s was slowly replaced by real fear. By the end of the 1970s unemployment had begun to bear down on those in work, the police were more assertive, the recession narrowed horizons and a new sense of selfishness was abroad. The political individuals to whom we now ascribe the changes are accidents – it was fortuitous that Thatcher overtook Whitelaw or Healey was defeated by Foot. But a new direction had been set in which the political weaknesses of the Labour Party and orthodox trade unionism, both in terms of personnel and ideas, were to become appallingly obvious. It was also apparent that an orgasm a day, as the enthusiasts of sexual politics had hoped, had not kept false consciousness away. And that drugs, if they had been emancipatory, were now very much part of the problem.

Although our politics had never been put into practice, we were blamed for the unsuccessful half-measures of the mid-1970s Labour interregnum with the bloated state bureaucracies, low production and stationary wages. The revolutionary Left, the home of the pedagogue, was accused of wanting to lower educational standards and censor books; we, ultra-democrats, were said to oppose the trade union elections for which we had long campaigned, and socialist critics of totalitarianism in East Europe were said to be making excuses for Stalinism. Instead of republican excellence, we got hung for welfare capitalist mediocrity and unceremoniously bundled out of Callaghan's frying pan into Thatcher's fire, no one much interested in our singed claims that we had wanted neither.

The rest is recent history and none too pleasant. Labourism's failure delivered us to the mercies, and they are few, of Mrs T. Once ushered into office by Callaghan's avuncular incompetence, she has consolidated confidence and power in a series of battles which she organised and understood better than her opponents. There is no need to invent a special theory for her predominance; she has simply, as the punks used to advise, dispensed with the bullshit. The rich have been enriched and the officers of the state rewarded for services rendered with an appalling candour. In the name of freeing the individual from the unwelcome state, she has cut welfare services, schools and hospital beds and tremendously strengthened the police, the armed forces and the secret and civil services. She has annointed with financial favour her 'angels in marble', the Tory-voting working class. Her re-election is made possible by the calculated split from Labour made by the SDP. Yet challenged by Labour, she unerringly repeats that her policy is the logical continuation of the approach of the last Labour government. She relies continuously, whether in the Nottingham coalfields or in the HGVs that ploughed through the Wapping picket lines, on workers divided against fellow workers. And that, in part, is the Left's own responsibility. Politics abhors a vacuum, and when socialist ideas and enthusiasm lose direction, people look elsewhere, to the sale of their council house, the chance of a privatised share issue or page 3 of the *Sun*, for inspiration.

But because I was stamped in the unruly days of 1968 with a socialism-from-below which regards with scepticism political evaluations based solely on opinion polls, membership rolls or even unemployment tallies, I do not feel as defeated as perhaps I should. Dear friends have perished: from suicide, AIDS and drugs, the ailments of the age, but no great war or decisive repression. Whereas, in Prague I'd be a janitor and in Durban, dead. Capitalism, although a more ingenious and inventive system than we allowed when tearing its blinds down in 1968, still fails to provide useful work for all, far less the ability to distribute the fruits of its production equitably within or between nations. It neither plans prudently nor produces usefully. And as my professional work constantly brings home to me, people continue to eke out a living in social conditions which are a disgrace because they are entirely preventable. Although claiming to stand for order, this system can only survive by violent, unplanned change. Marx wrote in the reactionary 1850s:

> The so-called revolutions of 1848 were but poor incidents, small fractures and fissures in the dry crust of European society. But they denounced the abyss. Beneath the apparently solid surface, they betrayed oceans of liquid matter, only needing expansion to rend into fragments continents of hard rock.

Now we live over a thermonuclear volcano.

In fact we did succeed. We succeeded in changing attitudes profoundly but did not have the strength to change the economic and therefore political power structure fundamentally. 'And those who make revolutions by half,' St Juste warns us, 'dig their own graves.' Or, in the case of reformists, dig other people's. Britain certainly was more monochrome and stilted before the Beatles, satire, the underground press and the May Events, a strange world of fretwork radios, college scarves, white bread and deference which the Left has done a good deal to alter. The irony is, however, glaringly obvious: at the same time as attitudes have broadened and expectations dilated, material circumstances have narrowed, education is far worse and much less egalitarian, jobs fewer and social advance is made at one's fellow's expense. Social crisis stares us full in the face. We have paid a terrible price for our disorganisation and failure of nerve in the face of an enemy which learns faster than we do from its defeats. Mrs Thatcher is teaching us a hideously expensive lesson but one from which we have to learn and from which we will emerge.

In the meantime we need forcibly to remind ourselves of a historical and an international perspective. In fact, in the two decades since 1968, now said to demonstrate the triumph of reaction and the irrelevance of Marx's political ideas, that allegedly extinct beast, the working class, has on at least five occasions taken mass action of revolutionary proportions.

In May 1968, Gaullism was rocked by the longest and most inventive general strike in European history. In Chile in October 1972 the first attempts by the Right to overthrow the Popular Unity government were met by an insurrectionary eruption based on the urban industrial belts, or *cordones*. In Portugal the 1974 revolt, instigated by junior army officers, led not just to the overthrow of Caetano but an experiment in 'popular power' which lasted eighteen months.

The regime of Shah Pahlavi with its lavish armed forces and ubiquitous secret service was toppled. In Poland, Solidarity developed from a protest by a handful of rank-and-file workers about victimisation in a single shipyard to a membership of 8 million and the potential to up-end the entire bureaucracy of East Europe. Once released from the mind-forged manacles of conventional parties and reformist trade unionism, these movements surged forward fast and furious.

Each case was characterised by the growth of workplace committees of occupation as centres of social power. For when those organisations combined, as in the Interimpresas in Lisbon, the *cordones* in Santiago's industrial zones or the Inter-Enterprise Strike Committee in the Baltic ports, they became capable of taking on the administration of civil society. And did so in Nantes, under workers' control in 1968, and Gdansk, occupied in August 1980.

This political form, called 'soviets' in Bolshevik Russia in 1905 and 1917, is exactly the 'true secret' Marx recognised in the Commune: the social basis of a new society. It would be fatuous simply to celebrate these moments. What Marx called 'the old crap' revives only too fast, especially in religious guises (crucial in Iran and Poland) and in the form of traditional reforms (instantly packaged as in Portugal). And those who designate themselves as revolutionaries were too often both grandiose and ineffectual. But it is in these social movements, their equivalent in Britain and political organisation geared to their potential which have the answer to Thatcher and her ilk. And a way forward to a new century.

Hackney, February 1989

PART I DAYS OF HOPE

1

Against Grown-Up Power*

I wrote this piece of period teenage Sturm und Drang in a morning of abject frustration in a hot London August. It's uncanny how acid, paisley shirts and day-glo headbands are once again putting the wind up the bourgeoisie twenty years later.

So this week it's the Hippies you've found out about. *Melody Maker*, the *Archiv für Sozialwissenschaft* of the flower-people, describes them as 'the young people of America's West Coast and London's Tottenham Court Road, complete with flowers, bells and incense'. If you go to Goodge Street Station, be sure to wear a flower in your hair. All you need is love, but a private income and the sort of parents who would have a Chinese smoking jacket in the attic help. Packaged cereals have gone psychedelic, there's pot in the psychology seminars and LSD at the better office parties. As soon as the young patent an experience, the Alfs, the grey people, the straight world are buying it in the big stores. Each generation has its own style and truth. But what's amazing when you are 20 today is the ruthless enthusiasm of the grown-ups. Whenever two or three flower-people are gathered together, there in the midst of them is a BBC 2 camera team, three *Observer* columnists and Bernard Levin being miserable about it all. While our own excesses are acted out in an elaborate self-aware mime, grown-up society falls for it all, beads, bells and bananas.

From the receiving end of this exercise in identification, it might be worth pointing out two of our elders' more falsetto voices. The first is the Establishment's enthusiasm for youthful energy as long as it is 'responsible', 'reasonable' and 'constructive', which in practice means uncritical acceptance of all received explanations and institutions, defined and thus controlled by them. The second is that of the anti-Establishment, that great pantomime of *Observer*-people, menopausal teenyboppers, Regent's Park psychedelics and novelists walking to

*First published in *New Statesman*, 1967.

and fro, talking of Pirate Radio, whose highest ambition seems to be the complete and perfect reproduction of youth styles and values.

At least the position of the Establishment is consistent. Missing the point, emasculating the dangerous tendencies of dissenting minorities and absorbing what's left, has been the central strategy of our rulers. In America, the spiritual Ronald Reagans and Chief Parkers have a more straightforward answer to their hippies, students, hell's angels, dope-fiends, ballet dancers and black revolutionaries: arrest, arrest. Here we are more sophisticated: minority dissent is ignored, insurgent dissent suppressed and social dissent de-fused more effectively with the gossip column than the billy-club. If dissent looks likely to cluster round the Stones' trial or the political incompetence that young people have been competently manipulated into, there is one of Her Majesty's Judges or the Latey Report to let off steam without changing the boiler. The changes are, however, in nomenclature and tone of voice. The Latey Report may look like a bombshell in Whitehall, but as a blueprint for our liberation, Miss Whitehorn's previous contribution, *Cooking in a Bedsit*, is a good deal more relevant. Between one pull of the forelock and the next, we are supposed to draw brief inspiration from Mr Levin's and Mr Rees-Mogg's concern for our well-being. But despite the liberal rhetoric from Whitehall and Printing House Square, the power stays very much where it is. There may be a transistor in every skull and free-range drugs on every other corner, but the power to define and change our lives stays emphatically in the hands of the boss and the schoolmaster, the executive and the don.

In the schools, the ruling institutions described by Brian Jackson and Robin Marsden remain dominant. The sad procession of speech-day, assembly, houses, prefects and external exams inflict their scars on the most tuned-in teenager. The grammar schools manage the rituals with all the more enthusiasm. My school even invented a Latin song about the school's airy position above the railway sidings, which we sang like so many housewives being introduced to Royalty. While the liberal universities invite the student hierarchy to participate in their own oppression, the notion of pupils participating, like anything else left of the Rotary Club, is unthinkable in school. In the universities, despite the odd outburst and TV militant, students are left in their common rooms, like so many heated goldfish, to talk about *The Hobbit*, milk bottles, North Sea Gas and anything else that's not 'intellectual'. The student's say over his personal freedom and union autonomy is intermittent; their voice in syllabus, planning and government of their university is unheard. If it does exist, it is donated from above and, like Richard Marsh's velvet glove to the steelworkers, is an offer to collaborate not participate.

In the shops, department stores, offices, factory apprenticeships and trainee schemes, the young people unable to learn their way out of the necessity to earn a living are exploited in the precise technical sense of the word. Tell an Islington shop assistant about the Love Generation and she will tell you about the last bus home. In Upper Street they have to make do with amphetamines and stolen scooters. In Barnsley or Leeds, it's a very pilled-up mod who wears a neck-scarf in a pub after 10. Try it with bells, beads and rhododendrons and you would start a holocaust that would make Detroit look like an argument with a waiter.

In fact the real breakdown has nothing to do with LSD or geraniums. It is that the grown-ups' language contains values which are no longer accepted or even relevant to young people. Just to take the public language of politics, though the gap is greater in social and cultural vocabulary, yours is the generation which calls concentration camps 'strategic hamlets' and supporting the oil sheiks 'a peacekeeping role'. 'Democratic breakthroughs' are things like letting workers at Fairfields actually talk to their boss or stopping students standing up when lecturers enter the room. These simple failures of meaning enlarge; you come to define democracy as the competition of élites for the periodically registered consent of voters. Politics becomes the business of managing a given industrial system to reward those it exploits at intervals which more or less coincide with elections. The bad joke at the Palace of Westminster represents the people, and together with the TUC, CBI and the bankers becomes something called 'The National Interest'. All questions are complex, all ideologies suspect, all larger passions fanatical. The peak of your vision is pulling in your belts to keep up your imperial pantaloons. Your passion is reserved for those parts of the politico-industrial machine most prone to breakdown: the unofficial striker, the demonstrating student, the advocate of black power, the drug-taker and the hippy – anyone who dares to rock the coracle of the state.

And when the Establishment takes a step backward the middle-aged trendies take three forward, nudging and titillating themselves with what they see from their car windows. Their approach is another attempt to embrace the mini-skirt revolution and be genuinely surprised if the same young people take a moral or political stand. It wants to make even revolution bland and photogenic; to take the flower generation without the nettle people, the Carmichaels and

Moses and Adelsteins and unspecified young people in Greece and Bolivia and Detroit and the Mekong Valley cut down by Grown-up Power.

What is frightening is not the trendies' flatulent prose and fake bonhomie. It's that your generation's radical culture has become quite flaccid. The cowlove determination to accept all that is young leads the grown-ups to admire pop products for precisely their banality, predictability and second-handness. Attached to society by their dog-lead, they caper about celebrating their own submission and defeat. Your Left-wingers are Judith Hart and Tony Greenwood, your satirists part of the paraphernalia of swinging London, as much artifacts of glossy society as their victims who long to be attacked in this painless gossipy way. You gave Lenny Bruce an overdose and David Frost a Golden Rose. Where are they now, the nuclear protesters and radicals, the iconoclasts and the rebels? In the Cabinet and the posh Sundays, every one. All a very precise tribute to society whose idea of moral outrage is to get its subscription up to date with Hampstead Majority Rule for Rhodesia Association.

So accept that flower-power looks like being the biggest gimmick since the hula-hoop. Accept that its chemical short-cuts and transplanted mysticism don't get much of a purchase on reality, and that if it did it would be distorted by your Agencies of Misinformation and Departments of Lies. But the Love Generation does aim at real community rather than boozy conviviality, a public total art rather than low culture, and gentleness and warmth rather than pre-heat love and a *Saturday Evening Post* family. Until they get there we can wait for *24 Hours* to choke on its rubber larynx, the *Observer* to become a Trappist broad sheet and start a feature called 'Design for Dying', and Malcolm Muggeridge, Bernard Levin and Jack Priestley to lock themselves in a cell with one typewriter.

2

When Harrods is Looted*

This was for the post-May events OZ, an Agit-OZ production with a cover of detachable sticky slogans in day-glo which in those days caused appalling production as well as political problems. I was trying to be serious and the effort rather shows: the mass conversion of a legion of hippies to my rather ill-understood notion of Bolshevism was, in retrospect, improbable. It was printed in violet on green, except for several passages reversed out into oblivion and accompanied by a complicated political diagram which indicated William Morris's affinity with Rosa Luxemburg and Mao's with Stalin. It was overprinted with a cartoon of Marcuse with a thought bubble containing a diagram of a brain – a hippy witticism.

1968 would be as good a year as any for the liberal intelligentsia to start taking politics seriously. Let's, for example, pretend that the Metropolitan Police are the Wehrmacht and the dockers are breaking the windows of all the Chinese restaurants in Gerrard Street. Or we could make believe in the National Conservative administration of 1971, the first shot striker and the Student Problem. Or perhaps the meat porters do find out that it's the bankers and not the blacks. Either way the elaborate parlour games of most of our political intellectuals could be broken up very fast by the realities of a world recession, concentrated economic and political power and eroded democratic institutions.

Fleet Street's chain of fools and their allies in the university have told us for years that the class struggle didn't exist or wasn't needed any more or that it was our business to be on the other side of the barricades anyway. When the students in Germany talked about overturning capitalism, they patronised them and put the rebels on the front of their glossies like cavemen-painted mastodons to show their mastery. When it happened in France, they talked of its 'style' and

* First published in *OZ*, 1968.

how we have a middle tier of oppression so it can't happen here. And when it does happen here and maybe it's no longer chic but brutal and muddy and the rubbish is burning and Harrods is looted, they will not still see it's about revolution and socialism and that for us all else is folly. The nice people will have to choose then between those who honked their horns around the Champs Elysées and shouted 'Cohn Bendit to Dachau' and accurately 'Liberate our factories' and the workers marching in the Place de la Bastille with the clothes they have stood besides machines in all their life. And if that's already too much like cliche, then you've already chosen your side. As for us, we should have chosen long ago. For until this struggle against capitalism and for popular power is finished, we remain in this log jam at the middle of the century – slung, as Arnold wrote, 'between one world dead and the other still powerless to be born'.

At least while the Labour Party is in opposition the myths of Fabianism might be maintained; for the intellectual that increased parliamentary representation of the Labour Party means the increase and then the achievement of popular power, for the worker that if there was a Labour Government as well as a Labour Council then rents would not still go up and houses would get built. But the vulnerability of the British economy to international capital movement and 'confidence' has revealed yet again the marked and unjustified optimism that social democrats have always had about economic and political power. The independent foreign policy, as beloved of CND as Douglas Home, is so many sweepings before the broom of American Power. The 'export-led boom' depends simply on for how long and how low working-class living standards can be forced, and the science of 1964 means the productivity of 1966 means the exploitation of 1968. Labour has simply been taking its pleasure too often on the bed of Capital, for us still to be crying rape. But the rewards of collaboration with capital have not been adequate to buy mass support with wages and domestic booms and Labour has been without mass support for four years now. But over the last two years even those party activists who remained have been finally sickened away from politics and gone back to *Gardeners' Question Time* and mild and bitter. Increasingly suitable undemocratic professionals of Transport House are wielding the dead weight of a party defined by the absence of militants or real strength from the class socialism is all about. In fact the students' emphasis on opposition outside Parliament is a precise expression of the options open to serious socialists in the face of the shift to the right which social democracy and European communism has made over the last twenty years. Coalition social democracy has abandoned even its verbal claims to equality and social reform, the rhetoric of Wilson, Brandt, Mollet and Nenni (and for that matter Sik and Lieberman) is now thoroughly state plannist, elitist, technical and manipulative.

The Communist parties have in turn occupied the reformist parliamentary programmes which social democracy has vacated. The drive towards respectability and the attempt to strip the tiger, ballot box by ballot box, has meant the isolation and frequent suppression of the CP's militants so that its functionaries could achieve the plush comforts of the Parliament. The Marxism they practise is for the most part the ruling class ideology of the Soviet Union, national and conservative and forced to express the most authoritarian elements of European socialism. The responsible CPers appealing for moderation at tenants' meetings are as fundamentally reformist as the French Stalinists who shopped the students and workers of Paris, just less successful. They are no more de-Stalinised than Globke and Oberlander are de-nazified. The cameos are plain; the leaders of the CBI welcomed to the leather chair of the Kremlin to complain about their workers over vodka aperitifs; the cautious and 'responsible' behaviour of the Moscow Narodny Bank Ltd in tiding over the last two gold crises.

But because there is no visible political institution which can be seen to represent student socialists and because loyalty to Eastern Europe is no longer an accurate litmus to the far Left, the political train spotters and student affairs 'experts' whose ideology is end of ideology have assumed that students are no longer interested in theory and analysis but are just in it for the punch-ups. If only lines of communication could be opened for full and free dialogue and the troublemakers eliminated, the universities could get back to the real and superbly harmless works of scholarship. Whereas in fact political students spend their waking, thinking, drinking life utterly bound up in politics and analysis. Those who are fond of asking why we don't join the NLF should not suppose that the workers and intellectuals of the Spanish War are the only people who meant what they said when they declared they would die for what they believed. Indeed, the very franticness of students, their capacity for outrage and hope, is an affront to the play ethic of late capitalism for which a flayed self-awareness wears so much better than conviction.

What is at the back of this urgency, what makes the anger last and deepen is the horror which must happen every day to maintain the US occupation of South Vietnam and the final horror which comes from the realisation that the Vietnams will be repeated until the US is either a fortress in mutiny or so over-extended that the final reckoning comes. But students' response is not just the contempt that any person with a sense of meaning must feel over the mouth disease of LBJ, Brown's righteous hypocrisy and Wilson's diatribes written in the Pentagon. It is not only the well-chronicled, familiar, glutinous lies, the genocide to save a civilisation, humanity's Incendergel, the fragmentation bomb of freedom. The mirror Vietnam holds up to the West illuminates precisely those myths that are at the centre of the status quo, the absence of class struggle, the inevitability of economic growth and thus increase in living standards, the post-colonial powers' benign international intentions.

International capitalism has obliged the triple anniversary of Marx with a life-scale demonstration of precisely why it cannot make the world liveable for its people. It is not just the war in Vietnam, but the needs of an economy which makes Vietnam the rule rather than the exception, an economy 'stabilised' only by high unemployment and massive defence-related expenditure, a system required to police the neo-colonial empire that it has, at least for a few more years yet, to expropriate economically and supervise politically. America, that fine citadel of democracy, needs its guns and buttresses; to get them Tom Paine must be bound naked to the stake of militarism. As the late Isaac Deutscher, whose magnificent witness against the new barbarism alongside Sartre and Russell was an initial inspiration to the movement which has grown up across Europe to defeat the Americans in Vietnam, wrote: 'About 60 years ago Rosa Luxemburg predicted that one day militarism would become the driving force of the capitalist economy but even her forecast pales before the facts.'

The helplessness of Wilson even to make a formal diplomatic break with America (and thus the helplessness of those on the Left whose sole aim was to pressure him into dissociation) illuminated the nature of our satellitism to the needs of imperialism as clearly as the bankers' budget, the gratuitous cuts say in the NHS for the foreign audience, and the shows of 'toughness' indicate the helplessness of national capitalist planning with capital international and irrational.

The world's on fire; all Wilson can offer is the nudging and anticipation of backward British capitalism into mergers, investment and what is known as technological advance. The carrot is his grim dedication to the task of depressing living standards to a level at which even British business cannot help but become more competitive in the bitter conflict over dwindling growth (perhaps even an absolute decrease in 1968) margin of world trade. The political drive towards state capitalism makes sense to Maudling and Shore as well as Robbins and is resisted mainly by small CBI firms. Its main political implication is the increased induction of the higher levels of the trade union bureaucracy into the state planning machinery and then the use of the unions themselves to discipline their own rank and file. The TUC leaders find themselves wandering the corridors of power without entry to any of the doors of control and having abandoned even the notion of a militant rank and file on their journey to the top.

In the 1950s, it proved easier for much of British business to pay wage drift rather than fight it and union officialdom was able to acclimatise to relatively automatic reformism from above. But the conditions which underlie the Gold Crisis mark the end of this era; wage increase must be fought and won in conditions which inevitably link the industrial to the political. It is in this promising situation and in the opportunities it provides for attacking the fact and the politics of freezism, that student socialists have tried to find a footing. But as the aprons and boots in St Stephen's Yard suggest, there is no guarantee provided that the turbulence and disillusionment within the union rank and file will turn to the Left, although similar vacuums in Germany, France and US have led to important achievements for the revolutionary Left. What is clear is that the Labour Party's roots in the working class are withered in the air; the MPs and intellectuals who remain must feel as far away from the young people who proudly carry NLF flags, as they do from the workers who are no longer ashamed to shout Keep Britain White.

The Sunday press waxes or rather wanes eloquent, the svelte Left cries into its whisky and the parliamentary Left continues to flog its dead horses in the Augean stables of Westminster, but none of them notice there's no one listening and nothing is revealed. Of course the taste for revolution is nothing new to the young middle class. Acid hippies, progressive school bohemians and bored pop entrepreneurs all like the language of liberation and the look of Che Guevara (and some can even spell his name right). But as for theory, history and ways of understanding these are all brain diseases. Indeed, the more the underground loons on about the revolution, the more obvious it becomes that pot serves roughly the same role that gin did in the 1920s, to enable the enlightened to sit about talking about their enlightenment. The club called 'Revolution' where youthful members of the ruling class whinny under the portraits of Mao and Che is typical. The hippies in Britain are about as much of a threat to the state as people who put foreign coins in gas meters.

As the traffic to Xanadu thins, it ought to become clearer which of the new orientalists are moved to ask or answer any serious political questions. But in the USA the generous dreamings of the acid Left has been overtaken by reality, hippies give away food but negroes take refrigerators and will hopefully leave the induction centres, police stations and tenements in ashes. Ginsberg did drink the water of the Ganges and he did have dysentery for a month afterwards. The intelligentsia seem happy enough treading the water of the Mall palaces, content in the knowledge that we live in a world of violently interacting bourgeois bric-a-brac. The whole thing makes you realise how much more important is a single busman on strike than five thousand critics campaigning to legalise pubic hair.

What, on the other hand, characterises the political militants is a strong sense of the impotence of seminar socialism, Marxist hash evenings and all the complicated rationalisations of the liberal intelligentsia which ultimately serve to limit all activity to discussion and contain all discussion within the magic circles of the academic middle class. It has made them wary even of the photogenic struggles within the university. For the result of such militancy is usually the collaboration within a few committees on the herbaceous border of power where a large amount of time is spent comparing the students' white with the administration's black and settling on a negotiated charcoal.

Those who are serious are increasingly aware that the universities and the technical wing of the binary system are essentially there, enlarged or otherwise, to provide specified amounts of predictable skills at the medium levels, to a given industrial system. It is this system and the ways of changing it which finally concern us; the JCRs are voting their money to the picket line not the pantomime, students spend as much time with Tenants' Associations as with their tutors, the spectre is still haunting Europe but its banners this time read 'Today the students, tomorrow the workers'. Unnoticed by the whispering gallery of the London Left, students and workers are making growing contacts, gaining mutual self-respect and through their activity and their experience of it retrieving something from the husks of Wilsonism.

For without these roots into and connections with working class life, the most scintillating critique of bourgeois ideology, the fullest of blueprints for student power, and the grooviest of anti-universities could all be paid for by the Arts Council for all the danger they present.

To wait for revolution by Mao or Che or comprehensive schools or BBC 2 is to play the violin while the *Titanic* goes down, for if socialists don't take their theory back into the working class there are others who will.

Similarly the solidarity with our German and French comrades was not just a vicarious gesture, but because we know our struggle is integrally linked to theirs and that we both face and are overcoming very similar problems. The spirit in which the students of Europe increasingly collaborate and meet politically is specifically one of socialist internationalism, not the remnants of the Fourth International nor the furniture of international Stalinism or the dining clubs of European social democracy but rather the invisible international which the great revolutionary Victor Serge wrote of.

It represents the beginning of a recovery of the tradition of European revolutionary socialism and the activist heart of Marxism within it. It is no accident that Luxemburg and Liebknecht were the faces paraded in the German streets and Trotsky's face that the students pinned across the courtyards of the Sorbonne. The rifle butt and the canal for Luxemburg, the ice axe for Trotsky and the pistol for Dutschke – these are different weapons of different ruling classes.

The message of this last year is that their imperatives are being taken up again in the cockpit of Europe.

3

Bomb Politics*

This article was directed at people who were drifting towards urban terrorism, in Britain represented by a group which remained small, called the Angry Brigade. The article became more influential than I had realised but was only a fragment of a much larger unrecorded debate which succeeded in heading off support of an English Red Brigade or Baader Meinhof Gang. Touchingly orthodox, really.

The bombings produce in me a scandalous contradiction. My heart feels a real and rare joy at physical attacks on a system I hate. Bullets shot at the US Embassy, petrol bombs burning in an Army Recruiting Office and gelignite in the Chamber of Commerce seem a necessary and overdue reply. But my mind remains quite unconvinced. And then, even as the well-rehearsed Marxist arguments against terrorism commence, there remains the private knowledge of my admiration and my fear. You can't argue with a bomb, but, emotionally, it requires you to define yourself politically. In a world where we are competently manipulated into incompetence, each explosion questions our own passivity. And the smoke and wreckage and perhaps the ambulances also ask 'How do you expect to fight an inhuman system and remain human?' How can the intensity of your hopes for the future be expressed in your hatred for the present?

Some questions are easier than others. After Algeria, Cyprus, Aden, Kenya and Vietnam, we have learned that the violence of the oppressed bears no relation to that of the oppressor. The refusal of the Third World to allow itself to be obediently pillaged has shown us once again that, in Trotsky's words, the end might justify the means as long as there was something that justified the end. To the coolie of the Mekong Delta, the tin miner of Bolivia, the trade unionist in Durban, pacifism is a black joke. It is our white Tarzans, our Kiplings and our Livingstones who took away their countries. As Ernest Jones, the

*First published in *INK*, 1971.

Chartist, said, 'The British Empire on which the sun never sets and the blood never dries.' And as we are being shown every night, the British Empire still means graves and bayonets, not Coronation caddies and Camp coffee. The terrorist refuses to accept capitalism's claim to be concerned with humanity: he has seen too many lives slowly or rapidly destroyed by its concern.

The programme of outrages undertaken by the Angry Brigades is a return to an older anarchist tradition; of propaganda of the deed where exemplary targets are attacked to demonstrate the possibility of action. The Angries have painstakingly linked their explosions to working-class issues, the 12 December one-day strike against the Industrial Relations Bill, the Department of Employment and Productivity, the home of Ford management. And despite some fairly harsh words to those comrades tactless enough to join groups, they have clearly seen their organised terrorism as parallel and contributing to militant mass action.

The bombers clearly see their actions as penetrating, by their audacity and violence, our feeling of political helplessness. But the Angries, even if they pierce the spectacle, leave the rest of us as spectators, only able to gawp at their courage and the police's hopelessness. It's clearly true that electronic capitalism is amazingly capable of invading our own subconscious. The anti-colonial, black American and women's movements have variously teased out how they are contained by their own ideas about themselves, the slave mentality of the Algerian, the self-hatred of the Uncle Tom, the passivity and inner-directedness of the woman. Capitalism does have ways of getting inside our brains – head-fixing the Wobblies used to call it – of consuming our own imagination, of assembling our own desires out of its commodities.

But the way outwards is connection, is politics. Only combination can make sense of and then disprove our isolation and incompetence. This discovery cannot be made for us by the Angry Brigade. And those examples which have actually served to reanimate a dead revolutionary movement in Britain have been simpler and more distant. The implacable, unbelievable insistence by the Vietnamese that against a capitalism of unimaginable power, humans still have the possibility to make history themselves. The looks on the faces of mothers squatting in Ilford and shipyard workers working-in, the tactics of direct action re-awaken in the working class via the student movement. The symbolic evidence that we are in a new era of crisis and socialist possibility once again: the barbed wire on the grass at Lords, the cannister of CS in the House of Commons, the police snipers on Government roofs protecting the Queen. They want to pretend it's still *Dixon of Dock Green*, but down at *Z Cars* they're all going oink oink.

For the Bolshevik objection to terrorism is neither moral nor conservative. Lenin's argument with the Old Russian conspiratorial tradition was that it had been made irrelevant by the rapid growth of the Russian working class and was bound to isolate, demoralise and disorganise. But in clearly defending guerrilla action in the Lettish territory, he insisted that the revolutionary does not repeat old tactics but rather prepares to observe what new forms – like the soviets which appeared in 1905 – the working class might use, and learn from them. Marxism had largely developed by Plekhanov's opposition to Russian populism which had first led a wave of intellectuals into the countryside to establish agrarian communes and then in the 1870s attempted a messianic transformation of the Tsarist autocracy by killing Alexander II. Most of those intellectuals succumbed to the terrible repression introduced by Alexander III, among them Lenin's eldest brother who had sold a school medal to purchase chemicals to make one of the last bomb attempts. Indeed, Trotsky attributes some of Lenin's severe centralism to his memories of the 1870s when 'the best of that generation went up in a blaze of dynamite warfare.'

The two upsurges of anarchist outrage in France also started and ended in despair, if more tempered by defiance. Between 1891 and 1894, Ravachol, Valliant and Henry became the heroes of the Paris proletariat by the bombs they hurled at bourgeois cafés and the Palace of Deputies.

Syndicalist workers whistled songs in their praise and employers began to ease the repression they had introduced after the fall of the Commune. Again, in 1913, the terrorist emerged from the lower working class districts of Paris. The Bonnet Gang, led by an ex-industrial militant, was like Robin Hood and Ned Kelly's bands of primitive rebels, essentially a group of political criminals who explained their ideas in socialist papers and sent letters of sarcasm to the bourgeoisie. This wave of outlaws shot the police and then blew their own brains out shouting nihilist slogans: 'One Against All', 'Damn masters, damn slaves and damn me'. Their politics reflected the wave of suicides which had swept through a despairing socialist movement after the joint suicide of Paul and Laura Lafargue, Marx's son-in-law and daughter, and the awareness of an approaching era of violence. Victor Serge, that remarkable witness, framed and sentenced to five years' prison, described these *bandits tragiques* as having the same exacting idealism in breasts of uncomplicated men, whose energies could find no outlet in achieving a higher dignity or sensibility because such an outlet is physically denied to them.

Serge's sympathy did not obscure his regret: 'Their energies were wasted in struggles that were bound to be fruitless.'

The fruitlessness is repeated (you have to pay to get out of going through all this twice) in the ghoulish history of Weather man as told in Harold Jacob's *Ramparts* book. The decline and fall through confrontation theory, overnight Maoism, stale socks Marxism, street-fighting man, Manson fan, 'heavy' politics, heroic will, radical gelignite and revolutionary self-immolation ends in the New Morning communiqué which winningly observes that going underground has made it difficult to meet and organise among people. Lenin's view that terrorism 'easily occurs to the mind of people who have a weakness for stereotype' is confirmed in pages of self-dramatising and contradictory rhetoric, all faithfully republished in an underground press apparently hypnotised by its repetitiveness.

The alternative route, outwards towards solidarity and towards working people is most carefully put in a new pamphlet, 'Why Miss World?'. It was written by sisters earlier involved in *The Woman's Newspaper* which had published a critique of the Angry Brigade action against Biba's, arguing that its meaning was unclear and didn't go to the roots of the problem.

> Our manipulated desires are left untouched; it's not going to stop your wanting to wear the dress because it's snatched out of your hands. The fears and insecurities that trap us can't be blown away by a bomb ... We see Biba's as an enemy, but don't think it can be destroyed by bombs; direct action like bombing is only effective politically when more people understand it and can see it as part of their struggle.

The pamphlet shows how an assault on the spectacle of Miss World, that most extreme example of how women are merchandised every day and night, unearthed the power just behind the spectacle: the police, the courts, Holloway nick, and finally the lethal process of being turned into a counter-spectacle, as distant to most women as Miss World herself. The collective's conclusion is this:

> For us, out of that vacuum and despair, we began to build ways of acting together which will make a movement over years instead of flash and disappear. We've worked more in the communities we

> live in – fighting for nurseries, playhouses for our children, working with unsupported mothers in Claimants' Unions, meeting in small groups. Some of us have tried to live in collectives, some have worked with GLF. Most of it has been slow, painstaking organising compared with the Miss World demonstration – but it's in the home around kids, sexuality, that our oppression bites deepest, holds hardest.

It isn't an easy way out. It demands theory as well as imagination, patience as well as energy, boredom as well as break through. To my mind, it requires a party, both democratic and revolutionary, capable of spanning the experience and the struggle of the shop steward, the claimant, the student and the housewife. With more possibility for revolutionary ideas to regain a footing among working-class people than at any time for thirty years, simply to throw bombs or, more likely, simply to admire those who do, is an admission of a terrible pessimism.

4

The Pilkington Strike*

In Britain student activism of 1968 fed into a rising arc of working-class struggle which was, in the early 1970s, to produce the highest level of strikes since the 1920s. This included long national strikes by unions like the builders who had never taken coordinated action before, the miners' strike which produced the Three-Day Week, and the Battle of Saltley Gate, the dockers' triumphant rescue of their imprisoned members from Pentonville Jail in Camden Town, and the UCS work-in on the Upper Clyde. Factory occupations against closure and job loss sprouted and developed national networks of support. Women workers were prominent. Even hospital workers, with hardly any trade union experience, started answering back. And rank-and-file workers developed their own newspapers, industry by industry, in which the International Socialists, which I had joined in 1967, had a genuine and creative influence. Ex-students, either as white-collar trade unionists themselves or as socialist organisers, had produced a revolutionary leavening in British trade unionism which heartened the existing militants and which the bureaucrats found impossible to contain. And many artists, especially in theatre and TV, added their impetus to the industrial movement. The Pilkington strike, with its almost accidental origins, its anti-bureaucratic character and in the marvellous film Allen and Loach made about it, embodies many of these elements.

The road to St Helen's in April 1970, to the explosion of working-class anger they said didn't happen any more, is a long and narrow one. Until the late 1960s, post-war labour history amounted to short, small and successful strikes. Their essence was cash, their impact was local, their conflict muted. Broadly it was the politics of Brother Kite in the Boulting Brothers' classic of Ealing snobbery *I'm Alright Jack* – among the militants a half-remembered loyalty to Russia, among the

*First published in *INK*, 1970.
Review of Jim Allen's TV play *The Rank and File*.

rank and file a political agnosticism. But across this period were superimposed a series of violent upsurges of class revolt, disputes which, for an instant, reached insurrectionary level only to burn out in their isolation. The 1958 bus strike, St Pancras rent strike, ENV closure, the Shell lockout, the Barbican strike, the Roberts-Arundel dispute formed a litany for the Left, a series of proofs of the revolutionary equation before the May Events proved the whole theorem yet again.

These disputes, recorded only by the pamphlets of the far Left and the court reports of the local press, were the dragon's teeth. *The Rank and File*, Jim Allen and Ken Loach's magnificent TV dramatisation of the Pilkington strike, examined what has grown out of them. It shows such a local conflict but now against the background of an open and declared war of attrition between the working class and the state, a battle which can only end in one side breaking the other's back. It lifts the smirk off the face of the world of 'Industrial Relations', where all claims are 'inflationary' and all strikes 'damaging'. It showed us a glimpse of the real world which smoulders behind TV 'reality'. As a film, its political effect, perhaps 'invisible to a superficial glance', will be far more than that of *The War Game*, Peter Watkin's H-bomb film which single-handedly extended CND's life by four years.

We live in a time dizzy with statistics. But we know that prices increased more in a month this year than they increased in an entire year in the 1960s, that we have already had more strike hours than any other year since 1926, and that rickets is being reported again after twenty years among the children of Liverpool and Nottingham. We know that British capitalism remains unable to grow at anything more than a quarter the rate of its main trading rivals. And that means, in the cool appraisal of one Professor of Industrial Relations, 'more and more managements seems to me to be becoming aware that the labour situation has drifted dangerously far and that they are faced with the need to reestablish control over their workers' (Allan Flanders). 'Reestablishing control' means a battery of attacks from productivity dealing through legislation and welfare cuts to that most successful incomes policy of all, 1½million unemployed. And as each sortie by the state is driven off, the next one is more extreme. Conversely, every victory of the working class strengthens its confidence ('if the militants succeed in imposing their will on this government, they would be in a stronger position to frustrate a reforming Conservative government', the *Sunday Times* fretted three years ago).

The features of the struggle may alter. Yesterday's Union Lord with his eyes on a Bank of England governorship is replaced on the 'Left' by the 'aggressive' union leader less liable to let his contempt for his men show. Beer, butties and midnight negotiations with Harold Wilson are replaced by Heath's deliberate seeking out of setpiece confrontations with ill-led unions. Old style Labour Party 'modernisation' of the social services is replaced by the Tories' flamboyant assaults on health and welfare rights. But the essence of class struggle over the last five years is its continuity and the break with the traditions of the preceding fifteen years' hibernation.

It is against this background that Jim Allen's remarkable transcription of the Pilkington Strike has such political value. It is a primal drama where a company whose profits rose in 1969 from £13m to £120m, and which boasts it's in the top 25 per cent of the big 300 companies in Britain, meets its town – one of the 30 most socially deprived areas in the country with 10 per cent of its occupied houses classified as slums. A town where, as a striker put it, 'People are always on about providing us with facilities for extra leisure. I can tell them where OUR leisure is spent – AT PILKINGTONS.'

Allen's life as an active trade unionist (he came to write for Coronation Street after coming to Granada's notice as a trade union journalist and before writing *The Lump* and *The Big Flame*) gave the detail of the outbreak of the strike its uncanny realism. He had demonstrated his quite unique skill at scripting the dialectics of negotiation in the opening scenes of *Big Flame* where dockers put the case against Devlin Stage Two. The speed of the outbreak from the Flat-Drawn Department's complaints over pay slips to a full strike for £25 for 40hrs was brilliantly developed. The snowball of self-confidence as the glassmen tasted their own power: 'It was fantastic, the atmosphere that afternoon. We could have done anything. We could have stopped the world. We didn't give a monkey's for the rain, the bobbies, the union. It was ... bloody great.'

Allen and Loach never allowed themselves to be trapped in the heavyhandedness which so often beckons Left-wing dramatisers of strikes. Rather it was the delicate understatement which gave the film its power. The brutality of a strike in such a tight community was shown as it must have been: muffled, ugly and nearly incomprehensible. The imprisoning web of TUC telegrams, TV cameras and phone calls showed how the committee was enveloped as the strike became a national issue. The tattered march and the ancient silk banner and the singing of *The Red Flag* explained so well the deep roots and instincts which give shape to the joyous spontaneity. The faces chosen by the director actually looked like the real people who inhabit mass meetings, with motorbike helmet kept on so no one will pinch it, long untidy hair, careful ears and the lines of age and work.

Some of the actors deliberately echoed faces from the actual strike – Gerry Caughey, the slight and intense strike spokesman, and Bill Bradburn, one of the old time GMWU stewards. The national officer, modelled on David Basnett ('probably one of the finest negotiators in the country') had the Robin Hood hat and boardroom manner of the species, strongly reminiscent of the Ford trade union whizzkid Moss Evans.

The impact of the strike on the old, the children and the strike leaders' wives, their incomprehension and their loyalty, was honestly if not optimistically stated. The agonised row between the ignored and excluded wife and her husband exhaustedly jabbing out a strike bulletin on an old typewriter was bitterly unsentimental. There was no happy resolution as in Biberman's comparable *Salt of the Earth* where the women fight equally on the picket line. In Lancashire that didn't happen. And even the comedy which seems to rise in the most austere political situations was there, the Laurel and Hardy scenes which arise when sticking up posters and the old gag to pinch the ticket on the bus to London.

Much had to be omitted, although if you want to see the 'management's point of view', it can in fact be seen twenty-four hours a day. Allen's insistence in spelling out the role of trade union officialdom in carefully stamping out the flames of a hundred years' anger and his determination not to let the scourge of the stockbroker belt, Hugh Scanlon, off the hook seemed an excellent decision. Post-Pilkington events, notably the collapse of any real TUC opposition to the Industrial Relations Bill and the defeat of the postal strike, vindicate Allen's politics. For the Tories are not out to smash the unions, they need its bureaucracy and want to strengthen it to work against the membership. The Feather-Cooper Right wing and the Jones-Scanlon Left wing both accept the indefinite continuance of capitalism and are arguing about their role within it. Cooper, leader of the GMWU, the Pilks union, has already broken ranks on the Croydon TUC decision and announced his intention to register with TORY BILL.

After a decent interval, and unless the militants hold them to the non-cooperation policy which they themselves have advocated, the Lefts will register too. As Scanlon's 'settlement' of the Ford's strike, condemned by the Ford stewards, showed, he is prepared not only to damage the fight for parity but to obey the Tory laws before they are even passed. The Communist Party are so short of excuses they had to hold down an I.S. car worker from Glasgow who wanted to propose defiance of the Bill by a strike on the day of its introduction and for his pains denounced him in the *Morning Star* as a playboy Trotskyist. It is in this situation that the rank and file, not as a hopelessly romanticised bunch of Spartacuses but as men often out of their depth and not unfrightened, are left with the obligation to give shape to factory struggle.

The Tories would much rather frighten the rank and file than jail them. Like the criminal who robs the bank with an empty gun, they would rather not pull the trigger, they prefer the union officials to do their work for them with some talk of voting Labour next time. It is in the rank and file and their own experience that the only real answer to the Tories lies. In answer to the question 'What have we won so far?', the Rank and File Committee bulletin issued at the end of the strike said 'First and foremost SELF-RESPECT – and the respect of the people of St. Helen's and the rest of the country. We have received an EDUCATION that money could not buy. We have seen the real face of Pilkington Brothers and the NUGMW.'

Plays like this have reached an audience some millions of times greater than the early morning salesman of the *Workers' Press* and *Socialist Worker* could ever hope to address. If a previous generation of industrial militants looked back on Jack London, Upton Sinclair and Robert Tressel as the writers whose vision of socialism captured their imagination, perhaps the young workers of today will find their images of the future and the suffering through which it comes in *Cathy Come Home*, *The Big Flame* and *The Rank and File*.

For those who still imagine the working class is a bribed, bamboozled and bewildered force, Loach and Allen's film has painstakingly traced how the creativity and solidarities of class struggle are constantly exploding out of the constrictions which surround it. Most of all their film points to the possibility of a future when St Helen's is run, not by the Lord Pilkington, but by the rank and file.

5

Union Blues: Harlan County USA*

When I first visited the fascinating and repellent US of A in the mid-1960s, politics were dominated by student radicalism, the civil rights movement in the Deep South and the Vietnam War. When I returned in 1974, I was determined to see more of that well-kept secret, the American Labour Movement. If, after all, it didn't exist or was assimilated completely, Marxism really didn't add up. Of course, there is a large and militant trade union movement with proud traditions, if you look outside of those bits of New York and Southern California Europeans mistakenly regard as archetypal. But Harlan County took a bit of finding, down among the beautiful, primitive and dangerous mining towns of Kentucky. Once found, it was familiar: the warmth of a mining community on strike and in their respect for song and history. It was a visit which made me feel *rather than just* assert *that the working-class movement knows no national boundary.*

Kentucky's main gift to Britain so far is Colonel Saunders's finger-lickin' chicken. But down in Harlan County, a mountainous area rich in coal, there's another kind of cooking going on:

Take a scab and kill it
And put it in the skillet
Fry it up golden brown
That's union cooking and it's mighty fine

For eleven months, 180 miners and their families have been on strike over the right to organise in the union of their choice, the United Mine Workers of America (UMWA). Brookside, the centre of the strike, is a small mine in a part of the American South where horses still drag ploughs scratching across dry fields, chickens pick in the dust and the jukebox plays solid, sad country music.

It's also a part of the world where votes can still be bought for a

*First published in *Socialist Worker*, 1974.

five-dollar bill, where the bootleggers have bigger houses than the preachers and where blacks keep themselves to themselves.

But it's here at Brookside that members of a union which has only just begun to untangle itself from twenty years of rusting and twisting of its democracy, face up to Duke Power, a giant North Carolina-based electricity supply corporation, the sixth biggest public utility in America, declaring this year profits of $26 million.

It's a battle with a history. For generations companies like Duke have come into the Kentucky Mountains looking for wealth. They have taken the mountain people's coal and timber, their health and sometimes their lives too.

Those who owned the coal have controlled the police, the legal system and the schools.

They are passionately anti-union and don't care a damn if miners go home battered and broken. For them, mining is non-union or not at all. And when they fight the unions, they do not use the velvet glove or the aristocratic embrace.

In the 1930s, the wife of a union organiser wrote a famous song on the back of a calendar when the sheriff, J.H. Blair, ransacked her home. It's called 'Which side are you on?'

They say in Harlan County
There are no neutrals here;
You'll either be a bosses' man
Or a thug with J.H. Blair.
Don't scab for the bosses.
Don't listen to their lies.
Us poor folks haven't got a chance
Unless we organise.

('Which side are you on?', Florence Rees)

A 60-year-old member of the Brookside Women's Club told me how Harlan got its reputation.

Harlan got called Bloody when they started this union, when they started to organise. The owner then had his gun-thugs – he's pretty much like Norman Yarborough. He'd just get him a good bunch of gun-thugs that weren't scared of anything. They'd just come up to the organiser. They was wanting to get rid of him. They wasn't having no organising. Three carloads of thugs eased across the road and stopped in front of his house. They meant to kill. They just shot up the house. The bullets made big streaks about a foot long. All through the house.

Today, the UMWA bumper stickers still carry the question 'Which side are you on?'

The strike is not about a wage increase. The contract put forward by the UMWA is more straightforward. It is about power, about the miners having some control of their union, their work and their lives.

Above all, the strikers want a decent health programme which would provide good care for the family and modest but reliable pensions for retired miners, especially those injured by dust and accidents. They want a proper procedure for grievances and promotions. They want payment from the time they go underground, not the time they start cutting.

Scarcely extreme demands. But in Harlan, where corrupt company unionism and police violence has kept the miners on their knees for a generation, this would mean a small social revolution.

Take safety, for example. First, there are simply no decent local hospitals or doctors or public services. The old and not-so-old who come down with pneumoconiosis, 'Black Lung', the disease caused by coal dust, are left to fend for themselves without a guaranteed pension from either company or union. Even after an organised campaign over Black Lung which did much to revive the miners' union in the 1960s, only one in three of the Kentucky miners who applied have obtained a federal pension or were awarded compensation.

Somebody said that's a strange tattoo
You have on the back of your head.
I said that's a blueprint left by the coal,
Just a little more and I'd be dead.

('Coal Tattoo', Billy Ed Wheeler)

Accidents are notorious in this area and the owners are proud of their indifference. A few years ago, thirty-eight men were buried at near by Hyden and a federal investigation found that the explosion that killed them was caused by illegal mining practices which the company knew were unsafe.

Brookside is said to be so dangerous that even the rats stay away. Limbless men and crutches are common in these parts, although you never know whether it's the mines or Vietnam. There's an artificial limb shop on Main Street, Harlan. Safety inspections are a farce and enforcement worse. Violations remain out standing for years. A miner told me he knew the very hour and the very day when the mines inspectors were coming: 'The boss would say, "Let's make it look pretty now".'

Among the pretty sights recently recorded by the miners at Brook side were missing fire alarms, missing brakes on the coal locomotives, areas of flooding which prevented inspection altogether, fire sprinklers that don't work and missing roof belts. But effective safety means effective organisation, and that means a continual challenge to management's absolute rights. Norman Yarborough, the mine boss, understands this well. 'I'm not going to abdicate the right to any final say on safety because I'm the responsible party. Ultimately, it has got to be a management decision,' he says. 'There's no such animal as a safe coal mine. It just doesn't exist.'

The miners don't agree. 'I don't want my son to go into the mines. But I firmly believe that by the time my sons are old enough to go to work, this mine could be organised so that it's as safe as any factory,' says Jerry Rainey.

> There's a man in a big house way up on the hill,
> Far from the shacks where the poor miners live.
> He's got plenty of money, Lord everything's fine,
> And he has forgotten the Mannington mine.
>
> ('Disaster at the Mannington Mine', Hazel Dickens)

The union would not be just something inside the mines. It is needed to change the whole way the miners and their families live. Houston Elmore, the union organiser, says:

> We have to start to make the union work for the people of Harlan, people we've let down badly in the past. But it's not just about coal. The education system, the housing, the courts and the political system have got to change if the miners are to get justice. The judge here, now he's a scab coal operator. So how can he be impartial? The teachers in the local schools, they are the sons and daughters of the owners because they are the only people who can get to college. It's sort of like a feudal system.

Brookside is laid out like a cross between a company town and a medieval village. Normal Yarborough's mansion looks out over his mine and his miners, separated only by a row of pine trees, a two-lane road and a little hill. Just beneath his home huddle the smaller but still luxurious homes of his managers and foremen, arranged by rank.

The miners' homes are wooden, temporary-looking shacks, in rows along dirt trackways. The wood is unpainted, the faces pinched, the teeth yellow. Their living conditions are a kind of grim joke. They have a colour TV but no lavatory. They have cars but no dentists. Large families sit on the porch, father in white T-shirt rocking backwards and forwards, mother in a beehive hairdo, and kids bathing in the creek. Behind them, the coal gleams and a canopy of firtree overhangs the mine shaft. It all looks quite idyllic from a distance. Until you look twice and see that underneath the veranda is a heap of shit and toilet paper which is only flushed away when the creek floods once a year. And you find that everyone boils all their tapwater because the last time the Harlan County Health Department tested the drinking water, it was 'highly contaminated' with faecal coliform bacteria (a count of 24: permitted level 4).

Harlan and the sprawling, grimy wastelands of the factory plants of Cleveland, Cincinatti, Akron and Minneapolis made us recall with mirth the New York intellectuals who had told us there was no longer such a thing as a working class in America and therefore socialism was an irrelevant idea. In the Mid-West at least, those who went in search of the American Dream were to be permanently disappointed. There is nowhere better to witness the unplanned squalor, pitiless pollution and sheer ugliness of free enterprise on the rampage.

In the summertime we didn't have shoes to wear,
But in the winter we'd all get a brand new pair
From a mail order catalogue
Money made from selling a hog,
Daddy always managed to get the money somewhere.

('Coalminer's Daughter', Loretta Lynn)

The schools are pretty foul, too. When one of the strikers' children went to school with a UMWA button, it was torn off him. 'When your father gets involved in the union, makes your brain go bad,' drawls another miner who has conducted his own survey to prove militants' children have got mysteriously bad grades at school since the strike.

Miners are locked into a whole series of social relationships which keep them down. Jerry Rainey says:

Now Mr Yarborough ain't no fancy dresser. To look at him, he might almost be a miner. But he sure does want to stand over us. He wants to stand over us like a mule master with a whip, he does. Well, I ain't no mule hauling a plough. Them's just slavery.

In this situation a union is both last hope and first chance.

Now the strikers' main enemy is time. The miners have been out for eleven months. The pickets squat, playing cards in the hot dust, listening to the car radio and building a heap of empty beer cans. At night, people whittle round camp fires and play mandolins and banjos. But if the management try to pull a fast one, a whistle will summon 150 miners in two minutes. The deadlock is tense. If they are beaten, the pickets will have to leave for the auto and steel plants of the north. In a town where mining is the only work, the owners' blacklist is an order to leave.

They also know that Duke is hungry for coal. Only two weeks ago, the president of the 'yeller dog' company union was photographed and taped attempting to bribe two strikers with $140 in cash with the promise of a $5000 pay-off if the rest of the men could be 'persuaded' back to work. Just underneath the calm and heat and the waiting is fear; Harlan is where the owners have always fought trade unionism with machine guns. It was in Harlan that miners' union reform candidate Yablonski was shot dead in his bed. So far in the strike, the only shooting has been some high velocity bullets into the back of a picket van. So far ... The union organiser has a revolver stuffed in the bottom of his briefcase of union business.

I can see the people stirring through the valleys and the hills,
I can hear the people stirring as I go, as I go.
I can feel the people stirring through the valleys and the hills,
Oh, I'm going home to Jesus, bless my soul, bless my soul.

(Traditional)

To get up spirits, the strike committee has equipped an old station waggon with loudspeakers, and this 'booster van' cruises between Evarts, Brookside and Harlan, cheering people up and passing on the news and gossip. But it is the demurely named Brook side Women's Club which has been the most successful morale builder.

In September, the male union members were prevented by a local court injunction from mounting effective pickets. This itself was a fraud, as a local doctor, himself active in the 'Black Lung' movement, snorted: 'I am sick and tired of rule by injunctions, by the big money in this country. Do you ever see an injunction given in favour of a poor person?'

But while the men were banned, the women stopped the scabs. 'At first they thought we were pretty funny, but finally they quit laughing,' says Minnie Lunsford. At first they tried talking, but when a scab pulled a gun, all hell let loose. The state police moved in with squad cars and truncheon charges, the women retaliated with two-by-two clubs and hoe handles. One woman shouted at the police, 'You're a coal owner and I resent you trying me. And that clerk beside you, her son photographed union men at Brookside for the blacklist.'

Their defence was clear: 'We had to picket ourselves to prevent the coal owners from getting round the law. We all know we are doing what is right.'

The women of Brookside looked uncannily familiar, sitting out on plastic garden furniture; they have heavily dyed hair, faces roughened with too much work and too much make-up; the quick penetrating glances and precise irony at first concealed behind what sounds a slow-thinking drawl. They are working women and proud of it. Their glances, if not their accents, can be observed in a Strathclyde saloon bar at lunchtime, or a Yorkshire coast holiday camp. Those eyes have seen a lot of suffering and crying ... and some joy. And when they decide to fight, heaven help any man who gets in their way. For mountain people of North America, like the communities in Wales and Scotland, and for that matter northern Spain and the Andes, union militancy and music have gone hand in hand and women have played a leading part in both. Men and women remain very different creatures still but, granted their separate spheres, there is mutual respect and sympathy. The women's particular emotional strength, their mixture of defiance and endurance, are qualities which have come to the fore as the lock-out trails on. It made the women of Brookside, in their quiet way, some of the most intense people I met in America, whose memory lingered on long after more spectacular sights and people faded, and whose reality made the glamour of New York and LA just tawdry.

In both men and women, the strike has awoken new capacities and determination. 'People listen better than they did before,' says one striker. 'We've met people who we didn't know existed on that picket line,' says another.

'Sure it's been worth it,' says Minnie Lunsford. 'It was just like a school. I've enjoyed every minute of it.' 'Sometimes I wonder if I knew anything before this strike,' mused Betty Eldridge.

The strike has shaken the county up. The union idea is spreading; employees of the Appalachian Hospitals have been out for union recognition. Waitresses in the town, including some of the strikers' daughters, are trying to form an association.

Personal relations have been changed, too. Women who have won their husbands' grudging admiration for their courage on the picket line and their insolence in court are not going meekly back to the sink. Some of the family scenes which we were told of, hushedly, of rising female assertiveness, of community wrath and revenge against back-sliders, recalled scenes in *The Salt of the Earth*, a semi-documentary film about a Mexican miners' strike where women had taken to the picket lines to beat the owner's legal injunctions. I had been involved in the showing of that classic, made by socialist film-makers run out of Hollywood by McCarthyism, in the Yorkshire coalfields. I wonder if we could ever show the film that is being made about Harlan, by 'a woman cameraman from New York, Barbara Koppel'. Even the movies were a'changin.

I ain't got much money, not much of a home.
We own our land but the land's not our own.
But if we all got together, we can work it all out,
We'll take over the country and run 'em all out.

('Black Waters', Jean Ritchie)

Newest of all is a sense of power. 'When miners move together, that's really something,' one striker said of the British coal strike in 1974. American miners took a close interest in the British coalfields and are amazed that British miners actually forced a general election.

The Brookside strike may not yet have Duke Power and Richard Nixon on their knees, but it does show again that if the working class doesn't change the world, even the world of East Kentucky, then nobody will. 'We've got the cat by the tail now, can't go but one way.'

6

Green Bans Down Under*

The self-confidence of the workers' movement in the early 1970s was infectious and international. In some ways the Green Bans in Sydney pushed the political dimension of workers' economic demands further and faster than building workers anywhere else. But Australian labour have far deeper radical roots than many European socialists realise ... and the Oz establishment far greater capacity for cruelty.

The Builders Labourers Federation organises the Australian building workers responsible for demolition, excavation, scaffolding, rigging and concreting. Until the mid-1960s, the union was Right-wing, dominated by full-time 'standover men' in informal liaison with the building employers. But as the Sydney building boom took off, fuelled by the investment capital of the insurance giants, a new BL leadership began to challenge the site bosses, the old gangsterism and the second-best mentality that many BLs themselves had developed. And in this challenge they were aided by changes in building methods. Off-site construction, continuously poured concrete and nailing machines had acted to narrow or make irrelevant the skill differentials between the labourers and the craft unions. And as the trade winds of speculative office building tore through the older parts of central Sydney, it was the BLs who were first on-site and who had to do the developers' dirty work.

To a Londoner ground down by the grime and corrugated iron of the last four years' slump in the British building industry, at first sight Sydney's new architecture is refreshingly elegant. But for all the copper-coloured glass and fancy fountains, it's still Centrepoint times ten. All the clichés of modern life are there, air-conditioned lifts, open-plan offices and cloud-level viewing platforms. But while the

*First published in *Socialist Review*, 1975.
Review of *Taming the Concrete Jungle: The Builders Labourers' Story*, by Pete Thomas, and *Black War*, by Clive Turnbull.

rows of unlet office blocks make money for their owners, they impoverish the city workers threading their way through the sunless, memoryless corridors that once were familiar, living streets. The social effects of speculative office building have been especially clear in Australia because the population is highly urbanised and the quality of public housing, even when the Housing Commission estates are given cheery names like Sunshine and Broadmeadow, is very low. A store-front balladeer wrote:

No war declared,
No storm has flared,
No sudden bomb so cruel.
Just a need for land,
A greedy hand,
And a sign that says 'Urban Renewal'.

The earliest BL strikes were aimed at 'civilising the industry' by direct action to improve on-site amenities and, with them, the labourers' own confidence. Its symbols were a shabby tin changing hut heaved into the foundations of a Bramble's job at the Cross in Sydney, a dented compressor which 'fell' into a Clarence Street excavation where many Mediterranean labourers had no place whatsoever to change or eat, not even a tap, and the Newcastle builders on the Civic Centre site who took a naked shower on City Hall's steps to dramatise site conditions.

Accident pay for on-site injuries was the next target. Building workers accounted for one in five of recorded work incapacities and averaged 20,000 compensation cases with 40 site deaths a year in New South Wales alone. BL excavators were prone not only to noise injuries but high silicone dust levels from Sydney's sandstone rock shelf. Of six Queensland union secretaries who signed a 'Stop the Slaughter' newspaper appeal in 1970, two were dead within three years. But, as always, continuous breaches of lax safety regulations were commonplace, until a strongly organised union tackled them with action on the job. As the *Australian Financial Review* reported an industry executive saying in a moment of truth: 'To the discredit of the industry, every major safety change has been at the initiative of the union. We have played no part at all.' A five-week wage strike in 1970 was followed by a united building trades stoppage for a flat-rate increase and injury payments. And by 1971 the construction trade unions edged the engineers into second place in the strike tables, with 1.2 million strike days won in dispute.

During these strikes the government-dominated arbitration courts were simply ignored when necessary and emphasis was placed on the organisation of the rank and file. Mobile 'de-scabbing' brigades inspected sites where strike-breaking was suspected. The scabs might disguise themselves by grabbing a broom, but their handiwork would be gently demolished. Just as British building workers in 1972 decided there was little point in hanging round the empty shells of solid strikes, so their Australian brothers put the emphasis on applying their picketing strength where it really had effect. Jack Mundey, a BL leader and Australian Communist Party member, put it: 'We did not set out on a wanton destruction rampage but attacked only buildings where the employers were attempting to use scab labour to break the strike. This had a devastating effect on employers, government and police alike. In this dispute it took the class enemy by surprise.' Further strike action tackled the problem of permanency on the sites and sought to establish union-controlled hiring halls to prevent the destructive effect on organisation and morale of short jobs and long waits for work. The Master Builders, who were doing well enough out of the boom, got more and more worried as the BLs attacked them not just for money but to break the features of the industry which put the site workers on such a permanently weak trade union footing.

The famous Green Bans also grew out of the union's determination to go beyond just bargaining about the price of labour but to consider 'the worker's life and not just the worker's day'. The bans were an extension of the blacking of goods to the blacking of socially undesirable demolition and building work. The building regulations are notoriously lax in Australia and local government weak and easily corrupted. So it was direct to the BLs that the conservationists appealed. And if the BL rank and file, after public discussion and a full vote of members, agreed, a threatened demolition or development would simply not be carried out. The first request came from a rich residential area, but Green Bans were soon in force in areas of central Sydney which had traditionally housed low-cost working class housing like The Rocks, Woolloomooloo and Victoria Street. In all these areas, residents, local trade unionists and squatters joined the BLs in enforcing the Bans. By 1973, there were 32 sites green-banned, holding up £1500 million worth of speculative building. The politics of the action became clearer as the first bite of the depression started to push up unemployment. 'Yes, we want to build,' said Mundey. 'However, we prefer to build urgently required hospitals, schools, other public utilities, high quality flats, units and houses rather than ugly, unimaginative, architecturally bankrupt blocks of concrete and glass offices.' In Melbourne, BLs introduced the 'amber ban' by refusing to knock down the few remaining 'water-holes for workers', pubs where you could go in working clothes and get a drink at normal prices which were otherwise being 'renovated' with high prices and dress rules. So much for the sneers of the *Sydney Morning Herald*, who had crowed, 'There is something highly comical in the spectacle of building labourers, whose ideas on industrial relations do not rise above strikes, violence, intimidation and the destruction of property, setting themselves up as arbiters of taste and protectors of our national heritage.'

The sustained campaign would not have been possible without an unusually democratic internal structure in the union, an insistence on democracy inside the union which was at least as shocking as the Green Ban concept. The union full-timers were all elected, earned wages related to site levels and were put off the payroll during strikes. A limit on tenure for full-timers was introduced. Full-time organisers held office for three years but many rotating temporary organisers were chosen from the rank and file. When Mundey and Pringle went back to the ranks, there were no expensive dinners and insincere speeches but an 18-gallon keg on the bar of the Sussex Hotel and two bunches of roses. This principle of election unionism certainly sent shivers up many of Mundey's CP comrades safe in permanent niches, and may explain the very obvious lack of enthusiasm with which the more powerful CP-influenced industrial unions defended the BLs when they were successfully deregistered.

The BLs are also one of the first all-male industrial unions to turn their commitment to sexual equality into a limited reality. Working class girls went into the industry, usually as 'nippers' (the odd-job person who cleans up and takes out the lunch orders) but took the building industry exam for forklift and hoist work and have worked as catwomen (the female version of dogmen, the crane hook leader). Most of the girls started for the money but got interested in proving the point. They got, as one woman said, 'a very quick education as to the rights of women'. There was a definite determination to break down the idea of what 'women's work' was, and a handful of Women's Movement activists, women BLs and women organisers managed to establish quite a firm base inside the industry.

The first wave of BL activity was eventually systematically crushed by the employers and the wage courts. The union was banned from representing its members on the basis of fabricated charges of on-site violence ... a Down Under Shrewsbury. Police moved in with formidable violence on the Victoria Street squat and several organisers. The Maoist Federal Secretary of the union hired thugs and armed organisers to systematically smash the NSW branch. For the last two years, thinly veiled gang unionism has reigned again and the Master Builders no longer have to worry about where or how they build.

The BLs are regrouping in Victoria and NSW and negotiations are in progress over amalgamation with the Industrial Union for the industry.

Pete Thomas's account is undermined by his inability even to admit the strength of the forces pitted against the BLs and is open to the general criticism that the CPA was obviously more interested in the electoral potential of the ecology issue than the political potential of the rank and file and union democracy issues. Green Bans were a tactic, not the mystique Jack Mundey now seems to make them. Like all tactics, they have to be jettisoned without sentiment if the conditions they once fitted alter. But the BLs' struggles must rank as one of the most advanced industrial struggles of the long boom, for not only did the rank and file push their industrial power to its political limits, but they were genuinely affected by the various currents of the revolutionary Left. To harp on the inevitable limitations of the leading militants would be to miss the creativity the BLs showed in this notoriously hard-to-organise industry.

In a recent enthusiastic survey of Australia, *The Economist* noted: 'It has to be added, brutally, that Australia has no race problem.'

And that, brutally, is because the settlers in Australia exterminated the black nomads who once wandered over the continent with more ruthlessness and success than was managed in Africa or North America. The aboriginals who now remain on the cattle stations, river banks and reserves, or cluster in slum-hut settlements on the fringe of the small towns and the black ghettos of the cities, are the memory of a race. Though their militancy stirs and rises, their culture has been pulverised.

Tasmania, the spice island off the NSW shore, is the most extreme example of the successful genocide that established Australia. A French explorer reported in 1802 on the warmth of the aboriginal islands: 'The gentle confidence of the people in us, these affectionate evidences of benevolences which they have never ceased manifesting towards us, the sincerity of their demonstrations, the frankness of their manners, the touching ingenuousness of their caresses, all concurred to excite within us sentiments of the tenderest interest.' The islanders were naked but without shame, emotionally open, loved talking, singing and especially dancing. But because they had little interest in making or accumulating things, they were seen as mental inferiors by the wise explorers who ran up a flag, fired off muskets and unloaded liquor, venereal disease and their fellows in chains. Because they disdained alcohol, did not know how to prostitute themselves and lived with an uncanny closeness to the land and animals of Tasmania, the settlers called them savages. Their occasional acts of self-defence as they were pushed off their tribal lands, dreaming places and water sources, became 'atrocities' and the first murders began, sometimes for as little as the 'brutal desire to see a Nigger run'.

Over the next seventy years, 5000 Tasmanian aboriginals were killed in the Black War. As the inefficient military governors sent back to London long-winded heroic dispatches in gentlemen's prose, the natives were hunted down. In the townships they were inefficiently strangled in public hangings, brained by musket butts, jailed and starved to death. In the Bush, with no one to call them to account, the pioneers of civilisation shot aboriginals after dinner along with kangaroos. They castrated men and raped women.

An eyewitness wrote, 'The wounded were brained, the infant cast into the flames; the musket was driven into the quivering flesh; and the social fires, around which the natives gathered to slumber, became, before morning, their funeral pyre.' Those few forced into religious settlements where they were strapped into strange 'civilised' clothing and forced to sing hymns to a god they didn't know, died too, only more slowly.

The *Colonial Times* put the matter quite frankly about 'the infatuated savages': 'We make no pompous display of philanthropy – we say unequivocally: self-defence is the first law of nature. The government must remove the natives; if not, they will be hunted down like wild beasts and destroyed.'

By 1869, the Christian gentlemen of Tasmania had succeeded. King Billy, the last male aboriginal, a souvenir of a race who had been introduced to HRH Prince Albert at the Hobart Town Regatta as a joke, died of drink aged 34. Even his death was brutalised. A surgeon acting for the Royal College of Tasmania entered the dead man's house, skinned his head and removed the skull, substituting another. Under his coffin draped with Union Jacks and a possum skin, his face was a mound of blood.

In NSW and the spreading mainland settlements where aboriginals' skills as guides, cattlemen, frontiersmen and domestic servants were useful, they were exploited, once they had been pushed off the best land. Tradesmen were, as in North America, adept at the old sport of selling them booze and raping their wives and daughters. The race was given an acquaintanceship with white society without any rights in it and were, in the process, stripped of their old culture and self-respect and introduced to the most corrupt of capitalist values. If the white settlers couldn't avoid them, they exploited them, and when that became a bit glaring, they improved them. Tight control was kept over the movement and supply of alcohol to aboriginals. The law-givers then expressed surprise that the nomads were demoralised and that, denied the right to buy alcohol, it became a revered item which made a fortune for white racketeers.

Aboriginals were by and large denied access to permanent employment and housing and then derided for being idle and unclean. In 1938, a manifesto of the Aboriginal Progressive Association said:

> You took our land by force .... You have almost exterminated our people, but there are enough of us remaining to expose the humbug of your claim to be civilised, progressive and humane. We do not wish to be regarded as scientific or anthropological curiosities. We ask you to teach our people to live in the modern age, as modern citizens.

Yet thirty years later the choice is still between being shackled to a reserve or cattle station as a sort of rural slave or to be destroyed in the towns, seeking solace in defiant bouts of drinking, another urban 'problem' that missionaries ponder and sociologists measure. On the shelves of the Sydney tourist shops, books wax on about the aboriginals' mystic culture and knowledge of the bush terrain, of Dreamtime and the Ceremony Places and the herbs they used. On the rims of the cities, aboriginal derelicts shelter in tin tanks among the milk cartons and the empty bottles, smashed by a society whose final insult is to make coffee-table books out of them.

There is still resistance. Ten years ago, Vincent Lingiari led 200 of his people of the Wave Hill cattle station through the bush wilderness to a place called Wattie Creek, saying simply, over and over, 'We want white fella to go away now.' The white fella was Lord Vestey who, besides owning 6000 square miles of Australia, has ranches in Africa and South America and owns 400 separate companies including Midland Cold Storage, the packing depot which the Pentonville Five London dockers were imprisoned for picketing in 1972. It wasn't just a strike by the black cattlemen, it was the first land claim, their demand for the land back. When they were told to get off Lord Vestey's land or pay for it in a white man's way, the Gurindjii elders pondered and then suggested they buy back the land in the currency that had been used to take it away seventy years ago – flour, sugar and tea. Now there are several stations being run by blacks, land claims that have worked. But they are still dependent on funds which Whitlam fuelled but Frazer is bound to attack, because the implications of successful land claims terrify the Country Party. Especially when the blacks object, as they did in Nabarlek, to the highly profitable mining of uranium, saying, 'Uranium rock is a dirty rock and people who muck about with it get dirty hands.'

There is also more organisation by blacks of blacks in the cities, with co-operatively run health centres, legal-aid organisations which can really fight the loading of the judicial dice and a Black News Service sponsored by the Australian Union of Students. But the condition of the descendants of the first tribes of Australia and the apparent inability of government, religious or charitable institutions seriously to alter it, is a constant reminder of the Dark People who had to be destroyed before white Australia's paradise could be constructed. A contributor to *Smoke Signal*, a duplicated magazine produced on an aboriginal island, wrote:

> Yes, all you dead friendly, helpful, thoughtless 'couldn't-give-a-stuff' folk out there, this is Palm Island. This is where wine is blackmarketed for £20 a flagon. This is where men, black naturally, work for peanuts. This is where poverty is at its lowest ebb. This is where the blacks' only release from heartbreak, oppression and the bastardies of life is to get drunk or gamble or to sit and shiver because he does not have enough warm clothes or blankets for the night. This is where the kids have legs, arms and their heads oozing with sores.

Reading that, white Australia seems not so much different to South Africa, simply more successful.

7

A World Revolution*

I really did write this while encircling the earth and so overflying many of the locations of Claudin's anti-history. It's perhaps not the soundest book on the fate of the Communist International but makes up for it with its intensely felt involvement ... nothing better than left-wing writers reworking their beliefs in public. The best reason for reprinting it is that it provided a test case for the policy of the then editor of Nation Review*: George Andrews's anti-national-chauvinist policy of rendering capital cities and countries in their own name, rather than an anglicised variant. For anyone stuck, Balgarija is Bulgaria and Magyarorszag, Hungary.*

I read Claudin's panorama of communist history on the flight from Sydney to Paris. As we floated past the desolate edge of Western Australia, the 1919 Berlin Spartakus uprising was brutally over whelmed; by Singapura the Spanish Republic was on the ropes and by Al-Bahrayn Churchill was shooting up Athinai with a wink from Stalin. As I dozed round the world, Claudin's study traversed 30 years of revolutionary endeavour in five continents.

Claudin's flight is not the glib trajectory of the cold war academic coldly computing names and data but the committed and self-critical account of an insider, forced painfully to work through his old loyalties, attached to some of the events he describes. He served on the political committee of the Spanish Communist Party from 1947 till his expulsion in 1965. When he painstakingly demolishes the strategy of the Spanish CP, he is taking himself apart. At the end of his narrative, it is impossible not to feel drained, exhausted by the sheer scale of the drama and dwarfed by the immensity of the human sacrifices. As Victor Serge, until Claudin probably the best chronicler/participant of this political timespan, put it, 'Behind us lies a

* First published in *Nation Review*, 1976.
Review of *The Communist Movement, from Comintern to Cominform*, by Fernando Claudin.

victorious revolution gone astray, several abortive attempts at revolution and massacres in so great numbers as to inspire a certain dizziness.' Yet one is saved from political vertigo by Claudin's sheer composure, his insistence on applying the Marxist method to Marxism itself and his determination to understand rather than to blame. This book and the planned two volumes which will bring the study into present time are a political event in their own right.

The account begins in 1943 with Stalin's decision to dissolve the Comintern, the international coordinating body of world revolution, in order to facilitate negotiations with Truman and Churchill. With characteristic dryness, Claudin notes that within days the Holy Synod was restored in the SSSR and the Internationale was replaced by a patriotic national anthem in praise of Great Russia.

The dissolution formally marked the end of the era in which Soviet foreign policy had even lingering revolutionary aspirations. Instead of being a part of a united international workers' movement, it became a power above it. Both Mao and Tito were to come to power without and despite Stalin's help. In post-war Europe, Moskva was to insist that the armed Communists who had led the resistance drop their revolutionary ideas and accept the limits imposed by the capitalist democracies for waging the struggle.

In 1927, Bukharin had ridiculed Chamberlain's request, 'We have no objection at all in trading with you but would you mind winding up the Communist International.' In 1943, Stalin was to do exactly that. The world revolution had become synonymous with the SSSR and the SSSR was personified in J.V. Stalin. If the possibilities for revolution in the West or East conflicted with Stalin's assessment of Great Russia's needs, they were jettisoned. But under the marble-thick political façade of the SSSR, there were no soviets left to defend just a machinery of pre-selected 'reliable' congresses, pre-written rhetoric, compulsory confessions and the organised insanity of the purges.

This line of argument is not new. It was mapped out at the time of many of the events with an icy precision by Trotsky, although to advance it publicly even as late as the 50s was to risk the most hair-raising psychological and occasionally physical attack from the established Left. What is new in Claudin's contribution is the thoroughness and fairness with which he presents the issues and his insight into the internal mechanisms of Stalin's rule, derived no doubt from his own past as a functionary.

After tracing the early setbacks for the Third International, perhaps rather too critically in view of the enormity of the obstacles, Claudin settles into a detailed analysis of the Spanish Republic, whose defeat was such a prophetic omen. Although initially very small in relation to the dominant anarcho-syndicalist tradition in Spanish labour, the CP's organisational precision and the prestige and power it derived from the SSSR propelled the party to a commanding position during the Civil War. This influence was continually utilised to insist that the Republicans fight the war first and consider the revolution afterwards. This policy resulted, as usual, in losing both.

'The real choice,' insists Claudin, 'lay not between the establishment of a counter-revolutionary dictatorship and the consolidation of the bourgeois parliamentary republic, but between a counter-revolutionary dictatorship and a proletarian revolution.' The only way to stop Franco was with Lenin, not the crew of sub-Kerenskys who presided over the disintegrating republic, continually blocking the only measures – land seizures, factory occupations, the independence of Al-Maghreb – which were worth fighting for. 'Instead of adapting Marxism to the distinctive features of the Spanish revolution, we tried to adapt the Spanish revolution to the particular form of Marxism that had served for the Russian Revolution,' Claudin admits. He goes on to argue that the French Communist Party, under Stalin's tutelage, did everything to help the struggle of the Spanish proletariat, except what would have tipped the balance decisively in favour of the Spanish revolution – to pursue a revolutionary policy in France. For the Popular Front movement of 1936 in France was overtaken by a wave of factory occupations which was the biggest mass movement since the commune, but whose potential was never recognised or explored by the French Communist Party.

If St Just's motto 'those who make a revolution by halves dig their own graves' is relevant to the Spanish Republic and the Popular Front, it applies even more dramatically to the political opportunities lost by the workers' movement in Europe at the end of the Second World War. In northern Italia, in April 1945, the working class controlled the main industrial enterprises, local political power and command of 300,000 organised fighters. On the eastern frontier was the Yugoslav army, on the Austrian border the Soviet. Yet that potential strength was simply handed over to the Anglo-American military administration who proceeded to dismantle the popular committees of the resistance, return all goods and land to the owners and disarm the partisans. And if the Yalta deal was an opportunity lost in Italia, it was a literal tragedy in Éllas where the resistance was as revolutionary as in Jugoslavia and had obtained comparable support.

The Yalta carve-up allowed Churchill a free hand in Éllas and a '50 per cent influence' in Jugoslavia in return for letting Stalin do what he liked in Rumania, Balgarija and Magyarorszag. The Soviet military attache, from the hotel he shared with the allied brass, surrounded by resistance fighters, insisted that the Greek partisans would receive no arms or encouragement whatsoever. The British forces, direly needed to relieve the allied position in the Ardennes under threat from von Rundstedt's successful counter-offensive, were given a free hand to machine-gun Athinai. The price was not simply the 13,000 Greek partisans shot but the loss of Éllas, its socialist Left annihilated, to permanent clienthood to first British, then American imperial power. There was an alternative road, as Tito showed, but it meant breaking with Stalin and the moral and facing the material persecution and vilification that went with it.

There is an air of unreality about revolutionaries re-running history, so that the good guys win and the botched and beaten revolutionary attempts start again. Claudin is most careful to avoid this vice. He argues a more subdued but actually more impressive case. In España and France in 1936 and in France, Éllas and Italia in 1945, the elements of genuine revolution from below were present but were stifled before they were born. The old capitalist states were collapsing like sandcastles, some measure of local power was already in the hands of the workers. What developed might have fallen short of revolution but would certainly have produced a completely different map of Europe.

Here Claudin is forced back to the very root of revolutionary Marxism, the idea that the emancipation of the working class is the act of that class itself. The working class, Claudin insists, must be seen as an active, self-conscious force, not some kind of optional ingredient which can be replaced by an army or a police force, even if the substitutes wear socialist insignia. The regimes which were set up at the end of the Second World War were police dictatorships based on forced labour, not commune-states resting on workers' councils. The fact that private capitalism was mercilessly compressed into state capitalism meant nothing if the workers did not control the state.

To come cleanly to this kind of view requires considerable mental effort. For someone like Claudin, whose life has been wedded to a professional political orthodoxy, it shows a capacity for self-critical renewal which is truly inspiring. Two decades ago, if your god failed, the only alternative seemed to be various species of lucrative liberalism. But Claudin has returned from his priesthood in Stalin's religion to restart on a secular Marxism which can ask the hard questions of itself and he does so in the company of a new generation of revolutionaries no longer pinioned to Moskva.

8

Alternative Lenin*

It is impossible to write anything new or original about Lenin and mad to try. But until another revolution in an advanced country of equal moment arrives we are obliged to look back at the Russian Revolution and sift through its ambiguous legacy, just as the Bolsheviks studied the Paris Commune. The post-1968 student-based Leninisms were sometimes farcical but often more honourable than the noisily anti-Leninist libertarian groups who, by the 1980s, all seemed to have found their way into social democratic parties anyway. The man who arrived at the Finland Station was perhaps the most gifted political leader and uncompromising radical our century has witnessed. But to unearth and honour that radical spirit takes some doing.

Lenin remains a difficult figure to bring into political focus. Austere, plain, down-to-earth, he possessed a rare combination of practical realism and soaring imagination.

The Russian Revolution saved the honour of Marxism. Yet what has become of the Soviet Union proceeded to lose it again. Official Marxism–Leninism is now a more conservative cult than the Catholic Church and Lenin's curt, bearded brand image endorses some of the most repressive, boring and un-revolutionary states ever to exist.

There are more 'Leninist' parties than inverted commas, covering every sin from the ascendent bourgeoisie of Malawi to the doctrinaire Trots of Michigan. We have to sneak past the Mausoleum guards to meet the elusive, unpretentious genius of 1917, a leader 'straight as rails, simple as bread'.

It would make life a lot easier to dismiss Bolshevism en bloc as inherently hierarchical and inevitably dictatorial (as do the libertarian and anarchist comrades). And more soothing to some how persuade yourself that the various heads of state who flank the nuclear missiles

* First published in *Socialist Review*, 1975.
Review of *The Revolution Besieged*, vol. 3 of *Lenin*, by Tony Cliff.

in Red Square every year are socialist revolutionaries-of-a-sort after all (as do most Communists, some social democrats and a fair few Trotskyists).

It requires more imaginative effort to comprehend that the Russian Revolution was both overwhelmingly and genuinely a mass social revolution and yet that it began to lose its authentic socialist character within months of the workers' seizure of power.

Yet it is exactly this agonising and contradictory process which Cliff studies in *The Revolution Besieged* with commendable honesty and clarity. The skill with which the author co-mingles the heroic and the tragic makes this the most moving volume in what was in danger of becoming a worthy but somewhat tedious biography.

For those of the orthodox Right and the libertarian Left who see the Bolshevik slogans of self-emancipation and workers' control as convenient camouflage for the ambition of a minority party, Lenin is again and again shown in his most radical light, coaxing, exhorting, applauding and congratulating the initiatives of 'the ordinary' in emerging from the wings of history to centre-stage.

'Let us suppose for a moment that the Bolsheviks do gain the upper hand,' speculated the Petrograd equivalent of the *Daily Telegraph*, 'Who will govern us then; the cooks perhaps, those connoisseurs of cutlets and beefsteaks? Or maybe the firemen? Or perhaps the nursemaids will rush off to meetings of the Council of State between the nappy-washing sessions?'

Lenin had his answer:

> Comrades, working people! Remember **you yourselves** are at the helm of state. No one will help you if you yourselves do not unite and take into your hands all affairs of the state ... Get on with the job yourselves; begin right at the bottom, do not wait for anyone.

Socialism was to him nothing less than displaying the abilities, developing the capacities and revealing the talents 'so abundant among the people whom capitalism crushed, suppressed and strangled'. Addressing the Second All-Russian Congress of Soviets at the moment of the seizure of power, Lenin declared 'We must allow complete freedom to the creative faculties of the masses.'

The statements are too frequent and too passionate to discount, the results too spectacular. Despite siege, blockade and invasion, in felt shoes, chewing black bread, banging rusty typewriters and shouting down crackling telephones, the ordinary people fought, organised, educated, entertained, improvised and loved as never before. The country may have been enfeebled by prolonged war, blasted by well-provisioned armies of invasion, betrayed and sabotaged by the Cadets, bled dry by the immense, suspicious steppes, but it was **their** soviet Russia, theirs at last.

It's this democratic control which is the key to real human free dom, not the occasional ballot paper or the wording of the statutes. Cliff states the matter plainly.

> The liberation of the working class can be achieved only through the action of the working class. Hence one can have a revolution with more or less violence, more or less suppression of the civil rights of the bourgeoisie and its hangers-on, with more or less political freedom, but one **cannot** have a revolution, as the history of Russia conclusively demonstrates, without workers' democracy – even if restricted and distorted. Socialist advance must be gauged by the workers' freedom, by their power to shape their own destiny ....

As Cliff says elsewhere, 'The workers can get many, many things from the top, they can get reforms. The cow can get extra grass, the farmer can give her extra hay. The one thing the farmer will never give is the control over the shed. This has to be taken ....' All the Red hydroelectric dams and the battleships named after the Commune come to nothing if the workers do not control them.

Yet this book also documents, virtually on facing pages, quite how fast 'the old crap revives'. Long before the banning of factions in 1921 or the defeat of the Left opposition in 1927, the Bolsheviks took measures which undercut that workers' democracy which Cliff sees as the essential, indispensable element in socialist revolution.

Already by 1919, 'the Red Army was undeniably as far from Lenin's idea of a workers' militia as chalk from cheese.' In a mere eleven months, the number of secret police grew from 120 to 31,000 and the Extraordinary Commissions (the Cheka) had their own chain of authority, over-riding the Soviets.

The civil war sucked workers out of the factories and pulled industry out of shape. As workers' control and various forms of centralisation and methods of factory management were debated, Denikin and the invading armies called the tune. 'Industry was turned into a supply organisation for the Red Army and industrial policy became a branch of military strategy.'

The first exuberant wave of workers' power was obliterated by the firearms of the invading armies. The Red Army won a kind of victory in the civil war, but at what a price: 'the destruction of the proletariat that had made the revolution, while leaving intact the state apparatus built by it.'

From her cell in Breslau prison, Rosa Luxemburg wrote in October 1918: 'Everything that happens in Russia is comprehensible and represents an inevitable chain of causes and effects, the starting point and end term of which are: the failure of the German proletariat and the occupation of Russia by German imperialism.'

True, but then almost anything – including Stalin – can be justified by 'the force of circumstances'. One notes from Cliff's account a tendency within the Bolshevik Party to redefine their political aims and retreat from the commune-state so decisively sketched in *The State and Revolution* which Cliff rightly calls 'the apex of Lenin's writing – his real testament'.

Mysteriously, the dictatorship of the working class shifts its location from the Soviets to the Bolshevik Party, indeed to the centralised officials of that party. And in reality, party members, bound by voting discipline, could dominate the Soviet lists even before their organised rivals were banned. The state was not merely fused with the party, the soviets were subordinated to the Politburo, the Orgburo and the Secretariat.

After 1920, Kamenev, Zinoviev and most outrageously Trotsky in March 1921, arguing against the workers' opposition who took up exactly this point, began to call on the party's 'right to assert its own dictatorship'.

In that critical debate, Lenin, head in hands and taking copious notes, remained silent. In his final months of semi-coma, he reproached himself, using expressions like 'the fault is mine', 'I am to blame' and, in his last dictated note, 'I suppose I have been very remiss with respect to the workers of Russia'. Nigel Harris notes in this period '... Lenin's purely pragmatic tacking between two extremes. He seems to have lost his moorings, to be aware of the problem but to see no social force capable of solving it.'

He attempts to quell the tide without challenging head-on the new theory of the dictatorship of the party or re-asserting the themes of 1917. His last speech to Party Congress, in March 1922, has a surreal quality. 'The machine refused to obey the hand that guided it. It was like a car that was going not in the direction the driver desired, but in a direction someone else desired; as if it were being driven by a mysterious, lawless hand, God knows whose ...'

It would seem that the Bolsheviks not only made virtues out of necessities but to some extent fell victim of their very organisational prowess. The very eminence and indispensability of Lenin made his loss so devastating, especially since, in the Cliff account, it is only Lenin's incomparable rapport with the workers which enables him periodically to overcome the conservatism inherent in the illegal and highly professionalised Party.

The all-important role played by the tiny group of exile leaders inherent in the Bolshevik mode of organisation left an enormous gap in experience between them and the rapidly changing party rank and file. 'The proletarian policy of the party is not determined by the character of the membership but by the enormous undivided prestige enjoyed by the small group which might be called the old guard of the old guard of the party,' Lenin admitted grimly in 1922.

The very dependence of the underground party on skilled revolutionary functionaries is part of the reason it succumbed so swiftly to the bureaucrats of the old order who, Lenin complained, 'wear a red ribbon in their buttonholes and creep into warm corners'. The technique of selective appointment from above, perfected by Lenin in the early faction fights, now re-appeared in monstrous form, used to debar party Congress delegates from Samara who supported the workers' opposition or to insist on the election of a 'loyal list' of candidates in the Metalworkers' Union, despite the fierce protest of the Bolshevik engineers.

The absolute Bolshevik hostility to any kind of 'utopian' speculation seems to have left Lenin a little dazed and disconcerted when the external changes of the revolution began to hit people's inner consciousness. Yet he seems to regard Kollontai, Mayakovsky and dear old Lunacharsky as slightly childish for being concerned, in their different ways, with this problem. Certainly, in his notorious interview with Clara Zetkin and his polemic with the Proletkult group, he adopts old fart positions on sexual and cultural questions.

Anyone who thinks it is 'Leninist' to denounce attempts to alter ways of feeling and living as part of the making of socialism and resolutely to postpone such problems till somewhere over the rainbow and After-the-Revolution will be challenged by the limitations Cliff demonstrates in this aspect of Lenin's thinking. None of this is to belittle a man Reich called 'the greatest mass psychologist of all time'.

Rather it is to identify conflicting and unresolved elements in Lenin's politics, two souls to his socialism. We have a responsibility to select the aspects we now need to emphasise rather than attempt to imitate a 'pure' Leninism to order, which would be both impossible and irrelevant.

Part of Lenin's political make-up is that of the orthodox materialism of the Second International, whose philosophy is strongly affected by Victorian positivism, whose economics predict inevitable crisis and immiseration and whose politics aim at socialist majorities in existing governing assemblies. It was a misunderstood Marxism and with the dialectic deleted in which 'Marxist symbolics were preserved' but from which 'the revolutionary soul took flight', as Bukharin put it at Lenin's funeral oration.

Although Lenin's explosive rediscovery of Hegel and Marx, and his and Bukharin's radical new analyses of the unstable nature of modern imperialism, were to topple that era of mock-Marxism, Lenin was, until 1914, a disciple of Kautsky.

Cliff does not stress enough the extent of the reappraisal which led to the production of *The State and Revolution* and the degree to which its view of the party, the revolutionary state and socialism itself revise the traditional Bolshevik formulae. The research in the famous blue notebook was undertaken to repudiate the 'semi-anarchist ideas' Bukharin had submitted in July 1916 in an essay called 'Towards a Theory of the Imperialist State'. At this time Lenin still held the orthodox view that 'socialists are in favour of using the present state and its institutions in the emancipation of the working class.'

But in reviewing Marx and Engels on the Commune and the sharp exchanges between Pannekoek and Kautsky in 1912, he comes to the view that what is at stake is not a contest with the bourgeoisie over the state but **against** the state. Not an effort to take office in old chambers but make power in new forms. He sums up with characteristically explosive punctuation, 'One could perhaps express the whole thing in a drastically abbreviated fashion as follows: the **replacement** of the old ('ready made') state machine **and of parliaments by soviets of workers' deputies and their man dated delegates**. This is the essence of it!!'

This re-assertion of the commune-state and the adoption of the Trotsky-Parvus theory of permanent revolution, itself inspired by a re-reading of Marx, make possible the *April Theses*. And at the Finland Station, 'State-and-Revolution' Lenin has to struggle against the legacy of 'What-Is-To-Be-Done' Lenin in the form of a conservative party who found his ideas scandalous. **This** is the Lenin we need to rediscover after a half century when the dialectic was frozen over far deeper by J.V. Stalin et al than Herr Kautsky could ever manage.

Yet the problem is that the species of Leninism which entered the vacuum on the European and North American Left after the collapse of the mass movements of the 1960s and early 1970s was too often of 1903 not 1917 variety. The leaders of these largely self-appointed 'vanguards' are really twentieth-century Kautskys, well-read, confident that they possess all the necessary socialist knowledge if only the damn workers would read their articles.

Post-graduate unemployment has supplied them with a labour force of functionaries and even surrogate workers, all of whom can be depended on for their loyalty to the official view. The party rank and file exists in a guilty limbo which has a very sketchy understanding of working class experience.

The 'discipline' demanded of members of such groups is the obedience of automatons. Luxemburg precisely pinpointed the ambiguity in Lenin's praise of discipline:

> It is not making use of the discipline impressed upon him by the capitalist state, with a mere transfer of the baton from the hands of the bourgeoisie to that of the central committee, but only by breaking through and uprooting this slavish spirit of discipline that the proletariat can be prepared for a new discipline: the voluntary discipline of social democracy.

Rather than educating and being educated by the discussion of real experience, proletarian hostages are grabbed, lectured and exhibited as evidence. Formulas from *What Is To Be Done* and much virile talk about 'building the Party' and 'iron discipline' wrenched out of context and ill-understood. Sexual politics are taboo, obviously since machine-Leninism can't face the intimacy of their critique of hierarchy.

Standing in the same place for seventy-five years does lend one a certain authority, I suppose, but it would have given Lenin, for whom things changed all the time, fifty fits. And of course, if the working class spurn the proferred copies of *The Spark* or whatever and go up the pub to talk about Jeremy Thorpe's sex life, this only proves the abysmally low level of consciousness, backwardness and economism the vanguard suspected them of all along.

The 'trouble with Leninism' is not that it has been fetishised or repeated mechanically or contains destructive or male-dominated tendencies. All these misfortunes can and will befall a theory of organisation within capitalism without rendering it irreparable. The real problem is that the flowering of 1917 was so swiftly nipped in the bud that the fruit we have inherited has been largely damaged and diseased.

The blossoming-blighting process which Cliff documents froze over Leninism and only mass revolutionary working class action is able to melt it from its icy limbo. Lenin is therefore trapped in his moment, surrounded by a thicket and awaiting political rescue: 'An old communist conceives an embryo of longing.' One day, his Modern Prince will come. Until he is woken with the proletarian kiss, the problem is not that Leninism has failed, but that it has not been tried. And 'alternatives' to Leninism are often old reactions in new disguises, forms of terrorism, reformism and anarchism which were politically surpassed by Marxism a century ago.

This is very sad because the revolutionary essence of the Lenin of *The State and Revolution* is profoundly emancipatory, heartily contemptuous of people who think in the past tense and deserves a lot better. But as long as Leninism remains on this pathetic level, it provides the perfect excuse for people to revert to its mirror image liberal-anarchism (the other big late-1970s political growth industry), give up any organised collective attempt to change the world and sit around and discuss their relationships.

It is even sadder because even if everyone started buying *The Spark* and suddenly a scale-model replica Bolshevik party were reincarnated on Clapham Common, as Lenin himself has warned, it would be most unlikely to fit our needs. In an important passage in 1918, Lenin suggested 'The whole difficulty of the Russian revolution is that it was much easier for the Russian revolutionary working class to start than it is for the West European classes, but it is much more difficult for us to continue.'

They have ways of making sure it never happens here, like Len Murray, *Crossroads* and the *Morning Star* (as well as the SPG and the army). But when it does, the problems of sheer need which crushed the Bolsheviks are less pressing and the comparative strength and confidence of the modern working class is immensely more promising. If we need to be much more sophisticated to take power, it won't be so difficult to hold it.

'Leninism', said Norman Mailer in one of his annoyingly insightful moments, 'was built to analyze a world where all the structures were made of steel – now the sinews of Dragon Lady could hide them under her nail.' We don't just need a 1917 rather than 1903 Leninism, we need a post-electronic Leninism whose politics can move with astonishing ease from the details of a strike to the problems of childrearing, which has the centralised striking power to win street battles but the imagination to create in spiring carnivals, which is seeking not Euro-Reforms but a new way of life, love and government.

9

Sylvia Pankhurst*

Sylvia Pankhurst is one of the few British revolutionaries to have publically debated with Lenin. Indeed, she is largely known for having come off the worse for it. But she was a link between the British revolutionary movement of the nineteenth century, the world of Engels, Eleanor Marx, Kropotkin, Louise Michel and William Morris, and the era of briefly triumphant Bolshevism and the Third International of Lenin, Gramsci and Bordiga. In her journey between the two, she collaborated politically with the outstanding revolutionaries and labour leaders of the time, Tillet, Thorne, Mann, Pollitt, Larkin and Grayson. And in East London she sought to build a 'strong self-reliant movement among working women' and succeeded in editing a genuine worker's paper, The Dreadnought, *perhaps the first British socialist paper to use the phrase 'rank and file movement'. So if I am allowed one hero, it is her. There is still no biography which does her political justice, but I was given invaluable help in writing this tribute by the historians Lucia Jones and Sheila Rowbotham.*

Three women of the Pankhurst family dominated the struggle for women's suffrage in Britain. Mrs Emmeline Pankhurst married into a family with a history of radical and suffrage agitation and moved towards the socialism of the Independent Labour Party in the 1890s. The Women's Social and Political Union (WSPU) was founded in her front room in 1903 with the slogan 'Votes for Women'. Christabel, born 1880, her favoured elder daughter, was her fiery lieutenant in the suffragettes' war of broken windows, slashed paintings and burnt-out churches as the Votes for Women agitation reached its crescendo. Sylvia, born 1882, middle, less glamorous and less well-known daughter, broke, painfully, from her mother and sister. Between 1912 and 1922, she attempted to remake the once intimate connections between socialism and feminism, not in the industrial north where the women's suffrage began, but in proletarian London.

* First published in *Radical America*, 1974.

My interest, affection, it's hard not to call it love, for Sylvia Pankhurst has grown over the last five years spent practising as a doctor not half a mile from her old home in the Old Ford Road. East London is different now, studded with tower blocks and fenced with corrugated iron. But curiously the same. Still solidly proletarian, still the sweatshops and street-fights and rent strikes and plenty of old lady patients who remember 'our Sylvia' with a twinkle. Still the migrants, speaking Bangladeshi rather than Yiddish, still the dole queues, longer now than ever. And still a revolutionary socialist minority, of which I'm part, spouting at street corners, dishing out leaflets, spreading union membership, occupying hospitals due for closure. Sometimes I feel Sylvia's presence so sharply, it's like a political ghost leaning over my shoulder to look with anger and compassion at the wheezy infants and cooped-up young mothers and panicky grannies who live in the council blocks the Council has had the nerve to name after Shelley, Morris and Zangwill.

From 1910 onwards there was growing unease within the Pankhurst family and the WSPU. After 1912, on Christabel's instructions, the organisation concentrated on direct attacks on the property and person of the male members of the ruling class, carried out with much melodrama. Yet only two years later the same women became the most fervent opponents of Germany and Mrs Pankhurst transferred her vitriol to new targets – 'conscientious objectors, passive resisters and shirkers'. Working men did have a role after all, to bayonet each other in the trenches of the Somme. Christabel had been early to complain at Sylvia's speaking at mixed meetings; by the end of the First World War, she had bundled Bolshevism, sexual intercourse, strikes and venereal disease into a unified masculine conspiracy. As the WSPU became more despotic, it relied more and more on rich women who appear to have combined a radical break with sexual orthodoxy with a fairly conventional upper-class mixture of patronage and loathing for the lower orders.

In 1914 the long-awaited breach between Emmeline Pankhurst and her socialist daughter was made public with Sylvia's expulsion from the Women's Social and Political Union. Sylvia Pankhurst reported that the split came because 'we had more faith in what could be done by stirring up working women than was felt at headquarters, where they had more faith in what could be done for the vote by people of means and influence. In other words, they said they were working from the top down, we from the bottom up.'

She had moved in 1909 to live at Bow at the house of the Paynes, who were both shoemakers, and began to build suffragette branches with the help of a handful of middle class friends who shared her politics. She first approached known radicals, but soon attracted a group of working-class women leaders who were born agitators. Women like Charlotte Drake, ex-barmaid, labourer's wife and mother of five; Melvina Walker, a one-time ladies' maid and, like many of Pankhurst's supporters, a docker's wife, whose scandalous tales of high society made her a favourite speaker; and Mrs Creswell, a mother of six and married to a paint factory worker who eventually became Mayor of Poplar, one of the most radical of the dock area boroughs of London. At first the message spread among the tailoresses, serving women, factory girls and wives of Stepney, Limehouse, Poplar and Bermondsey, by word of mouth. The East London Federation's minutes record: 'Membership is growing through afternoon tea parties. The outdoor meetings were not successful; too cold.' But the colours of the East London Federation, the old suffragette purple and green with red added, were soon seen at early morning dock-gate meetings, Mothering Sunday marches, the traditional speaking sites at Victoria Park and Gardiner's Corner – where the male listeners raised the traditional cry, 'Wot about the old man's kippers!' – and on street pitches and outside picture places.

Pankhurst's constant and hectic political activity in those early days taught her details of the life of East London people. She got to know her way round the blank walls of the docks with their fortified entrances where the wealth of the empire passed through the hands of the very poorest. She sold papers outside gates which became an early morning parading ground of the workless desperate for casual labour. She was at home down the mean backstreets with their barrack dwellings, hard to keep clean, dangerous for play, costly to heat in winter and airless and dark in summer. She knew how hard it was to keep up the rent when work was uncertain. She sheltered in the blackness of Blackwall Tunnel at night, the only underground shelter during the war's bombing raids where mothers and babies huddled next to munitions wagons awaiting shipment to the Front, with the horses shivering and rearing with terror at the noise. Describing a 22 bus ride through London ending in the Isle of Dogs, she wrote:

> Leaving the broad river in its quiet. Leave the wide sky, mount again to the narrow streets, to the mean streets, to the tumbledown hovels among the massive factories, to the lovers with nowhere to go, who clasp each other in gloomy doorways. Great chimneys,

gaunt, great chimneys, fantastic shapes of elevators, and Venus that shines up there in the quiet sky. Majestic sadness. Stores of wealth kept here in bond amid the poverty.

East London, then as now, presents particular problems for political organisation. Its long history as a national port and merchant capital defined the geography of the city before industry grew up. Londoners remained divided according to trade and transport, with most manufacturers small, and many service in dustries. Paper flower-making, hat finishing or driving a cart was more likely than factory work. There are no mines and little shipbuilding in London. There were pockets of high capital investment where working conditions and union politics were more like Glasgow or Yorkshire (the Beckton Gas Works was the world's largest and employed 20,000), but light engineering, wood working and clothing manufacture in small workplaces were much more general. One in three working women were in service, mainly as cleaners. London trade unionism had been weakened by the 'commuting artisan', by the conservative outlook of the skilled craftsman, the isolation and powerlessness of the unskilled casual worker, by the relatively large proportion and poor organisation of the migrant and women workers. Nonetheless, in the national patchwork of pre-war militancy, London workers of both sexes were as active as those in the provinces. There were long strikes of women cleaners, biscuit makers and jam packers in 1909 and 1910.

With Pankhurst's leadership, these problems were addressed by the *Women's Dreadnought*, newspaper of the East London Federation, established in 1913. It exposed the conditions of women home workers, campaigned on behalf of single mothers and the victims of hat-pin abortions, published articles on 'The schooling of the future' and international affairs. It sold about 8,000 copies, with the Bow branch holding the record with a regular 800 a week and a claimed 1,600 in one week. Some sellers complained of the police, the difficulty of selling to immigrants who could not speak English and of male hecklers who 'crowded but did not buy ... giving us a very rough time'. But these problems were countered by determined and imaginative publicity campaigns with late-night *Dreadnought* 'chalking parties', 'red sticky-backs' and the hiring of a pleasure boat in Victoria Park from which were unfurled parasols spelling out DREADNOUGHT.

Pankhurst found her first real happiness among the Cockneys, who despite her middle class background took her to their hearts, calling her 'Our Sylvia' and providing her with a bodyguard called Kosher Hunt, a local prize fighter. From 1912, Mrs Pankhurst and Christabel, while stepping up the apparent militancy of their campaign for the vote, were moving to the right. After years of public organising and exhausting constitutionalism, the WSPU was transformed into an upper-middle-class urban guerilla army, commanded from a secret HQ in Paris.

By contrast, Sylvia Pankhurst's efforts to build an independent working women's movement in East London brought her in contact and co-operation with the revolutionary Left. In 1914 she intended the *Dreadnought* to widen the East London Federation's political interests. But by 1917 the paper was more concerned with the unity of the Left and full of optimism for the Russian Revolution. In October 1917, it was re-renamed the *Workers Dreadnought*. But the insistence on women's issues continued, both on local matters and in re-publishing articles by Alexandra Kollontai, Clara Zetkin, and Zinoviev on the necessity for women's councils and a Woman's International Congress. The extent and the sophistication of socialist feminist agitation carried out by the women's organisations of the Third International in the early 1920s remains curiously neglected even by feminist historians.

The War had effectively put a pistol to the political head of every political organisation and interrupted the steady growth of the causes of women and labour. It enabled state-organised official obedience to push back the initiatives being taken by the women, the workers and the Irish. The overwhelming majority of the socialist organisations, with various complicated rationales, ended backing the most pointless and brutal military slaughter in history, even those who had pledged, at conference after conference, their utter opposition.

The suffrage movement also fell first obediently, then enthusiastically, behind the war effort. Just as Pankhurst moved away from the women's vote issue towards general political agitation, so in 1915 her mother, financed by leading industrialists, went on a speaking tour of industrial and mining areas of Britain appealing to wives to resist Bolshevism and stop supporting the shop stewards. The polarisation was to gather speed; just before Pankhurst arrived in Moscow eager to debate with Lenin, her mother had been in the same city trying to rally support for the dying Kerensky regime. But even by 1914 the ways were parting. The prospect of martyrdom and glory did not appeal to the working women who had until then supported the suffrage campaign. The ladies broke the windows but the working women hung back.

Sylvia's sustained community organising in East London tried instead to get to grips with their more immediate problems – food, rent, and working conditions. The East London Federation campaigned against government calls for food rationing. When bread prices went up, they suggested: 'Someone should go into the shop and ask for it at normal prices and if it were refused, go and get a number to back her up and then take it.' They tried to start a 'No Vote, No Rent' strike but the idea was rejected by the WSPU because 'it was impossible to work it through their organisations as their people were widely scattered and it is only in working class homes that women pay the rent.' They also suggested to the Poplar Trades Council that 'the Russian example can be followed and the empty houses in any part be commandeered for people now in the workhouse.' The Federation was accustomed to working with local men trade unionists. They joined the general campaign against the 'sweated trades' and particularly took up the cause of women finishers who sewed buttons and seams on soldiers' trousers and demanded that 'if a woman does a man's work she shall have a man's pay.' Equal pay was of particular importance because women were sucked into traditionally male jobs when those men were sent to war. Union branches of the Stratford and Bromley railmen heard women speakers on adult suffrage, and the trades councils turned their members out on suffrage demonstrations.

The Federation was also adept at disguise and decoy so that Pankhurst and others could defy the 1913 Prisoner's (Temporary Discharge for Ill Health) Act, the 'Cat and Mouse' Act aimed to neutralise the tactic of hunger strike by allowing for temporary release and return to prison once health improved. Once out, Sylvia Pankhurst resisted re-arrest and made a defiant speech to the faces of the police in Trafalgar Square. The Federation also took up a campaign about the conditions in Holloway Jail where the women succeeded in getting the garters and proper teaspoons they had pleaded for, tiny victories that meant so much to women crushed by well-regimented pain. The scale of this East London agitation challenged the government. In 1920, during the intervention into Russia, the British Socialist Party, the Workers' Suffrage Federation and the shop stewards' movement led a united campaign for 'Hands Off Russia'. Dockers refused to load munitions for the Polish army of invasion and the heavers refused to coal the ship. The Workers' Suffrage Federation called on dockers' wives to support not only their husbands' campaigns but also to agitate at their own workplaces and on the public housing estates. This activity, which at one point had public speakers operative at over thirty open-air speaking sites in East London, did much for the Hands-Off-Russia campaign. British support for the Poles was stopped in its tracks.

Sylvia Pankhurst spread her ideas to other industrial towns in Britain and lectured in Denmark, Norway, Budapest and Vienna on socialism, suffrage, education and child care. In America she spoke on 'the garment workers' strike, drug fiends and juvenile delinquents, the Negro question'. She had particularly close links with the male engineering workers in Glasgow. But the activities in East London were in continual danger of caving in under the sheer weight of misery. The Federation had to create places where working class housewives could meet and support each other practically before it led them on to the streets and into the grim cells of Holloway Jail. A toy factory was started in Bethnal Green for workless women and run under a kind of workers' control with equal pay. From it sprang a creche where 'working mothers can leave their babies for the day at a charge of 3d a head. For this the children receive three meals, the loan of suitable clothes and are cared for in every way.' A pub, The Gunmakers Arms, was converted to a maternity centre, The Mothers Arms, with a resident nurse, cheap maternity foods and hygiene and health talks. By 1915 mother and baby clinics had been set up in Bow, Bromley, Poplar and West Ham, connected to *Dreadnought* readers' groups. Cost-price restaurants linked to the paper served stew and rice and meat pie and potatoes in Bow and Poplar. In Walthamstow a League of Rights was set up by the wives of soldiers and sailors to compaign for better treatment for servicemen.

It is true that by 1917 the East London Federation had not produced great results. The distress relief always tended to become a disguised form of charity instead of the working women's self-activity that was intended. What with people running off with the cash, the co-operative factory being bankrupted by commercial firms and the maternity nurse watering down the milk, only bits of the Federation's private welfare schemes remained to be taken up by Poplar Council. The Federation was aware of the danger of merely providing services as a form of political charity, but certain that without collective provision for some of the working woman's burdens, it was fanciful to demand she step forward and emancipate herself. And the creches, kitchens, choirs and clinics were themselves organised in a radical fashion. Socialist doctors and psychologists gave talks on sexual matters, the nursery nurses practised Montessori methods, advice on contraception was almost certainly given informally. During the war the Federation spread itself from its East London heartland to form branches in Birmingham, Nottingham, Glasgow and Wales. By 1918 it had small groupings in twelve of the major towns which emphasised day-to-day women's issues within a wider framework of socialist demands.

Sylvia Pankhurst's fierce and consistent opposition to the war, although applauded by the Scots engineers and Welsh colliers, in fact cut her off from her old friends in East London. Hope came only from afar, from the Bolsheviks and the Soviets in Russia. It was to them and the Communist Parties being organised throughout the world in the glow of the Russian Revolution that Pankhurst and her supporters turned. Like most British socialists, she was probably unsure what exactly Bolshevism was and certainly unclear about its relationship to her feminism, but she was to adopt wholly for the next few years its aim, the revolutionary overthrow of capitalism. As she told the judge who tried her in 1919 for agitating among the forces:

> I started four clinics and have sat up night after night with the little ones. I also set up a day nursery but all my experience shows me it was useless to try to palliate an impossible system. It is the wrong system and has got to be smashed. I would give my life to smash it.

When Pankhurst drew up the agenda for the Rank and File convention which met in 1919 to discuss the theories of Soviet power, and to which she proposed her idea of the 'social soviet' which would organise workers where they lived, far from abandoning her feminism, she was attempting to relate it to a new political era. For example, in an article on the shop steward movement published in Gramsci's *L'Ordine Nuovo*, she explained to Italian readers the meaning of the foreign phrase 'rank and file movement'. Her perception of the potential of the rank and file movement and the need to link the factory council with the social soviet, the need to 'translate' the Soviet experience into Western European conditions, are a contribution which make her a founding mother of today's revolutionary movement, even if she was fated to make connections in her theory which she couldn't forge in practice.

10
The Kerouac Connection*

The Beats are at present doing well in the laundromat of style and a complicated and scholarly circle of enthusiasts meet and correspond, in part through Dave Moore's excellent little mag The Kerouac Connection. *Whether this leads to people actually reading Kerouac rather than attempting to dress like him, I don't know. But he was a prodigiously gifted writer quite apart from the myth. And his premature death was a much deeper shock than the regrettably predictable death of the various rock stars our generation is supposed to have spent the 1970s mourning.*

Ti Jean, Vanity Duluoz, Sal Kerouac, you're gone now. You died age 46 in your house in Lowell, Mass. where you lived with your crippled mother and suspicious wife of one year, Stella, and they decided to do to you the American death thing and have you mummified, thread your veins with formaldehyde, tie a bow tie in position and clad your face in certain deathly cosmetics. And though Ginsberg, Orlovsky and Holmes stayed by you gently all night, dawn was soon and a Massachusetts funeral.

Marmite and Bop

To read Kerouac when you were 15, scrabbling through the Ks of Slough Public Library, was a coded message of discontent; the sudden realisation of an utter subversiveness and licence. He legitimised all the papery efforts of a child writer, dream books, pretend novellas, invented games, planned and described walkouts. He expressed a solution to the pent-upness, exitlessness of youth, that feeling of wanking off inside all the time. Everyone I know remembers where they were when they read *On the Road*, whether newly expelled from

* First published in *OZ*, 1969.

school, public librarians (trainee) in Hammersmith, car park attendants in Dorking, knowledgeable Eisenhower drunks or hospital porters, because of the sudden sense of infinite possibility. You could, just like that, get off out of it into infinite hitchhiking futures. Armed only with a duffle coat, you could be listening to wild jazz on the banks of the Tyne or travelling east–west, across the Pennines. Mostly we never actually went, or the beer wore off by Baldcock High Street and you were sober and so cold. But we were able to recognise each other by that fine, wild, windy prose and the running-away motif that made so much sense. I, like ten thousand other fifth formers, wrote series of letters in imitation of Kerouac, spiralling indiscriminate word patterns and being able, in his shadow, to write thewordstogether if I so wanted to. A Canadian friend who thought he was Dean Moriarty sent me a notebook bound in smelly red cellophane about his runaway with an autocycle and packet of Marmite sandwiches which he was forced to abandon in a snow-drift after two miles. The notebook was about 80 pages yet seemed proper and as it ought to happen and all accountable within the terms of spontaneous bop prosody. Jazz was the other part of *our* underground because it meant beer and beards and arguing about the 4th trumpet in Kenton's reconstructed front line like stamp collectors.

We would get three-quarters drunk and listen to Charlie Parker who seemed to be trying to sound like Kerouac too if you listened to the breath sounds and the oral punctuation. 'Yes, jazz and bop, in the sense of a, say, tenor man drawing a breath and blowing a phrase on his saxophone, till he runs out of breath, and when he does, his sentence, his statement has been made ... that's how I therefore separate my sentences as breath separations of the mind ... there's the raciness and freedom and humour of jazz instead of all that dreary analysis and things like "James entered the room and lit a cigarette. He thought Jane might have thought this too vague a gesture." When Hoagy Carmichael heard Bix Biederbeck, he fell off his chair. When Tom Paine was in hiding, he found shelter at the home of William Blake. 'Now I'd been getting bored with the stereotyped changes that were being used all the time and I kept thinking there's bound to be something else. I could hear it sometimes but I couldn't play it. I was doing alright until I tried double tempo on Body and Soul. Everyone fell out laughing. I went home and cried and didn't play again for three months.'

Red Shift, Big Bang

Kerouac's writing started with home-drawn comic strips, home-made comix, whole childhood exercise book novels, long systems for horse racing and basketball games in the comfort of your front room, played with symbols and pieces of paper money.

> At 18 I read Hemingway and Saroyan and began writing terse little stories in that general style. Then I read Tom Wolfe and began to write in the rolling style. Then I read Joyce and wrote a juvenile novel like *Ulysses* called *Vanity of Duluoz*. Then came Dostoevsky. Finally, I entered a romantic phase with Rimbaud and Blake which I called my 'self-ultimacy period', burning what I wrote in order to be self-ultimate. At the age of 24, I was groomed for the Western idealistic concept of letters from reading Goethe's *Dichtung und Wahreit*. The discovery of a style of my own based on a spontaneous get-with-it, came after reading the marvellous free narrative letters of Neal Cassady, a great writer who happens to be the Dean Moriarty of *On the Road*.

Cassady might, reluctantly, be compared to Trotsky in his historical span. Just as Trotsky is the sole link between Bolshevism and the post-war revolutionary movement, so it was Cassady who was the only human link between the West Coast beats and the post-Leary hippies, acting as the driver of Ken Kesey's acidic bus 'Further'. He stayed magnificently the same. In Kerouac he's this incredible talker, lost into a blue streak that's going to last all his life, pulsating even when silent,

> where once Dean would have talked his way out, he now feels silent himself, but standing in front of everyone, ragged and broken and idiotic, right in front of the light bulbs, his mad face covered with sweat and throbbing veins, saying 'Yes, yes, yes' as though tremendous revelations were pouring into him the whole time now, and I am convinced they were, and the others suspected as much and were frightened. He was BEAT-the-root, the soul of beatific.

And 10 years later, when drug-casseroled ex-novelist Kesey makes his American migration, there Cassady sat driving the bus.

> Cassady had been a rock on this trip, the totally dependable person. When everyone else was stroked out with fatigue or the various pressures, Cassady could be still counted on the move. It was as if

he never slept and didn't need to. For all his wild driving, he always made it through the last oiled gap in the maze, like he knew it would be there all the time, which it always was. When the bus broke down, Cassady drove into its innards and fixed it. He changed tyres, lugging and heaving and jolting and bolting with his fantastic muscles popping out striation by striation and his basilic veins gorged with blood and speed.

Now Cassady's dead too. His body was found beside a railroad track outside the town of San Miguel de Allende in Mexico. It was said that he had been despondent and felt that he was growing old and had been on a long downer and had made the mistake of drinking alcohol on top of barbiturates. His body was cremated.

Bullet Beat

Cassady's writing had started, like Kerouac's, in the slow, painstaking, creative-writing-course-by-post way. Then he wrote *The First Third*, a novel about his childhood with his alcoholic father in the Denver alley wineshops and Greyhound station johns and the way they talked to each other (like Kesey's acid-soaked *Pranksters*) with 'minds weakened by liquor and an obsequious manner of existence, seeming continually preoccupied with bringing up short observations of obvious trash, said in such a way as to be instantly recognisable by the listener, who has heard it all before and whose own prime concern was to nod at everything said, then continue the conversation with a remark of his own, equally transparent and loaded with generalities.' Cassady sent Kerouac a 40,000 word letter (now called the *Joan Anderson* letter) which Kerouac describes as 'the greatest piece of writing I ever saw, better'n anyone in America, or at least enough to make Melville, Twain, Dreiser, Wolfe, I dunno who, spin in their graves' and which disappeared overboard into the sea. Kerouac and Cassady could talk each other into a state of semi-trance where their unrepressed word-slinging hotted up into a big shoot-out, bullet words whizzing backwards and forwards with words that were slippery without being gelatinous and made you tremble when you read them. 'We did much fast talking, on tape recorders, way back in 1952 and listened to them so much we both got the secret of LINGO in telling a tale and figured that was the only way to express the speed and tension and the extatic tomfoolery of the age.'

Kerouac/Cassady learned from this to curve and move their acoustic prose in the air, sustaining the long line by breath, rubbish image, riff, dazzling phrasing making an awkward tightrope walk like Chaplin about to fall but never quite doing so since able to 'add alluvials to the end of your line when all is exhausted but something has to be said for some specified irrational reason.' It's Kerouac's sound , not the coterie poetics of Creely/Olson that is behind Ginsberg's rush on language. And from all three Americans the florid young British poets of the 1950s fed, snatching bootlegged copies from Ferlingetti's *City Lights Press* and the other artistic contraband which made possible the dense undergrowth of the British small poetry magazines (especially *Poetmeat*, early *Underdog*, and the shortbreathed and 'substantial' *New Departures*). Mike Horovitz, whose mattress prose, too, is interior sprung, describes the impact of the American orals on off-the-page British poetry wonderfully well in his afterwords to Penguin's *Poetry of the Underground in Britain*.

Ferlingetti had always been social and political – 'all this droopy corn about the beat generation and its being "existentialist" is as phoney as a four dollar piece of lettuce ... only the dead are disengaged. And the wiggy nihilism of the beat hipster, if carried to its logical consequences, actually means the death of the creative artist himself.'

Ginsberg increasingly became political after his decision to 'expose self and accuse America'. But sez Kerouac, 'I agree with Joyce, as Joyce said to Ezra Pound in the 1920s, "Don't bother me with politics, the only thing that interests me is style".' Nowadays he seems to dismiss the holy goofing groin cats and wine lips of the San Francisco poetry gang: 'Ferlingetti and Ginsberg, they are very socialistically minded and wanted everyone to live in some sort of frantic kibbutz, solidarity and all that. I'm a loner.' Kerouac was the lonesome traveller jumping out of cars, into fruit waggons, merchant holds, going and going as if by his movement alone he could became a molecule in a marvellous unity. He deeply wanted to believe in a total unification of the Golden Buddhist eternity; his religion was his ultimate resource and he saw it mostly in nature; the misty swelling and blooming of the seasons, sea and redwood trees he watched over for a spell. This was the wonderful still centre within all his energy; the baby Ti Jean with kitten and candy bar on a pillow while the absolutely evil Dr Sax caused the swollen oily river to rise sucking and slapping in the streets of Lowell.

It is said that as a child Kerouac was discovered trying to fuck the world; found with his prick buried in soil.

What Happened

This handsome travelling man who sings and writes across the hugeness of the States is a great figure of the real migrant American. In the false America of the 1950s of Ike and Perry Mason's fight against freedom, in the symbol-worshipping, silent, bad sociology writing, thick 1950s, his very existence was a protest. Against that world's addiction to the inanimate, Kerouac's response was not political or critical – just damned them with his energy. Against the moral ruin of the world, he replied in every second of his hour with the creative act. He insulted them, almost without knowing it himself, with his exuberance, his wonder, his emotions, almost crazed by the torrent of experience and finally devoured by its own appetite. Compared with him, the alleged novelists of dissent on this side of the Atlantic look and were mean, conservative and trivial.

But he seemed imprisoned within his wonder and his age, the 1950s. He doesn't so much develop as a writer as accumulate, reworking the themes of his witness of the Beats, of his brother Gerard and family, of Mexico City and Paris with a steadily growing intensity. The compulsive nature of his writing could turn pathological; drugs and writing were the organising principles of his life, and death. 'Notoriety and public confession in literary form is a frazzler of the heart you were born with, believe me.' He was unable to alter the pace set by his mind which was as out of breath at 45 as it was at his hallucinated 15. He wrote, like Victor Serge, single spacing on a continuous typewriter roll at a punishing rate (in Tangier he typed *Naked Lunch* for Burroughs). *The Subterraneans* was written in three days, a physical feat much harder than the athletic struggles of the windy field, leaving him as white as a sheet and having lost 15 pounds and looking strange in the mirror. His babble-brook book *Sartori in Paris* was written on cognac and malt whisky. *Tristessa*, the fine mystic novel about a Mexican girl faint for morphine, and the remarkable Mexico City poems, were direct from his life in Mexico where his life and writing intersected dangerously. The vain records of the pageantry of the West-Coast Beats *Desolation Angels*, *Big Sur* and *The Subs* indicate the pace at which he lived, the tension level at which the books are charged. *Book of Dreams* used even his sleeping life for material 'in a style of a person half awake from sleep and ripping it out in pencil by the bed ... yes, pencil ... what a job, bleary eyes, insaned mind bemused and mystified by sleep, details that pop out even as you write them, you don't know what they mean till you wake up, have coffee, look at it and see the logic of the dream from the language itself.' He was the last American to write quite like this: the great Romantic, a naked sheet wound round experience and registering it in wonder – 'the true story of what I saw and how I saw it.'

As he grew unrelentingly older, he grew, logically, patriotic and sentimental. A rare public meeting he spoke to in Southern Italy was broken up by dumbfounded Italian kids when he defended the American war in Vietnam. His drunkenness, male adventuring, lumberjack clothes (now looking uncannily like the handsome Ronald Reagan) were of a different world now. He must have sensed it was impossible to keep hold of his old human universe when he retreated to his bungalow in Lowell. Like Dylan, his quietism is only objectionable if you interpret it politically; which of course you have to. When people started fighting back against the monster America, the nutcase radicals, Trotskyists, Black Panthers, they do so in a way that excludes him ... even disgusts him. For now protest is nowhere near enough. It's too conventional and we need to fight America with all the science it is using to destroy us. And we must win.

We have to blaspheme against Kerouac's religiosity and be wary of his colossal nervous system. He is a precious voice but from the past. When we win we can name streets and stars after him.

11
Lennonism*

John Lennon is the ultimate missing link. Not only was he a great artist but, unusually, he moved to the Left as his art matured. Had he stayed in Britain, he would have stayed alive and maybe involved with Rock Against Racism and the Great Miners' Strike of 1974/5. However heartening events like the Mandela Concert are, it is sad that the rock musician who first made the music and modern politics play together isn't there.

We already know the story. A lad from Liverpool seized black rhythm and blues and transformed it. The sound that white America found too funky for its clean earlobes was re-synthesised by the Beatles and ricocheted out of Matthew Street and the Reeperbahn to recapture Teensville USA. J.W. Lennon, grammar-school dissident and art-school yobbo, used the idiom of rock and roll to charm London into cultural submission, drive Britain half-crazy with excitement and enchant the world. But then saw through the corporate pantomime and, with Yoko Ono, turned the tables on his prodigious fame, discovered Art and Politics and mixed them with feminism to become, in a swift series of transmogrifications, a cynic who spoke for utopian socialism, a roughneck who pleaded for peace, an anti-sexist sex symbol and an advocate of the one male role never mentioned in rock and roll – that of father. Self-exiled in a country which idolised him without beginning to understand his talent, he was treated to that great nation's highest reward for achievement – assassination. *Sic transit gloria mundi*. Or, as the motto of the Quarry Bank Boys Grammar School put it, 'Out of this rock, you will find truth.'

But what truth does such a cruelly truncated life tell? If judged artistically – which is what he always wanted but seldom got – it is clear that Lennon and the Beatles transformed the face of post-war

* First published in *London Review of Books*, 1985.
Review of *John Winston Lennon*, vols I & II, by Ray Coleman, and *John Lennon, Summer of 1980*, by Yoko Ono.

popular music, establishing a new sort of audience, pioneering the stereo LP as a new form, and introducing avant-garde material into the mainstream of what had been a limited and conservative genre. If Lennon had done nothing after *Sergeant Pepper's Lonely Hearts Club Band*, he could still be compared, without facetiousness, to Bob Marley or Duke Ellington as a popular musician who was able to transform his own music from within. But what of the work he was planning in what he called, in an interview shortly before his murder, 'another forty years of productivity'?

For the musical purist, Lennon's music had been declining for years, its rock and roll wellspring poisoned by an excess of conceptual art. For the Beatle fan, still longing for a miraculous reunion, the fall from grace had been the break with Paul McCartney engineered by the wily Oriental Ono – dislike of whom was powered by racism as well as philistinism and envy. For the socialist, Lennon was irredeemably disorientated by his isolation from the realities of working class life. For the aesthete, he was stultified by the permanent juvenility of the rock world. For the moralist, a man who could never be forgiven for ditching his wife. For the sociologist, an example of the perils of vertical mobility. And for the numerologist, proof of the malevolence of the number 9. But had he lived, would he have entered 1985 rocking around the pit villages of Wales and South Yorkshire – or making a repentant celebrity appearance on *Stars on Sunday*?

It cannot be said that the volumes under review offer much aid to understanding what was happening inside John Lennon's mind. Of those people who should not attempt to write biographies of Lennon, Ray Coleman heads the list. A trade editor who might as well have been writing about agricultural machinery as music, he embodies everything Lennon had to fight: social conservatism, intellectual shallowness, gravestone prose, and the sheer boredom of the showbiz mentality. Coleman clearly admires Lennon and has conducted some routine interviews with him (in which Lennon's animosity is sometimes ill-concealed). He has the confidence of Cynthia Lennon, the first wife, and has spoken to Yoko Lennon after the murder. Indeed, this is a concise and accurate account of a complicated life, a workmanlike job. But when Coleman attempts to understand the conflicts within Lennon, and their relationship to political and social events in the outside world, he flounders rapidly into nervous platitudes. 'What Beatlemania had brought John, above all, was freedom. Or so he thought.' Ironically, Coleman's ostentatious deference to the authority figures in Lennon's life – William Ernest Pobjoy, the luckless headmaster of Quarry Bank Grammar School, once tannoyed at Goodison Park to deal with an outbreak of Lennonist insubordination, Aunt Mimi ('the guitar's alright as a hobby, but you'll never make a living'), and the teachers at Liverpool College of Art – draws inadvertent attention to the conflicts with authority that honed Lennon's famous 'edge'.

In some of the *Summer of 1980* photos, Lennon wears an interesting clue round his neck: it is nothing less than his old school tie. For one is forced by reading this book to concede that Lennon's particular talent is as much a tribute to the post-war grammar school as it is to the wonders of Little Richard. Brought up by the bookish and financially comfortable Aunt Mimi, Lennon was shaped by the conflicts of the bright working-class kid in the grammar crammer. Selected to make social progress and clearly intellectually able, he instead devoted his entire talent to in discipline – notably 'answering back' and the production of the Daily Howl, a fantasy satirical newspaper. It was exactly the people like Lennon who ought to have been grateful, working for good references and university entrance, who remained tenaciously loyal to their real class identities but expressed that loyalty in intricate 'apolitical' sarcasm and satire: inventive, intelligent indiscipline being the most comprehensive response to a system which 'hates you if you are clever and despises a fool'. In the course of his engagement with sabre-toothed schoolmasters, Lennon polished the anarchic, 'sarky' wit which made *In His Own Write* such a genuine, if overpraised linguistic pleasure, and bowled over the American news reporters.

Lennon himself sidestepped neatly into Liverpool Art School: in 1967 he sent a hallo 'even to Pobjoy who got me into art school so I could fail there as well.' Coleman does give a sense of the contradictions at this stage in his account: mini-skirts, but weeping in the Ladies over missed periods, 'drainies' carefully tightened by girlfriends, hungover mornings in a coffee-bar called the Jacaranda, the whole mixture of fierce ambition, drunken sarcasm, pretentiousness and authenticity lived to the point of self-laceration. Lennon humps his way into lettering classes, guitar over his shoulder, no doubt muttering fiercely to himself: 'No one I think is in my tree.' And this experience of growing up artistically is set, not in Jagger's Dartford or Bowie's Bromley, but in the heart of Liverpool, still an Atlantic port, still a centre of syndicalist militancy, and, after the 1956 split in the Communist Party, a base of the Socialist Labour League rather than the university-based New Left, home of Jerry Dawson's Merseyside

Unity Theatre, where the classics were translated into Scouse, seedbed of poetry and stronghold of music hall as well as of the high culture of the Walker Gallery and the orchestras. Arthur Ballard, one of Lennon's teachers at the Art School, has rightly said that it took twenty years' work to create the culture which produced John Lennon. A deeper study of this period would show Lennon systematically accumulating subversive influences and then sealing them in the irresistible sound of black American music, as translated into Scouse.

For, in an almost exact reversal of the golden triangle of the slavers, the Liverpool rebels in the age of affluence took from the black musicians of proletarian North America exactly those songs which, under nonsense codicils like 'Be Bop a Lula' or 'Bonie Maronie', most urgently reflected the rhythmic intensity and emotional drama of the music of Africa. In a curious way, the experience of belonging to a subordinate culture was a common element.

Lennon certainly rejected the dominant art-school affection for a jazz which had mysteriously removed blackness and which Lennon associated with 'all those bloody musicians and their GCEs'. In an interview with David Scheff, he insists again that although rock and roll first came into his consciousness through white singers like Bill Hayley, Elvis Presley and the most marked white influence on the Beatles, Buddy Holly, it was the original black music which 'changed our lives when we heard it' and knew 'it was something strong and powerful and beautiful.' And the particular R and B Lennon favoured went unreported in the *Melody Maker* and unplayed on the BBC (although with luck available on Radio Luxembourg's uncertain airways), and was obtained, not in record stores, but in the quayside pubs from visiting seamen. Just as dub was a *sine qua non* for punks in the halcyon days of 'Louise's' and 'The Roxy', and the sound of bebop storming the Winter Palace of jazz is once again the badge of dance-floor radicalism, so Lennon's adoption of the R and B originals was a statement of defiance – part of the process of putting imperialism into reverse which was later to produce the black-led uprisings in the great slave ports of Liverpool and Bristol in 1980 and 1981.

But it was in the port of Hamburg that Lennon says he finally grew up. There the band worked out their combination of R and B roots, rocker swagger and art-school chic. They were still kids, and exploited kids at that. Their promoter, Bruno Koschminder, forced them to live in three filthy rooms behind the Star Club's cinema screen, and to play six forty-five-minute sets each night, exhorting them with the vehemence of an ex-Panzer trooper to 'Mak show! Mak show!' and getting them deported for unauthorised jamming. Here Coleman busily defends the Beatles against claims of debauchery but is tantalisingly brief about their contact with their first intellectual fans, the group of Hamburg bohemian radicals around Astrid Kirchherr and Klaus Voormann whom Lennon called 'the exis'. Stuart Sutcliffe, the painter whom Lennon had recruited to play bass, fell in love with Kirchherr, a fashion designer and photographer.

In most cases, the pop star's rebel pose is laughable hypocrisy: successes in the pop world are egocentric, ignorant and conformist. Lennon's radicalism had more tenacious roots: in the particularities of Liverpudlian class consciousness, in the authentic music of the North American ghettos that he sought out and refashioned, and in the ironies and ambiguities of a European existential attitude. These influences explain his otherwise inexplicable dissatisfaction with what the Beatles became, and they explain his love affair and artistic collaboration with Yoko Ono, which both saved his life and, by Americanising it, brought to an end what was most durable and important in his artistic make-up.

The meeting with Ono which begins Coleman's second volume is legend. Whacked out on psychedelics and lack of sleep, Lennon succumbs to a piece of cutesy-pie conceptualism by Ono in the dreaded Indica Gallery, headquarters of druggy pretension. And the glimpses Coleman gives us of this period are a nasty mixture of the pseud and the ruthless, with the Beatles giggling at their toes while George Martin organises the aural shifts of *Sergeant Pepper*, and with Lennon first ignoring his first wife and then citing her non-existent infidelity to get custody of his son Julian. It would have taken a Manhattan avant-gardist brought up as a scion of the Bank of Tokyo and educated at Sarah Lawrence to cut through this bedraggled but corrupt crew. But what Ono seems to have told Lennon is only another version of the sort of advice Arthur Ballard seems to have already given him. Ono insisted that he was an artist and ought to be proud of it, that his bewildered aggression unsuccessfully concealed a wounded soul, and that the voracious masculinity of rock and roll would kill him. She also told him that she loved him as a brave, hurt, talented, confused human being and not as the most witless of people, a pop star. Whatever one feels about her art and her political philosophy (and I loathe them both), her intelligence and bravery are not in doubt, and she more than anyone prevented Lennon from making the traditional rock star exit as either a bloated drug-raddled corpse or a bloated Tory.

Rather than some dreadful deviation, his creative relationship with Ono was a return: a new equivalent to the camaraderie of the Quarrymen, Liverpool School of Art and the Exis and a relationship with a woman who could collaborate with him artistically. Lennon and Ono succeeded in creating music which was at the same time popular and avant-garde, stylised and expressive, candid and artful. In *Plastic Ono Band* and *Imagine* he at last reveals the full scope of his voice – alternately raucous, tender and disturbing – using language and ideas which are precise and harrowing. And in the socialist stompers and revolutionary anthems of *Some Time in New York City*, he brilliantly brought his rock-and-roll method of composition – 'Say what you mean, make it rhyme and put a backbeat to it' – to a political subject-matter. Agitprop dates quickly, but Lennon's subjects were well chosen and of real importance to the insurgent American Left in the early 1970s: the massacre of Attica State Prison, Angela Davis's persecution, the punishment of the radical leader John Sinclair with a ten-year sentence for possessing marijuana, and the Bloody Sunday shootings by the British army which had brought the situation in Derry to international attention. The personal monologues like 'Crippled Inside', 'Jealous Guy' and 'Working-Class Hero' – which has been brilliantly re-recorded by Marianne Faithfull, one of the very few singers who persists with Lennon's range of emotional and sexual-political reference – permanently expanded the range of the pop song. And the other statements – the bed-in, the films on rape and on James Hanratty, the solidarity with *OZ* magazine, the stunning performance, at twenty-four hours' notice, by the Plastic Ono Band at the Toronto Peace Festival – added up to a remarkable, if uneven achievement.

But this collaboration had a price, and that price was the permanent and, one must conclude, highly damaging exile. Although ostentatiously draped in the colours of Manhattan ('New York,' he said quite wrongly, 'is like a Liverpool that has got it together'), *Some Time in New York City* is in spirit the most Liverpudlian record he ever made, with its promiscuous allegiances, its poetic-political passion, its sheer jauntiness. But that section of the American Left which they encountered in New York was heading for catastrophe, making their stoned plans for cultural insurrection as SDS splintered into Stalinist sects and the Black Panther Party was systematically gunned down. Partly in reaction to the Yippy fiasco, and after a series of reproductive disasters, Lennon steered himself into a well-upholstered isolation which he devoted to bringing up his second son,

Sean, while Yoko moved from performance art to the administration of Lennon's business empire, plotting – to great effect, apparently – the purchase of breeding heifers by means of the horoscope. The man who had looked for a moment like the Lenin of the Rock and Roll Party seemed to have succumbed to the rock star grandiosity which the punks were, by 1977, so effectively denouncing.

Coleman's chronology increasingly features whinge-worthy entries about birthday presents of vintage Rolls-Royces, diamond hearts and mounds of fresh gardenias. The remnants of radical conceptualism consisted of having love messages sky-written over Central Park. If Ono rescued him from one kind of disaster, he appeared to have landed in another: the uncritical admiration of an entire generation of Americans – photographers oozing unction, self-promoting interviewers, minor pop stars with alcohol problems, and the battery of servants who showed the depth of their devotion by filching and flogging off Lennon memorabilia and memoirs after his death. In Lennon's circumstances, flattery is as dangerous as heroin, and Coleman's account of his circle shows him as almost wholly lacking contact with any intellectual or artistic equals. Almost all the photos in Yoko Ono's sad assemblage give the impression that he doesn't really know where he is.

It is remarkable that white rock musicians who pay exaggerated homage to the roots of their black musical heroes are so offhand about their own. Lennon's music was successful internationally, but what gave it its originality was his response to the very specific origins: the anglicised R and B, the intensities of the grammar and art schools of the time, the insubordinate popular culture of the North of England. Detached from its source-materials, and never relocated culturally, his work was eventually to turn into the vacuous soup of *Double Fantasy* and *Milk and Honey*, albums recorded just before his murder. There is an insistent sense that, against one's hopes, corporate America had killed Lennon long before Mark Chapman got to him.

12

Billie and Bessie*

A paid-up blues fanatic, I have never managed to understand the depth of my own obsession. This essay was an attempt to try. I think it was Dennis Potter's brilliant TV series The Singing Detective *which is about, in part, the allure of sentimentality in music, which finally explained it. The cynical ballard singer-cum-detective played by Michael Gambon, whose sexual self-repression is a kind of psoriasis, muses at one point, 'There are songs to sing. There are feelings to feel. There are thoughts to think. That makes three things. And you can't do* three *things at the same time. The singing is easy. Syrup in my mouth. The thinking comes with the tune. So that only leaves the feelings .... But you're not going to catch me feeling the feelings.' Which was exactly what Holiday and Smith did. It was also an attempt on my part to write about the rise of black music in this American century and to recall my own shock of seeing segregation in the Deep South in the mid-1960s. And, hopelessly, to understand the power of women.*

The blues is a feeling. For most of this century, music has been the only vehicle black America has been permitted to tell its story, to say what it feels and what it wants. From the harshest of slave systems has come the most moving art produced by modern America. And the source of the power of the blues singers has been their ability to empty out their experience of suffering and longing in the most direct and emotionally forceful idiom.

For what Bessie Smith and Billie Holiday have in common is not their victimhood – it would be sentimental so to suppose – but their understanding. They knew why America needed victims like themselves. They both could understand not only what it meant to be black when that was a considerable liability, but that it was white society which was deformed and lacking and not themselves.

They knew about capitalism, racism and sexism and sang about

* Shortened version first published in *The Wire*, 1984.

them, obliquely, subtly, from within, in words that didn't, mercifully, end with -ism.

The starting point for understanding the blues is the social system of slavery which, first in West Africa and then in Southern United States, created the tonal patterns and the rhythms which remain alive today. The blues have never lost the connection to the condition of being a slave. The chattel slave system began when Europeans used their ships and guns to bring tens of millions of West Africans to work as slaves on the sugar, rice and tobacco plantations of the Deep South of America. But after the discovery of milling methods which could pull the seeds from cotton, it proved possible to extend the types of cotton profitably grown and the trade spread into the coastal lowlands further across America. The Northern states bred slaves to send back to work in the South. Although these Northern states were more democratic in flavour, they too depended on the theft of land and slave labour. Slavery was therefore a national system which indirectly benefited the Northern merchants and created the capital for America's initial industrial expansion. American slavery was one of the most repressive slave systems ever. The slave was utterly powerless. The only provider the slave knew was the master who was also the source of all punishment, privilege and wealth. Slaves could not assemble unless a white man was present. Blacks were systematically cut off from education; a white woman found guilty of teaching a slave to read in 1855 was sent to prison for five months.

Within slavery had existed a ghastly kind of sexual equality, in that both sexes were equally powerless. Because the white master was the only provider, he became collective father for the whole plantation and the slave father's patriarchal authority as head of his own family was correspondingly weakened. Black women were raised to work outside the family, as field labourers, domestic servants and providers of child care for the white owners. And their reproductive work providing future workers was only too obvious on plantations whose declared purpose was slave breeding. Under the slave system, the black woman was legally the slave owner's personal property, he had power to do with her sexually as he pleased. Even after the formal abolition of this property relation, the sexual authority persisted. It was usual for the father to relieve himself and for his sons to gain their sexual experience with their black domestic servants, the colour of whose face was considered sufficient invitation to seduction. Black women were painstakingly denied both the big and the little rights and privacies essential to their sexual dignity. There were white ladies and coloured women. On the doors of the toilets it read 'Ladies', 'Gentlemen' and 'Coloured'. Laws forbade intermarriage so that no permanent sexual relationship could ever be established with white men. Black women customers were not allowed to try on clothes lest their imagined smell, condensation of their imagined sexuality, might stain clothes whites might have near their white skin. The black woman was not allowed to be modest. Her man was barred from protecting her, she was forced to live without dignity. Then the white man proceeded to announce she was a slut and therefore sexually to assault her because that was only to treat her as she deserved. Having seen to it that neither black man nor woman had social power, they were attributed with an abnormally developed sexuality as a macabre consolation prize.

Specifically sexual sorts of terrorism, justified by general myths directed at all blacks, were used against both men and women. The Ku Klux Klan was formed to organise acts of terror against blacks who attempted to make use of the voting rights won in the Civil War. The midnight raids, murders in broad daylight, pack rapes and the lynchings were justified as protecting the virtue of white women who were said to be under constant threat from black men, roused but not satisfied by their lascivious women and too primitive to control their sexuality.

The right of young, or drunk or Niggerhungry whites to rape black women was forcibly re-asserted as simply the most extreme symbol of the political defeat of the Southern black people after Reconstruction. Not only did it remind the black woman of her state of sexual nothingness on the plantation, it rubbed her man's face in his own powerlessness. To the whites it was morally legitimate to violate a black woman casually because they were all at the moral level of prostitutes. But the black man who defended her or attempted any sexual relation with a white woman was still more severely and publicly humiliated. The white Klansmen who seized blacks from the county jails they had fled to for protection, inefficiently strangled them with a rope over a tree, blew them into lumps with bullets and swigged Jim Crow bourbon from flasks, while white women soaked the dying body with kerosene and set a flame to it all, justified themselves in the name of Southern chivalry.

Nor were such rapes and lynchings rarities or isolated excesses. A total of over 10,000 lynchings are said to have occurred by 1920. The first mass black civil rights organisation, the National Association for the Advancement of Coloured People, was formed to combat it. It was black women who led the campaign against lynching, surviving firebombings of their homes and destruction of their printing presses. In doing so, they challenged head-on the myth not only of the rapist black man but of the loose, red-hot, sex-object black woman which buttressed it, answering wild prejudice with dossiers of painstaking evidence and lives of ostentatious propriety. Black life in the South was very far from high-kicking, high-living, heavy-drinking carnival portrayed by Hollywood dramas of jazz.

The musical traces of this time reflect that inner sadness: the heavy repeated chants of the convict labourers and the melancholy high-pitched near-howl, rasping mouth harp and harsh metallic fingering of country blues singers following work across plains, silent except for train whistle or the creak of wheels. The racy jolliness was confined to the official popular music of the day, the sheet music for the parlour piano, that symbol of respectability in the big houses, the waltzes, quadrilles, mazurkas, polkas and hymns recorded for the European settlers. For black music, which was to outlast all this jaunty rubbish, was not considered even worth recording until the 1920 Okeh recording of Marie Smith's 'That Thing Called Love' proved money could be made from it. Until then it did not even have the status of novelty value. 'Every race has a flag but a coon,' said a music publisher; 'Negroes just sing about what they eat and who they fuck,' thought a Republican senator; and Ralph Peer, business manager of Okeh records, admitted in 1936, 'We had records by all foreign groups: German records, Swedish records, Polish records, but we were afraid to advertise Negro records, so I listed them as "Race Records" and they are still known as that.' The New Orleans instrumental music called jazz, once recognised as commercial, was swiftly imitated for nationwide sales by an all-white band which had the nerve to call itself The Original Dixieland Jazz Band.

The classic blues were the first blues on record. They originated with women singing in the minstrel tradition as one of the acts in a touring variety show which, like the English music hall, might mix serious singing with freaks, jugglers and sword swallowers. But in the 1920s and early 1930s, under the impetus of the record industry, these women singers became performers in their own right, shaping a distinctive body of singing associated with the names of Gertrude 'Ma' Rainey, Bessie Smith, Clara Smith, Bertha 'Chippie' Hill, Lucille Hegamin and Victoria Spivey. Miss Spivey, the Texas-born pianist and singer, was an especially prolific instrumental blues songwriter. Her 'Dopehead Blues' is one of the first songs to deal with cocaine addiction, and 'TB Blues', recorded in 1927, is an open protest against racism. It was she who 'discovered' Bob Dylan, strongly influenced his writing and issued his first recording on the Spivey label. She died in October 1976 in Brooklyn.

The classic blues was not and could not be imitated. It caught a unique moment in the history of the American black on the move from rural, Southern, mainly peasant and small farmer life into the factories and the big cities of the North. 1914 saw the start of the first mass exodus northwards hankering after factory work (like Mr Ford who could pay you US$5 whatever your colour), in search of Jobs, Homes and, most important, Dignity. It caught the South as it was unsealed but before it dispersed. It captured the blues as they were changing from a folk music directly linked to work to a performed art, but before it was smothered with the showbiz gloss applied for the benefit of a commercial audience. The women singers of the classic era had taken the spirit of the blues but shaped the form into organised performance which had elements of a church but which was quite pagan in its encouragement of sanctified self-expression. Not only did it express black women's social power, it came at the time of the first wave of twentieth-century racial self-assertion, the black risings which followed the First World War, the founding of the National Association for the Advancement of Coloured People and the rise of Marcus Aurelius Garvey. And, despite the fear of the singers that it would lead to copying and the backstage signs 'Recording harms your throat', they are on record, in quantity.

Bessie Smith had begun in poverty as a child singer in dives and tent shows at the edge of a small cotton-gin town for a few pence. She had been taken up and taught by Ma Rainey, the queen of the classical blues, whose records reach back to a more open countrified sound. From that circuit, Bessie worked through minstrel shows, played the black theatres of the deep South towns and fronted orchestras in Cleveland and Chicago.

In towns like Memphis, she would give occasional concerts for white people only, complete with pearly smiles and rolling eyes. But singing to black audiences sometimes, as in the Avenue Theatre, Chicago, in May 1924, in the midst of near-uprisings, she could parallel the race pride which in the 1920s took the political form of Marcus Garvey's Back To Africa movement. She sang to the lonesome city migrants the stately blues of their childhood. For though her songs don't mention colour, her performance and repertoire radiated black pride.

As Bessie Smith's records and radio appearances spread her fame, she took on something of the life of a black opera star, dressing at great expense, travelling with a circle of assistants and drinking in quantity and with insistent generosity. She was a queen on her own terms, black and a woman who made her own sexual life. In one of her finest songs, first recorded in 1926 when she was aged 28, she states her independence in an upright, stately but unanswerable voice.

I'm a young woman and ain't done running round
Some people call me a hobo, some call me a bum
Nobody knows my name, nobody knows what I've done
I'm as good as any in your town
I ain't no high yeller, I'm deep yeller brown
I ain't going to marry, ain't gonna settle down
I'm gonna drink good moonshine an' run these browns down.

In the 1937 version, the song is slightly slower with a softer ring and more elegiac tone. But saying as proud as ever: 'I am woman.' She takes bawdiness from the vaudeville and the old ribald dozens of the medicine show and turns it into something else, a sort of magnificent frankness, insistently physical, proud and defiant, though sung in a slightly funereal and very serious voice.

After a serious but not fatal car accident in 1934, she literally bled to death while segregated hospitals and so-called doctors shunted her from pillar to post in search of a ward lowly enough for the black body of one of the greatest singers of the twentieth century.

The classic blues had died as dramatically as Bessie. The depression had devastated the South; the only way blacks could escape was North aboard the single rail line which ran the 1,000 miles from the Delta to Chicago, the home of Sears Roebuck, the *Chicago Defender*, and maybe a job. But women could not easily ride freight or work in the steel mills or car plants, and although they arrived in the North in equal numbers, the move squeezed them out of work. They were forced back into traditional jobs as cooks, nurses and cleaners, or the familiar options as whore or mother of children you couldn't afford to keep. In the same way, women singers seem to retreat into more conventional gospel or pop-romantic styles. Almost none found a footing in the raucous bar blues which developed with such ferocity in Chicago's South Side ghetto or the piano boogie woogie that thundered out of the rent parties.

In a very short musical period, an almost complete sexual reverse had taken place. Chicago blues is bouncy, raw and male. It held the blues line in the cities and spread by radio to the country blacks. It's an edgy, violent music where the electric guitar is more expressive than the voice, belted out in the cramped, tough bars of the overcrowded, workless slum belt of the South Side where police made captures almost at random and Sunday in the hospital was regularly followed by Monday in the court. All but the most remarkable of women were excluded.

In lots of ways the apparent vitality of R and B was, like the booze that accompanied it, a prop against the unbearable present. And the sexual blues became a male escape rather than a female celebration.

It was into this world Billie Holiday emerged from nowhere, eight years after Bessie Smith died in 1937. On the radio, the white well-made song and the creamy orchestras of Miller and Dorsey were easing the listening public through the Depression. It was a confusing time for a black woman. Bessie Smith could be strong but it was within clear limits, in a musical form which was established and when performance was face to face with a black audience. The record industry and music business was at an early and regionally organised stage. Billie Holiday faced the business and sexual pressures with more force and less protection. And while white society was now officially desegregating and would be civil to your face, it was a sham and the state of being a slave was still a close memory, even if you were wearing a silk gown. When Billie sings about lynching, it's real, not a metaphor, and when she sings about sexual humiliation, it's about her own life and the sexual cross-fire she was under every time she went on stage. Because of her autobiography, *Lady Sings the Blues*, much of which was censored at the time of publication, we know at least something about her own attitudes. It's one of the most political books ever written by a musician, which insists on going beyond the cliches of jazz tragedy to the economics of the music business and the pressure of Jim Crow.

Though she came from a show family, her mother was a maid for a white woman. While pregnant, her mother scrubbed the floors in the maternity hospital to pay for Billie's hospital delivery. Her grandmother had been a slave and an Irish slave owner's mistress on a big plantation in Virginia, having 16 children by him. 'She told me how it felt to be a slave, be owned body and soul by a white man who was the father of her children.' Billie remembers her first job was as a maid for a woman in Long Beach who would ignore her all day until about 15 minutes before her husband was due back. She remembers first being called 'nigger' with an electric clarity. 'Instead of telling me what she wanted me to do, she'd get all excited because her husband was waiting, start hollering at me and calling me "nigger". I had never heard that word before. I didn't know what it meant. But I could guess from the sound of her voice.' All her life, however successful she was as a singer, racism dogged her, whether it was the drunk at the bar who just had to shout 'nigger' at her, the sheriff who came up on the bandstand to drawl 'When's darkie going to sing?' or the countless casual taunts and jeers. In 1944, in an integrated club in St. Louis, she was refused permission to leave by the front entrance of the building. After a naval officer had called her nigger on 52nd Street, she cried for some time, and when soon after a friend asked, 'How are you?', she replied, 'Well, you know, I'm still a nigger.' Touring with Count Basie's band in Detroit, she had to put on special dark grease because the theatre management thought she looked too white. And in the same city, when having a drink with Chuck Petersen, another drinker came up and said, 'What the hell is going on? A man can't bring his wife in a bar anymore without you tramp white men bringing a nigger woman in.' On tour, eating was difficult, sleeping harder and going to the lavatory impossible. With Artie Shaw's first band, 'It got to the point where I hardly ever ate, slept, or went to the bathroom without having a major NAACP-type production.' The band supported her and were prepared to go hungry too if Billie was refused service. Being seen with a white man was a special problem; if she'd been a prostitute and he had been paying there would have been no problem. It was because she wasn't a whore that they disapproved of her. Nor were racial attitudes better in the North, just better hidden. At least in the South, Billie noted:

> when they insult you they do it to your face, and you know it. A cracker just wants you to clean up his house or take care of his kids and get the hell out. The big deal hotels, agencies and networks in New York were giving me a fast shove behind my back. This makes life a constant drag. Not only for me but for the people I meet and like. You're always under pressure. You can fight it but you can't lick it. The only time I was free from this kind of pressure was when I was a call girl as a kid and I had white men as my customers. Nobody gave us any trouble. People can forgive any damn thing if they did it for money.

Race was always wound up with money. The New York club scene was still like being on a plantation for all the freedom it offered her. To be recognised as an artist and not just a singer was too much to ask. She was forced into a gruelling touring regime to sing before people she often didn't care for to raise the money to pay her lawyers and cover expensive addiction cures which didn't work. 'If it had been left to the managements and promoters I could have shot myself long ago,' she ruefully remarked.

Billie probably got involved with heroin through Joe Guy, and drugs became the third party in all the subsequent sexual encounters. The police used her as a bait, bust her at the end of a residency and got a kick out of her misfortune. There was no remorse. They even made it their business to arrest her on her death bed.

Nor was her sexual life easy. She had been seduced by her brother and then raped by her uncle when she was 12. When she and her mother reported the crime and asked the police for help, crying and bleeding, 'they treated me as if I had murdered somebody and proceeded to snigger and give dirty looks ... no wonder I was scared to death of sex.' She acquired her name Lady because she didn't like showing off her body.

Billie Holiday sang relatively few recognisable blues songs and much of her recordings are of straight pop or the svelte anti-blues crafted by lyricists like Hart, Gershwin and Porter. Her involvement in cabaret settings is sometimes denounced in the same way as Bessie Smith's vaudeville connection, but for both it was about a way of connecting to a black audience. But she battled not to compromise artistically. 'People don't understand,' she said, 'the kind of fight it takes to record what you want to record the way you want to record it. I've fought for as long as ten years to get to record a song I've loved or wanted to do.'

Almost all her songs are about being a woman and being in love. Most are about sexual love, about surrender, loss, need, the moments when feelings make a fool of brains, about coming out with your sexual hands up. She wrote only a few of her own songs but somehow could unwind more personal meaning from other people's lyrics than many modern singers can extract from their own.

It was as if she needed the subjectivity of these songs to regain herself from the constant bruising battles against segregation, the music business and her men. There is almost revenge in the way she creeps up on the words of a song and tips them up. But it is in 'Strange Fruit', a classic of political lyricism, that the power of her own experience to rush through her voice is most easy to hear. The song was brought to her when she was playing at a club called Cafe Society, one of the happiest residencies of her career. The club was one of the first in New York to be genuinely racially mixed and the drink was cheap. Its slogan was, 'the wrong place for the right people'. There were many socialists in the audience and Frankie Newton, the trumpeter, could be found lecturing his band on the Economics of Marcus Garvey and the Soviet Five-Year Plan. Billie didn't like the discussions and, since the owner was obliged to run a strict anti-marijuana ruling, used to go out to smoke in the park in intervals.

One of the Cafe Society's regulars, a schoolteacher called Lewis Allen, offered her a lyric about a lynching down South. She was at first suspicious but then took to it with a passion. 'I worked like the devil on it because I was never sure I could put it across or I could get across to a nightclub audience what it meant to me.' The song awoke some of the raw political feelings that Billie often hid behind her elegance. It reminded her, she said, of how her father died and she felt it her duty to go on singing the song because of what she knew. 'I have to keep on singing it, not only because people ask for it but because twenty years after Pop died the things that killed him are still happening in the South.' He had caught pneumonia in Dallas, Texas, on tour with the Don Redmond Band and had wandered delirious from hospital to hospital trying to get help from white-only hospitals who wouldn't do as much as take his temperature. He eventually found a veterans' hospital who admitted him to their segregated ward when he proved he had served in the Army. Just in time to die.

The song is simple but allowed the full dramatic power of her voice and its richness of texture to blend with the passion she always felt every time she sang the song. It was because it moved her that she could so move an audience, almost flay them with the last eight lines with their mounting of sound, until inside the last elongated, swirling few words you can hear the gallows rope twisting and the wind curling.

Singing live, Billie Holiday exercised a mysterious command over her audience; eyewitness after eyewitness recalls the thickness of the silence, and the live records bear witness to the closeness of their attention, breathing, gasping and laughing to her turns and twists of phrase and weaving of rhythms, then erupting with fierce clapping.

And in the singing of 'Strange Fruit', her voice remembers the state of being a slave still, not a chattel slave like her grandmother but a woman who is always owned by another; by men who started as lovers and stayed as businessmen, by managers who cared more for cash registers than music, by the dope that at first had given relief and euphoria but became just a habit. She lived in a formally desegregated but still racist America where black women had in some respects even less social power than they possessed earlier in the century. There was no longer the musical protection which absolute segregation had, ironically, given black music. Her place was in the market place. Even as a success, she was always made forcibly aware that celebrity was conditional, provisional, precarious.

She wanted something quite simple: the right to be honest. Her epitaph might be her comment in *Lady Sings the Blues*: 'I plain decided one day I wasn't going to do anything unless I meant it .... You have to be poor and black to know how many times you get knocked on the head just for trying to do something as simple as that.' Male critics have a habit of making remarks about Billie's 'difficult' character, her 'unreasonable' need for reassurance, 'inadequacy' and so on, which, though intended sympathetically, are an insult. Her life as a black woman started and finished in pain, she had to fight constantly for the right to be herself and express her feelings. Her difficulty was that she wasn't dishonest about this, her unreasonableness was that she refused to conform, her inadequacy was simply the erosion of any one, however gifted, or brave, who takes on the social system alone. And although insecure about her lack of education and suspicious about politics, she felt instinctive solidarity with those who resisted the system. Jimmy Davis, the pianist and composer who wrote 'Lover Man' for Billie and served a year in jail for fighting the racial segregation in the American army, recalls a performance which in some ways sums up her political feelings. 'She came to Paris during the time of the war in Algeria when the Algerians were fighting for their freedom. She went to a clandestine meeting, to sing to encourage the fighters. This is something very strong.'

Bessie Smith and Billie Holiday are separated by twenty years, in different parts of America, with the music business in a different phase of its development. But the same collective history and the same personal experience soars behind their singing. Both women sufficiently commanded their art to take charge of the music and transform it. Both were proud to be race women, who did not need to flaunt their blackness but did not deny it either. Both insisted in every note they were women, not men's playthings, committed to passion in their own right. Billie and Bessie were left very hollow and sad at the constant effort of keeping up that exterior alone, drained by constantly giving outwards, haunted by nameless inner insecurities which they unsuccessfully fended off with booze and men. On stage they were acknowledged as outstanding but that was still not enough to entitle them to ordinary rights off it. Just by being black they were non-conformists. By being women and proud of it, they were asking for trouble, and when they got it, deserved it.

It was not having been oppressed that made them great. But their greatness lay in their ability to press past a world which battered and denied their beings and turned those bruises and denials inside out. To deny and dwarf the hurts inflicted on them by opening themselves out so completely and profoundly in their singing. Out of that bitter experience came forth something unsurpassingly sweet.

13

The Streets are Our Palettes A Tribute to Vladimir Mayakovsky*

One of the delights of growing up politically lies in discovering one's own traditions. In art they were nearly obliterated by Stalin ism, declared redundant by the long post-war boom and generally buried in a 'modernism' which was often apolitical and trite. It was exhilarating to unearth in Soviet Russia the most genuinely modern of modern art movements and Mayakovsky the original 'hooligan communist'.

Vladimir Mayakovsky, the poetic loudspeaker of the Russian Revolution, came to socialist ideas with the enthusiasm of youth. He began to read Engels and illegal pamphlets under his desk-lid when he was 12. When later the same year his school was closed by military edict because of the 1905 uprising, he became chief school leaflet distributor. When he made his first contact with the illegal Bolshevik Party, he immediately presented them with his forester father's shotgun. Aged 15, he was arrested in Moscow for helping to organise the escape of political prisoners from jail and was himself held in Novinsky Prison where he began to write poems. For the following twenty years he served the Revolution as a poet-agitator with the same audacity and passion. And when he shot himself in Moscow in 1930, he died a Bolshevik, brandishing his poems:

When I appear
    at the CCC
        of coming bright decades
above the band of poetic grafters and crooks
I'll lift up high,
        like a Bolshevik party-card
All the hundred volumes of my
        ComParty books!

* First published in *International Socialism*, 1970.

Mayakovsky's communism was, like him, broad shouldered and larger than life, impatient, rude and necessary:

> Proletarians come to communism from the depths beneath
> the depths of the mines
> sickles
> and factories.
> I plunge into Communism from the heights of poetry above,
> because for me
> without it
> there is no love!

But his passion was neither sentimental nor cosy, like the cliches of modern Soviet art; those cheery collective farmers, the harmonious choristers and the agile folk dancers. In his complex love poems like *A Cloud in Trousers* and *About This*, he explores the nature of revolutionary love, trying to untangle his private passions from his larger love of the Revolution as the expression of human solidarity and vitality. Through his poems, we can gain a glimpse of boisterous spirit and feverish energy of the real Russian Communism so deeply buried under the false images of Stalinism. As his last poem insisted:

> I abhor
> every kind of deathliness
> I adore
> every kind of life.

Mayakovsky also abhored literary pretentiousness and adored being rude and down to earth:

> I know
> a nail in my boot that's hurting
> is more nightmarish than all the fantasies of Goethe.

'I've become a terribly proletarian poet,' he wrote to Lily Brik, the woman he loved, in a letter covered with cartoons of himself as a bear, 'I've got no money and write no poems.'

The Russia Mayakovsky grew up in was still paralysed by its own political and economic backwardness, its industrial potential locked up in its under-development, its possibilities imprisoned by the absolute power of the Tsar and the vast empty plains of the East with their huddled villages of thatched wooden houses. But by 1900, Russia's very backwardness had acted to suck in new manufacturing techniques from the advanced capitalist nations of the West. Cheap mass production began in a few large factories and Moscow and

Petersburg became familiar with telephones, bicycles, irons and wirelesses, the new products of the machine age. To Mayakovsky, perhaps over-optimistically, the new forces of steam and electricity represented a promise of a new future and required a new form of art. Previously, the Russian Left had admired the realist novelists of the nineteenth century; Lenin's favourites and inspiration were Pushkin and Tolstoy. Systematic Marxists writers on art like Plekhanov and Lukács were aesthetic conservatives. But Mayakovsky wanted to alter the form of his painting and writing to suit an age of advertising and electricity and the altered perceptions of citizens of the twentieth century.

The Russian tradition of the realist novel sat in his way, 'like enormous bronze backsides'. So in the first Manifesto of the Futurist Group, characteristically entitled *A Slap at the Public Taste* and issued in 1912, it was denounced: 'Let us throw Pushkin, Tolstoy, Dostoevsky from the steamship of modernity.' In the name of Futurism, he and fellow poets and sculptors travelled Russia, reading poems, denouncing the Tsar and unfurling their manifesto. In many towns they were banned on sight and they remained unpublished. 'Publishers do not touch us. Their capitalistic noses sensed the dynamiters in us.'

And in Italy too, which had also experienced violent and abrupt industrialisation in a backward mainly peasant country, Futurism emerged with its explosive language and fierce hostility to old forms. But while Mayakovsky's hatred for poetic marzipan and literary dust was linked to a movement to socialise art, the Italian Futurist poet Marinetti wrote with jagged, bombastic phrases and his destructive spirit led him to press towards war as a means of artistic gratification. Italian Futurism became openly fascist. As the German critic Walter Benjamin put it, 'Its own self-alienation has reached such a degree that it can experience its own destruction as an aesthetic pleasure of the first order.' Marinetti and Mayakovsky met only once and hated each other's guts.

But in Russia, the Futurists were the first organised grouping of artists clearly to devote themselves to the October Revolution and to express the ambition of those years. Mayakovsky became involved in a series of magazines, *Art of the Commune*, *Lef* which he edited, and *New Lef* which championed the most avant-garde of the Russian art movements, Constructivism, which aimed at an artistic counterpart of the social revolution. The Constructivists differed sharply from the traditional defenders of realism who were grouped round the magazine *Krasnaya Nov*, edited by a supporter of the Left Opposition, Voronsky, and the Proletkult magazine *On Guard*, which had grown out of pre-revolutionary working-class cultural institutions and stressed a fairly crude and agitational art (these tendencies had permanent bombastic quarrels and repeatedly demanded the censorship of their rivals). The Constructivists wanted an end to old elitist forms of art; the novel in its morocco binding and the oil painting with its bulbous gilt frame. They demanded instead a motivated art in new forms which related to industrial techniques in a workers' state. As John Berger says, 'Their works were like hinged doors, connecting activity with activity. Art with engineering; music with painting; poetry with design; fine art with propaganda; photographs with typography; diagrams with action; the studio with the street.' They wanted to be master-executors of social command, not priest-creators awaiting inspiration. At its most extreme, it was an attempt to bulldoze down the wall between art and life, subordinating aesthetics to the actual needs of the workers' state. As the sculptor Gabo announced in his Realist Manifesto of 1920, 'In the squares and on the streets we are placing our work convinced that art must not remain a sanctuary for the idle, a consolation for the weary, and a justification for the lazy. Art should attend us everywhere that life flows and acts, at the bench, at the table, at work, at rest, at play; on working days and holidays; at home and on the road; in order that the flame to live should not extinguish in mankind.' It represented the release of artistic energy from the cages which boxed it up under capitalism, the energy in Mayakovsky's triumphant poem *The 150,000,000*:

We will smash the old world
wildly
we will thunder
a new myth over the world.
We will trample the fence
of time beneath our feet.
We will make a musical scale
of the rainbow.

Roses and dreams
Debased by poets
will unfold
in a new light
for the delight of our eyes
the eyes of big children.
We will invent new roses
roses of capitals with petals of squares.

The movement tended towards an over-simple anti-art feeling similar to Dadaism which had exploded in the West as a response to the First World War. And it was also magnificently unrealistic. As the Constructivist architect Lavinsky wrote, 'We are condemned to aestheticism until a bridge towards production can be found. But how can this bridge be built in a country where production itself is scarcely alive?' But amazingly, the Constructivists managed to alter the artistic means of production in fundamental ways which the capitalist 'avant-garde' has yet to come to terms with. In Russia of the Revolution amazing things *were* possible. Mayakovsky meant it when he pronounced, 'The streets are our brushes, the squares our palettes.' Tatlin was quite serious when he demanded the movement 'into real space and real materials'. Tsarist cinema, for example, had been dominated by foreign production companies who took themselves and most of their equipment home on hearing of the Revolution. Censorship had been comprehensive, even scenes of hard work and mention of the French Revolution were banned. But after the Revolution, what cinema industry remained was nationalised and new equipment procured with which to make feature and news films. The way films were made was revolutionised. The camera was emancipated from being merely a version of the human eye and film makers explored the possibilities of editing and re-organising the rhythms and images on the celluloid. Vertov produced revolutionary news reels; 'a swift review of VISUAL events deciphered by the film camera, pieces of REAL energy brought together at intervals to form an accumulatory whole by means of highly skilled montage.' Eisenstein began his series of epic feature films and Mayakovsky wrote amazing movie scripts featuring, as usual, himself as the hero. He worked alternatively on plans to re-organise the nationalised film industry (Sovkino) and on denouncing it for underestimating the masses.

Russian architecture had previously been oblivious to working class housing and produced only rhetorical and over-decorated impersonations of Western styles. Constructivist architects, organised around the magazine *Sovremennaya Arkhitektura* or *SA*, stripped away the larded decoration and disguises and used glass, aluminium, steel and asbestos frankly and elegantly. They invented the ideas of integrated design, as used on the new Pravda offices, flexible homes with interchangeable units to alter homes as families grew and shrank and 'new towns' like the one planned at Magnitogorsk. They stressed communal designs which aimed at maximum pooling and collectivisation of domestic duties and the socialisation of housework. Ginsburg stressed 'The Constructivists' approach to the problem with maximum considerations for those shifts and changes in our way of life that are preparing the way for a completely new type of housing ... that is to say, for us the goal is not the execution of a commission as such, but collaboration with the proletariat in its task of building a new life, a new way of living.' The Soviet Pavilion in Paris in 1925, on whose design committee Mayakovsky had sat, staggered the bourgeois world by the use of Constructivist principles. In the theatre, Constructivists produced mobile stage settings, hung the auditorium with placards and bombarded the audience with leaflets during the interval. Meyerhold produced Mayakovsky's play *Mystery Bouffe*, a *Pilgrim's Progress*-like account of the Revolution for the international delegates to the Third International. The storming of the Winter Palace was re-enacted and the streets, squares and monuments were dyed and re-decorated to celebrate revolutionary anniversaries. Printing presses were hugely expanded and poetry jostled with posters and edicts to be printed in cheap editions with experimental typography and photo-montaged covers. Art academies were turned into polytechnics and student numbers increased. 'We have taken by storm the Bastille of the Academy,' the students claimed. But, as if to strike a note of realistic warning, Tatlin announced in 1925, 'We must look neither to what is old nor what is new but only to what is needed.' He was to follow his desire for fusion of art and in dustry into the design of 'maximum heat, minimum fuel' stoves, collapsible furniture and utensils, reflecting the needs of a virtually nomadic proletariat.

Of course, Mayakovsky was in his element: 'the work of the revolutionary poet does not stop at the book; meetings, speeches, front-line limericks, one-day agit-prop playlets, the living radio-voice and the slogan flashing by on trams.' He travelled and declaimed on the agit-prop trains and boats which linked Moscow and Petrograd with the war fronts. He wrote slangy poems abusing the Whites and rhymed advice against drinking unboiled water and kissing ikons. He drew and wrote simple and direct story-poems (which echoed the old Russian 'lubok' picture and text street literature) to be displayed in Post Office windows. These ROSTA posters were printed daily in thirty-four towns by poster collectives and became immensely popular. He wrote advertisements for state-produced matches and sweets, held auctions of his manuscripts to raise money for the Volga famine, planned a book to answer the 20,000 questions he had been asked when reading, wrote nineteen children's books, conducted incendiary debates with rivals and fell in love several times.

Highly popular among workers and the young, he gained enemies elsewhere. Lenin disliked Futurism and did his best to halt publication of *The 150,000,000*. Since the Commissar for Culture Lunacharsky protected the Futurists (he had called them 'the virtuoso drummers of our Red Culture'), Lenin sent a memo direct to the Head of the State Publishing House: 'Isn't it possible to find some dependable anti-futurists?' But Lenin seemed to warm to Mayakovsky, whom he had called on first meeting 'a hooligan communist'. In a 1922 speech to the Communist Faction of the Metal Workers' Union, he mentioned a Mayakovsky poem, *In Re. Conferences*, which satirised Bolshevik obsession with meetings. Lenin said, 'I don't know about the poetry, but as for the politics, I can vouch for it that he is absolutely right.' In some of Lenin's more lyrical phrases, 'Socialism equals soviets plus electrification' and 'Revolution is the festival of the oppressed,' one can almost sense Mayakovsky's presence.

But as the heady days of war communism were followed by the compromises of the New Economic Policy, Mayakovsky became bitter against 'the academics, singly and in bunches beginning to knock at the door' and suspicious of 'the old familiar face of the aesthete peering out from under the mask of the engineer'. His plays, *The Bedbug* and *The Bathhouse*, satirised the arse-licking and pomposity of the NEP men and Red bureaucrats. 'From the philistinism of living comes the philistinism of politics,' he wrote. He hated the dishonest obituaries, writing after the death of a friend, 'Stop once and for all these reverential centenary jubilees, the worship by posthumous publication. Let's have articles for the living! Bread for the living! Paper for the living!' In his extended political poem *Lenin*, he warns that if Lenin is turned into a God figure,

> I'd have found enough curse words for blasting ears
> and before they could smother my cry and drown me
> I'd have hurled to heaven blasphemies,
> and battered the Kremlin with bombs.
>
> Down with!

And in 1923, a poetic leading article in *Lef* speaks concretely against what was to be called 'the cult of the personality':

> We insist
> Don't stereotype Lenin

Don't print his portrait on placards, stickybacks,
plates, mugs and cigarette cases.
Don't bronze-over Lenin
Don't take from him the living gait and countenance.

And in a 1929 poem, Mayakovsky characteristically imagines himself delivering a poetic report to the jovial ghost of Lenin:

Many
    without you
        got right out of hand
So many
    different
        rascals and blackguards
Prowl
    round and about
        our Soviet land
There's no end
    to their numbers
        and aliases
A whole assembly belt
    of types
        are unloaded
Kulaks
    bureaucrats
        and red tapists
Sectarians
    drunkards
        and toadies.
Chest sticking out
        they arrogantly strut;
pocketfuls of pens
        breastfuls of Orders

The Bathhouse was attacked and boycotted. *New Lef* came under fiercer criticism, most sadly from the poets of RAPP, the newly formed Writers' Union which Mayakovsky eventually agreed to join. His photograph was cut out of the printed copies of *The Press and Revolution* for April 1930. He was prevented from visiting his new love Tatiana in Paris and could not persuade her to come to Moscow. He told an audience at a Mayakovsky exhibition, 'I demand help, not the glorification of non-existent virtues.' He wrote:

I'm fed
    to the teeth
        with agit-prop, too
I'd like
    to scribble love-ballads
        for you
they're profitable
    charming and halcyon
But I
    mastered myself
        and crushed underfoot
The throat
    of my very own songs.

It was as if he realised what the future held, that the Constructivists' enthusiastic application to 'social command' and the principle of utility would be used by Stalin and Zhdanov to trim all which was revolutionary and truly modern down to tidy slabs of a 'socialist realism' which was in fact a nineteenth-century naturalism. For by 1930 the Constructivist impetus was faltering, a safer art which was prepared to lend dignity to socialism in one country was better received by the artistic authorities. While Constructivists' designs were halted on the drawing board, their new towns remained unbuilt and their journals were closed down, an ornate and pompous 'Palace of the Soviets' was constructed to house a 'Soviet' which no longer met. Dignitaries were now taken to the Bolshoi Ballet and the Grand Opera instead of Meyerhold's theatre and the street exhibitions. Oil paints, smocks, easels and Professors of Fine Art found their way back to the studios. Stalin ruled.

On 14 April 1930, Mayakovsky shot himself with a revolver. In his suicide poem he said simply enough,
'... the love-boat of life has crashed upon philistine reefs ...'

14

Motherhood Myths*

The pamphlet The Myth of Motherhood *was one of the earliest products of the Women's Liberation Movement in Britain. It was principally an attack on the work of the influential psychologist John Bowlby (now back in vogue). But its impact, which must seem remarkable now, was that it questioned whether the conventional nuclear family (mum busy being mum, dad out to work and 2.3 children beaming at them) was really the only way to live and bring up children. Wife battering was hardly acknowledged, child sexual abuse unknown and homosexuality only just out of the closet. Far from cold-shouldering the ideas of women's liberation, this review in* Socialist Worker *is evidence of the socialist Left's enthusiasm.*

The family is the most basic and the most ancient of groups. We are all born into one and may never leave it.

In a public world dominated by competition and ambition, the family and the home provide a private retreat, a world of kids, of love and the release of sex.

For the child, it is the place where he or she first learn the rules of society and find out that little boys must play with guns and little girls with dolls, that boys can't be cissy and girls can't be tomboys.

Strains

For the housewife who never leaves it, it can be a slow hell of repeated but unnoticed labour. There's a Weetabix commercial that puts the mother's role in society all too clearly. Against cosy pictures of glowing fireside faces, a mother is there to give:

* First published in *Socialist Worker*, 1972.
Review of *The Myth of Motherhood*, by Lee Comer.

Grace to her girl children,
Boisterousness in her boys
and strength in her man.

But every month thirty or forty happy well-cared-for Weetabix kids are brought into casualty departments as battered babies. Kids, usually under three years old, who have, in the words of the Ministry of Health, 'received non-accidental violence at the hands of an adult'.

The mythical happy families in the adverts just can't match up to the strains of the real world of over-crowded housing, shift work and low wages. Most families still get by, grumbling. But in some the pent-up frustrations explode into physical violence.

Hinged

It has taken the Women's Liberation Movement to press the question of the family back into the centre of socialist concern. Originally, Marx and Engels, who automatically assumed that the family would disappear after a socialist revolution, tried to anchor marriage and the family in the need to protect private property.

Marriage was based on economics: the wife was part of the man's possessions and was treated accordingly, they said. And since the subordination of women hinged on the male-dominated family, it must have arisen before capitalism itself.

Both Marx and Engels hated the hypocrisy of Victorian men who divided women into wives and prostitutes, the first maintained for social reasons and the second for erotic needs. Love, which Marx described as 'the experience which really teaches man to believe in the objective world outside himself', was and still is continually distorted by cash ... or lack of it.

Modern Marxists in women's liberation have continued to see the family as necessary for capitalism and mainly responsible for the oppression of women.

Within the home it obliges them to work round the clock, without pay or strikes. The sexual division of labour is so ingrained that most people assume that a woman's life will be spent looking after the children and feeding and caring for the male breadwinner.

Housewives just have to accept that their life will be devoted to somebody else's happiness. They must live their lives through their children, at second hand.

A wife's economic dependence on her husband means that she has to accept his petty tyrannies and assumed superiority even if she realises that he is just taking out on her the strain of his work. But if she manages to get a job, she is constantly discriminated against because of her position in the family, forced to accept 'pin-money' wages, the lowest jobs and the lousiest conditions.

And if she has no husband, the sickly clichés of society's concern for the sanctity of motherhood are transformed into contempt for 'unmarried mothers', and she has to suffer high rents, nosy parkers from the Social Security and the continual threat of prison and children being 'taken into care'.

Deny

An especially destructive myth, unconsciously accepted by too many socialists, is that child-rearing has to be women's work. This argument has its origins in the ideas of Freud, who was first to draw attention to the intensity of mother-child relationships and who emphasised the importance of the first years of a child's life in moulding its personality.

From this discovery it was deduced that the mother needed, biologically, to stay with her child for at least the first five years of its life. After the Second World War, many child psychiatrists blamed the rise in juvenile crime on mothers' failings.

From John Bowlby to Evelyn Home, it became usual to warn that a negligent mother would be punished by her deprived child becoming a teddy boy.

Lee Comer painstakingly examines the standard, male-authored, accounts of child care and shows that they almost completely deny the father's role in child-rearing, except when he pops up as a substitute mum when the real mum goes out to bingo.

She asks the obvious question: why has no one got so hot and bothered about paternal deprivation, the damage done to kids who only glimpse their father as he comes home from necessary over time and they are going to bed?

She shows how biased and shadowy Bowlby's evidence is, how he assumes as 'natural' a child's strong attachment to its mother, a child's yearning for love and affection and a child's constant need for understanding and guidance. But this is no more 'natural' than a black person behaving like an Uncle Tom. It is really social.

As long as our sort of society brings kids up in small, isolated, competitive, nuclear families, children are bound to be treated as possessions who must do well in exams, football and good looks compared with next door's kids. The controversial film *Family Life* was actually a lot better at showing the intolerable pressure that parents load on to their children than it was at explaining mental illness.

Lee Comer reckons that the working-class mother's tradition of 'healthy neglect' of kids is far better than the middle-class mother's suffocating adoration.

She concludes: 'When we have learnt to disengage ourselves from the pressure to conform to our image of them, we will be loving them without violence. In the process we will be going some way towards liberating ourselves.'

15

The Other Love*

Don Milligan's self-produced pamphlet The Politics of Homosexuality *was one of the first British attempts to define gay liberation from a socialist point of view. After the initial horror, the idea made a lot of sense politically, although not at this time to the editors of* Socialist Worker, *which explains why this review was published in the independent journal* Gay Left. *Still,* Gay Left, *like so many sexual politics publications, is long gone now, while* Socialist Worker, *if a little slow off the mark, is nowadays a resolute and reliable defender of the threats against gay rights which have materialised in the 1980s.*

Homosexuality has been a taboo subject on the Left for 100 years. It's always been somebody else's problem; something to do with bourgeois degenerates or Stalinist spies. Socialists who wanted to go to bed with lovers of their own sex have done so in great secrecy or simply become celibate and submerged their sexual longings in political activity. Although homosexual writers like Edward Carpenter, active in the Sheffield labour movement early this century, were very widely read in the movement (*Love's Coming of Age* went through twelve editions), their analysis could never advance beyond a desperate pleading for their form of love to be tolerated.

Radical homosexual writers who were drawn towards socialist ideas because of their own experience of the hypocrisy of capitalism were seldom welcomed. Oscar Wilde, openly prosecuted in an atmosphere of pre-Boer War patriotic hysteria, was unmentioned by the socialist press of the day. Walt Whitman, the American left-wing poet, whose proletarian following in Yorkshire corresponded and sent money to their hero, was never able to openly link his homosexuality to his political feelings, although privately they were inseparable.

Of female homosexuals we know only sneers and silence. The Left has occasionally included homosexuals somewhere in its list of

* First published in *Gay Left*, 1974.

oppressed minorities but the perspective has been reformist and legislative. For example, a warm-hearted article in *Socialist Review*, commenting on the Wolfenden Report which made homosexuality legal between consenting adults, still saw homosexuality as an evil and perverted form of love, a product of capitalist society which would be cleansed after-the-Revolution. In the meantime, queers are supposed to keep their heads well down and wait for more tolerant laws to be passed from above. And although the Bolsheviks acted to legalise homosexuality, since 1934 in Russia and in most of the state-capitalist regimes, especially Cuba, homosexuals have been singled out for the most vigorous persecution.

The emergence, out of the political Pandora's Box of 1968, of the Gay Liberation Movement has altered the whole terms of the discussion. A movement of homosexuals of an entirely new kind was born in collective struggle (literally in a fist fight with New York cops attempting to make arrests in a New York homosexual bar). They asked not for integration and tolerance but shouted defiance and challenged heterosexual society to examine the seamy side of its own 'normality'. A sexual minority, apparently contained in their own guilt-ridden ghettoised sub-society, suddenly in the late 1960s began to organise politically and look for radical explanations of their own situation. Seldom has Engels's remark that 'in the fore of every great revolution the question of free love is bound to arise' proved truer. The reaction of socialists has been embarrassed and uncertain. At one extreme the freak Left, by giving uncritical support to every whim of Gay Liberation (and they have been many) in fact took a liberal and also a rather patronising attitude.

At the other extreme, those socialists who denied that homosexuals were a 'genuine' minority, and suspect it's all a middle-class problem anyhow, ended up utilising revolutionary phrases to cloak straightforward prejudice (at the World Youth Festival 1973, for example, socialist homosexuals were beaten up when they attempted to raise a GLF banner). Milligan's pamphlet documents quite clearly how homosexuals are oppressed by law prejudice, the specific attacks made by psychiatrists and queer-bashers and, most importantly, the personal self-denial of a life of furtiveness and enforced secrecy. In reply to those who argue that this oppression has no relation to the class struggle, he quotes the words of the Bolshevik Central Committee member Alexandra Kollontai who wrote in 1919, 'the problems of sex concern the largest section of society – they concern the working class in its daily life.'

It is hard to understand why this vital and urgent subject is treated with such indifference. The indifference is unforgivable. Milligan argues that homosexuals are an affront to capitalism because they challenge the system's division of people into small competitive family units of obedient producers and consumers house-trained in obedience and rigid sex-roles. For, like the Women's Question, any adequate Marxist analysis of homosexuality is bound to deal with sexuality, child-rearing and psychology, topics not raised within the Marxist movement since the late 1920s. These questions are not being raised again in the working class movement by accident; it is inevitable they will be asked once again in new guises as we transform our revolutionary socialism from the dogma of the few into the faith of the multitude. Indeed, a modern revolutionary party unable to come to terms with feminism and the Gay Movement is storing up trouble for itself.

The struggle for a Marxist theory of homosexuality will continue and will only finally be made by working class homosexuals them selves. As Connolly says, it is those who wear the chains who are most qualified to begin throwing them off. In the meantime, socialist homosexuals are entitled to expect the active support of their heterosexual comrades. Socialists who are weak on this question will undoubtedly show themselves weak on other perhaps more important questions of principle. For it is not a question of moralism but one of class solidarity. For a male worker who sneers at queers, just like one who talks of niggers and slags, is finally only sneering at himself and his class.

16

Imprisoned by Chauvinism*

The publication of Norman Mailer's attack on Women's Liberation The Prisoner of Sex *was not just important because of Mailer's previous record as a political radical. It also raised, perhaps unintentionally, the question of how men who thought they supported Women's Liberation might then act, a subject which has produced a great deal of subsequent heartbreak.*

We left Mailer driving his Land-Rover through the mud and tide of Provincetown Bay, mourning his marriage and the moon, now both gone. Prose exhausted, weary in every comma and colon with inventing metaphysics for the sex-stripped mysteries of the moonmen and their machines. Well known for his well-knownness, celebrated for his fame, Aquarius was running out of eponyms. The Mailer who had uncannily foreseen the Black uprising guided us through the living heat of Beat, comprehended and fought the advancing order of brutality of Vietnam, seemed emptied. In *Cannibals and Christians* he had promised 'this country is entering the most desperate nightmarish time of its history. Unless everyone in America gets a good deal braver, everything is going to get a lot worse,' and in *The Armies of the Night*, he recognised the future as a twenty-year battle for the soul of America. But now he seemed to have caught weightlessness, the ideas he had been juggling for fifteen years were floating out of his reach, his moralism had turned sanctimonious, his paradoxes anaesthetic, his toying with a pop Marxism and a mock Existentialism simply a whim. His break with James Baldwin was the first clear sign. Mailer was prepared to offer the blacks an abstract right to liberate themselves. Baldwin understood that one of the first things it was necessary to be liberated from was people like Mailer, projecting their own unrealised desire for animality on to them. Mailer loved the revolution as long as it remained an enigma. Baldwin could no longer afford to make a

* First published in *OZ*, 1973.
Review of *Prisoner of Sex*, by Norman Mailer.

mystery of politics: 'If they take you in the morning, they will be coming for us that night,' he writes to Angela Davis. Now Mailer, who has always led with his prick, was finding women, too, less grateful for being sexually exploited to fit his fantasies.

The publication of *The Prisoner of Sex*, his frontal attack on women's lib (as they cosily and diminutively call it, those admen and novelists who thought it would be all over in a year) marks the end of any kind of sympathy for the revolutionary movement in America. His picture of women is not flattering, so clearly designed to shock, so sad. He says women are goddesses or sloppy beasts, they should live in temples or in cages, and he is showing off, desperately. It's a classic 'masculine' doublebind, a 'real man' hates piety and so denies himself the possibility of many of his feelings. Mailer likes to prime his thoughts with viciousness, but the pain explodes in his own face. Or conversely, he lays a mawkish mysticism on to women in a way that obliges them to become tangled in false versions of themselves, if only in escaping his. He glories in a picture of woman stripped of cities and corruption where she can do little else but act out the Christian symbolism of flesh, animality and fertility.

It's nothing new. Olive Schreiner, the nineteenth-century feminist, knew such 'lofty theorists before the drawing room fire in spotless shirt front and perfectly fitting clothes' who talked so passionately of the wonders of childbirth. Does, she asks, the same man say 'to the elderly house drudge who rises at dawn while he sleeps to make him tea and clean his boots, "Divine child bearer! Potential Mother of the Race! Why should you clean my boots or bring up my tea?" ' No, not Norman. 'He would love a woman and she might sprain her back before a hundred sinks of dishes in a month, yet he would not be happy to help her if his own work would suffer, no, not unless her work was as valuable as his own' ... and you can guess who decides that. Woman's work becomes miraculously no work at all. Mailer leans across a nation of invisible women on all fours to treasure 'femininity' and 'love', so obviously the projections of his distorted masculinity. For from the Women's Liberation view, the traits of women rolled out by Mailer, the passivity, the inner-directedness, the proximity to eternity, are not timeless mysteries but historically determined, no more mysterious than the grinning nigger. Step'n Fetchit became Stokely Carmichael, so die, 'woman', die.

His old megalomania is now reinforced by a new condescension towards women: 'obviously no journalist could have done the job – it was work which called for a novelist'. The job is selecting a kind of

Debrett of women's writing which he congratulates on being penned 'in no way women had ever written before' (has he read Mary Wollstonecraft, Flora Tristan, Emma Goldman, Eleanor Marx, Sylvia Pankhurst ... a whole submerged and passionate feminist literature?). He builds up a parody picture of the women's movement, all bras, Solanas and Scissor women, designed to be easy to beat. Greer's 'liberal heart' and Atkinson's extra-uterine plans are neither central to Women's Liberation (except in the media's eyes) or dangerous to Mailer's Right Conservatism. He grudgingly quotes a pamphlet which argues that 'women will not respond to an appeal to live the kind of lives they see men living and if they tried to do so in large numbers, they would cause a crisis in society.' Mailer is stunned by this 'echo of Bolshevism' (the Bolsheviks apparently being an all-male organisation) and concludes that it is probably true that men and women will not get anything fundamental without changing the economic system. He immediately drops the point. He's bored with statistics anyhow.

Never serious about Marxism, Mailer did have a period of thinking of himself as a 'Marxist existentialist'. Now his existentialism is just a poetic conceit, everything has consciousness, even his snot, and the Marxism is just a belief that technology, not the men that control it, is anti-human. The ideas he borrows, unacknowledged, from Reich, are those of cancer being caused by a failure of the psyche, the obsession with molecular forms of energy, the fear of homosexuality and the insulting tones of his last persecuted days. What gets left out, as so often, is Reich's personal and practical commitment to working-class struggle and socialism as the only true route out of the Weimar sexual hypocrisy. Reich's intransigent advocacy of Marxism in the Freudian front-parlours, the work of SexPol, his scientific use of the psychoanalytic method, began the study of how it is that the values of capitalism and imperialism take root inside people's heads. Marxist thinkers like him and Fanon, Sartre, de Beauvoir and Laing may be inaccessible and exceptions to the general conversion of Marxism into the doctrine of the Russian ruling class, but their work has been crucial to the black and women's movements. All that lies behind Mailer's heaps of adjectives is theology. Underneath the talk of 'science', a dreary catalogue of the biology of illiteracy from thoughts on the emotional life of the sperm to Eysenck on psychoanalysis.

Kate Millett has clearly wounded the old prize fighter, he can't stand a serious woman and so he sneers at her precision and brandishes his hornyness. He has not the beginning of understanding of how great is the effort of breaking through the silence, to what extent the ideas which make up the intellectual world are all seen through men's eyes ('We must learn to see the world through women's eyes,' wrote Trotsky). Millett's book is an attempt to begin the re-interpretation of sociology, anthropology and literary criticism's inadequacies from a feminist view point. For in every bourgeois science and a good deal of Marxism, women are made into invisible objects. We are only beginning to understand the process of the social education into femininity, the learning of how to 'please' men. It is beginning to be possible to see how men's notions of their own masculinity (derived, in my case, not from Lawrence and Miller but Blonde on Blonde and Belmondo) act to divide women sexually, to prevent their solidarity, to force them to police themselves in our 'interest'. Even in orgasm, Mailer is reasserting the domination of women which exists in the outside world, 'a man can become more male and a woman more female in the full rigours of the fuck'. It's a soap opera, even in the come. Perhaps we should assert the reverse, that women's liberation allows the possibility of man discovering his own femininity, anality, and the memories of sex before puberty, almost before birth.

For Mailer sex stays defined at the anatomy of the genitals; a woman's passivity from her 'damned sponge' of a womb and her narcissism from her ova, man's ambition from his penis and his wealth from his semen. Whereas the kind of sexuality which might be hoped for once man and woman have finally laid down their last false demand on each other would be truly as William Blake longed:

Embraces are cominglings
from the head
even to the feet
And not a pompous High Priest
entering by
a secret place

The lineaments of gratified desire are quite contradictory to Mailer's rigid semen economy which sees disaster in every wasted sperm, whether it be in a gay rectum, a schoolboy's hanky or a woman wearing a diaphragm. Mailer refuses to see that contraceptives increase woman's control over her body. Like Orwell, he hates rubberwear (Orwell ends a poem by accusing the cash nexus of being responsible for 'the sleek estranging shield/Between a lover and his bride'; in that fantasia of studhood, *American Dream*, Mailer-Rojack brings the nightclub hostess Cherie to her first orgasm ever only after removing his Durex). The definition of a successful fuck is that it produces offspring. He hates the fact that abortion is at last being made available early enough to make it an operation no more serious than a big dental job. He actually hankers after the era when puerperal fever made childbirth always pass close to fatal risk; 'sometimes the Prisoner thought it likely that women had begun to withdraw respect from men about the time pregnancy lost its dangers,' a remark of such offhand sadism that there is little indignation left to recall that Simmelweiss's discovery of the cause of puerperal fever was prevented from saving women's lives for years because of all-male doctors' refusal to introduce elementary hygiene. The extreme violence of man on woman could not be put more beautifully; Mailer still wants his sperm to have the possibility of causing the death of its recipient – it will have 'respect' that way. And if his victim dies, the streptococcus will kill other women simply because doctors are too proud to wash their hands. Just as the syphilis of the prostitute was the reality of the Victorian salon's waistcoats and crinolines, so what underlies Mailer's sexual delicacies is the power to kill, the mentality of My Lai. The religious respect for mystic womanhood becomes the reality of sexual punishment of the actual woman who must fall short of male fantasy; the anal rapes of Mailer's novels, the phallic murders of Cleaver's writing, the use of female genitals as ashtrays, urinal and punchbag in Henry Miller, Mailer's 'Old Master'. The hatred and the hypocrisy for women who won't accept their own subordination.

When the Paris Commune was finally destroyed a hundred years ago, the women, accused by the victorious aristocracy of free love, were treated with special sadism. As middle-aged women were marching to prison, a young aristocrat Hussar – how Mailer would have admired him – bent over from his horse and shouted at one, 'When we get you to prison, you red bitch, we will fuck you with a hot iron.'

But in a way the extremism of Mailer makes it too easy on the rest of us. Most men on the Left and the Underground are more like the male Communards who visited the women's clubs of the Paris Commune and whose rowdy interventions caused their closure. We oscillate between smugness and fear; it is to men much like us that a female Communard said, with dignity and perhaps more patience than we deserve, 'We don't want to act as playthings or entertainment for anyone ... behind your catcalls despotism is strengthened. You know very well that we don't want to lower you in any way but you are afraid to see us rise.' Men in movements against capitalism often find their own definition at the expense of women. At one level the Underground's sexual fantasy is a threat to the kind of pornography which actually caters for self-hatred. And it's clear that Lord Longford's miniature McCarthyism will do nothing about the 'pornography' in existence precisely because of the sexual hypocrites so well represented on his panel. Instead he will attack the subversive use of sexuality. But the Underground just can't go on seeing every nipple and grunt as an attack on capitalism. *INK* shows how little is really left when *OZ* is shorn of the porn. It's simply not enough to publish a perfunctory 'Woman's Issue' and still be saying, like Tony Elliott, 'an extra 5000 copies if we put boobs on the cover'. The Underground can no longer go on evading the issue with the aid of token women and the whole reactionary super-groupy sludge, any more than the Left can think the promise of a socialist revolution then is a reason to stop Women's Liberation now.

17

The Dialectics of Liberation*

In all the initially welcome but rapidly rancid recollections of 1968 which have taken place, not only were the great industrial battles into which they fed omitted but the intellectual exploration which preceded them was neglected. The Dialectics of Liberation Conference, although not very important politically, was a wonderful example of the ideological collisions which were taking place in the late 1960s. Like the London School of Economics, it became a symbol of possibility quite out of proportion to anything actually happening there. And it was one of the many auditoriums (the Anti-University in Shoreditch, SocSoc at Houghton Street, Living School at the Conway Hall, John Hopkins's Free School in Notting Hill Gate were others) where the contending ideologies of non-Stalinist Marxism, emergent feminism, anti-psychiatry, Blakean anarchism, Black Power, orientalism, situationism, hippy consumerism and high-art elitism were swirling and dancing before our eyes.

We are now midway through a sequence of twentieth anniversaries which began with the psychedelic revival, gained momentum with the Sgt Pepper promotion and will, no doubt, climax next May with the publication of the *Collected Works of Danny Cohn-Bendit*. The influence of the late 1960s on LP sleeve design, sexual mores and costume will be widely canvassed, and many children will be bewildered by their parents' indignant gesticulation at TV documentaries. However, the political ideas that animated the period will not get much attention. These will be reduced to the usual photogenic platitudes illustrating the sinister progression from flower power (nice but naive) to violence (demonstrator-kicking-police-horse-cut-to-hijacked-airliner-being-blown-up-at-Mogadishu).

In fact, contrary to the popular belief that the decade was spent in a state of groovy benightedness, it was the ideas that mattered. 'It was a period,' Pete Bruno of the pioneer agit-prop troupe CAST remembers, 'in which everybody was prepared to get a bit intellectual about

* First published in *New Society*, 1987.

things.' Radicals and revolutionaries of previous eras, Sartre, Russell, Deutscher and Marcuse, found new audiences. There was a passionate re-examination of older philosophies from gnosticism to Trotskyism, and the genuinely new syntheses like Black Power and Women's Liberation were busy being born. Anti-Stalinist Marxisms of various lineages mingled with a cultural upsurge which was anarchistic and sometimes millennial, and they all united in protest against the Vietnam War.

Few gatherings illustrated this confusing process as well as the Dialectics of Liberation Conference organised, twenty years ago today, by a group of then not very well known British psychiatrists in an engine shed in Camden Town. It is not, as far as I know, being reissued on CD.

That the instigators were psychiatrists was characteristic of an era in which unpredictable people did unpredictable things. British psychiatry is, in general, intellectually conformist and empirical. It would be difficult to imagine even a nineteenth-century radical doctor like John Conolly, after the completion of *The Treatment of the Insane Without Mechanical Restraints*, calling a public conference which linked mental ill health with imperialism, and inviting to the platform Chartist veterans and Indian nationalists who advocated armed risings.

Yet R.D. Laing, David Cooper and their collaborators, known mainly for their exegesis of Sartre and work on the families of schizophrenics, announced that the aim of their conference was to link the internalised violence said to be characteristic of psychotic illness with the mentality which fuelled the American war on Vietnam. The conference was to be nothing less than 'a unique gathering to demystify human violence in all its forms', the intellectual equivalent of levitating the Pentagon.

Earlier in the summer of 1967 a group of university socialists, stalwarts of the old New Left, had convened a conference with the aim of launching 'a self-organising, self-financing socialist organisation', the *Mayday Manifesto* group. The manifesto itself, especially in the expanded form published by Penguin, was a careful, cogent and beautifully written reproach to Harold Wilson's corporate vision of socialism. Its stress on meaning (and the loss of it) suggested Raymond Williams's hand, but clearly the other two main editors, E.P. Thompson and Stuart Hall, had contributed much drive and impetus.

The manifesto launch, however, and the organised intervention implicit in the issue of a manifesto, were less successful. The platform was heavyhanded and formal, the practical proposals ranged from the plaintive to the vague and the audience was disparaging. 'Another left reformist trip,' I remember a psychedelically inclined International Socialist stage-whispering.

The Dialectics of Liberation conference which began on 15 July that year was more abstract, more international and had the wisdom to set itself no future tasks, sidestepping the problems which had stalled the Mayday group. It was entirely happy to inhabit a political vacuum and suck into it half of London – bearded, bell-laden and often bewildered. The stated aim was to link the worlds of mass politics – political economy, class struggle and national liberation – to the individual psyche and the way authority is learnt and internalised.

The conference's real patron saint was neither Sartre nor Fanon (as often suggested) but the Marxist Reich of the interwar years. The late David Cooper stressed that neither Russia nor eastern Europe provided personal liberation although, characteristically, he was more optimistic about China. And the speakers sought to enlarge what were then the conventional Left's account of capitalism's destructiveness to include its ecological crimes and the repression of instinctuality as well as the violence of racism and of imperialism.

But what made the conference so much more exciting than its separate constituents was the controlled collision between the eternal verities of veterans like the philosopher Herbert Marcuse, the anarchist writer Paul Goodman and the Marxist economist Paul Sweezey, with the fire of the new forces of opposition; the magnificent sarcasm of the Black Power figure Stokely Carmichael; the unrelenting denunciation of American foreign policy by John Gerassi, a member of the Vietnam War Crimes Tribunal; and R.D. Laing's poetic and wry discourse on the difficulty of comprehending the obvious.

As a first-year medical student whose principal source of political education thus far had been Socialist Labour League lectures under canvas on 'Five Reasons J.P. Cannon Betrayed the Fourth International', I was intellectually bowled over, not least at the sight of large numbers of people, often several thousand strong, listening intently to complex speeches on Marxist philosophy.

In retrospect it is easy to see the omissions. There was almost no interest in what workers were doing, despite the fact that there was an important all-London rent strike going on and bitter victimisation disputes at the Barbican and Roberts Arundel in Stockport. Despite its pro-feminist themes, it was entirely and unconsciously male-dominated and it was hopelessly and inexcusably naive about Third Worldism.

But it was a true political expression of the great waves of subjectivity which were to shake the world in 1968. Prone to idealism and voluntarism, Maoism and wowism, it was uncannily prescient about the events of the next twelve months; the Vietcong's Hue Offensive, that *tour de force* of guerilla strategy; the May Events with their savage exuberant mockery of capitalist rationality; and the beginning of the economic slowdown which was to surface as the oil crisis. Certainly it was a lot nearer the mark than the predictions of the LSD-soused acolytes of Sgt Pepper who saw the future, if at all, as an infinite progression of people being beautiful in geodesic domes.

It was of course the Summer of Love, days of dope as well as hope. And it was to the hippies who had garlanded him with flowers that Marcuse addressed his opening comment: 'I am very happy to see the flowers here and that is why I want to remind you that flowers, by themselves, have no power whatsoever, other than the power of men and women who protect them and take care of them against aggression and destruction.' Marcuse then proceeded to propose an exacting vision of social revolution, an unapologetic defence of Marx's 'utopianism': 'Utopian because it is precisely the form in which these radical features must appear if they are to be a definite negation of the established society.'

And so it went on: Sweezey decimating the representative of orthodox developmental economics, Walt Rostow; Gerassi dilating on William Walker's conquest of Nicaragua, Bateson analysing imperialism through St Paul, Jules Henry on the role of anti-communism in the American psyche, Lucien Goldmann, speaking in French, transposing the worlds of Racine and Robbe Grillet, Laing's description of the Milgram experiments to cries of mounting disbelief, Carmichael's great oration which wove in Lewis Carroll, Machiavelli and Sartre and concluded with a poem by an SNCC organiser, Worth Young, which ended: 'We have found you out, four-faced America, We have found you out.'

Someone a great deal wiser and more objective than I will have to plot the ups and downs in the twenty years since the conference. My own account of the tremendous set-backs as well as the great break-throughs achieved by the revolutionary Left over the last twenty years would centre on questions of tactics and organisation, areas for which the dialecticians of the Round House had scant regard. But the feelings reawoken by reconsidering the conference are Hegelian: ideas have the capacity to become a material force and there is, as Hugo not Marx said, no force that can stop an idea whose time has come. We started losing when we stopped arguing for our ideas. I therefore like very much Marcuse's conclusion, which adapts well to less optimistic times: 'Let us continue with whatever we can – no illusions but, even more, no defeatism.'

18

Rocking Against Racism*

I'm never quite sure whether Rock Against Racism was the last gasp of the 1960s or the first wave of the music–politics alliance which has gone on to produce Band Aid and Artists Against Apartheid. Probably, like Janus, we were facing both ways. It was a lot more proletarian than the May Events ever were in Britain but had some of the visual and theatrical flair of Les Évènements plus a hefty dose of the Russian Art movements. In the book I wrote about it, Beating Time, *I argue that understanding racism and opposing it on the political and the cultural terrain are only the beginning of unlocking our present nightmarish notion of 'being British'. Alas, we are no nearer that than in 1977.*

E.J. Hobsbawm has recently noted that 'the advance to socialism depends on mobilising people ... who remember the date of the Beatles' breakup and not the date of the Saltley pickets.'

To judge from the puritanical and pessimistic professor's other prognostications, he himself might have difficulty in precisely recalling either event. But his point remains. In my view, 'Our Great Movement' has very nearly succeeded in boring a generation to political death by its narrow definitions of what is political, its enslavement to institutional ritual and its lack of skill and cultural variety in communicating its ideas.

As socialists in the Women's Movement have been arguing for over a decade to very little avail – and the Situationists, the Surrealists, Mayakovsky's Lef Group and Uncle Edward Carpenter and All have been saying for nearly a century – when socialist politics become dislocated from the experience of everyday life, they lose their ability to inspire, to convince or to make marvellous.

Likewise, if the institutions of labour fail to meet the real needs of the class (which are emotional as well as economic), people will vote

* First published in *New Socialist*, 1981.

with their feet and leave a dwindling body of irrelevant zealots burnishing the rule-books and moving the points of order.

And it is no answer to bleat on about media bias – colossal and impudently blatant as it is – if the Left's own press imitates, badly, the graphic style of that media and aims itself at a hypothetical male, white, happily married union activist heavily into carpet slippers, Brylcream and whippets, a figure who bears very little relation to anyone in the modern working class.

If socialism is transmitted in a deliberately doleful, pre-electronic idiom, if its emotional appeal is to working class sacrifice and middle class guilt, and if its dominant medium is the printed word and the public procession, it will simply bounce off people who have grown up this side of the 1960s watershed. And leave barely a dent behind it.

The stakes are high. If we cede the difficult but necesary ground of the politics of everyday life – of the world of the cultural, the emotional and the sexual – it falls by default to the Right. The British ruling class has an almost unique sophistication and continuity. Not only does it possess immense material resources but it has on file several centuries of the imagery of subordination, patriotism and xenophobia to call on as required. It appears to possess history itself, to define 'common sense' and therefore to make the rules about what is funny, normal and entertaining.

To make a radical joke (as Richard Prior is able), a subversive TV appearance (as Arthur Scargill can) or produce a revolutionary Number One hit single (as the Sex Pistols did in Jubilee Week and the Specials did during this summer's riots) is to literally turn the tables on them. And it requires as much skill, timing and attention to detail as a successful bullion robbery.

There are ominous precedents if we fail. As Trotsky's luminous commentaries on the rise of National Socialism in Germany argued, Hitler's success depended not just on reformist paralysis and the tactical disasters of German communism, but on Hitler's brilliance at cultural and emotional manipulation – 'soul-massage', as Goebbels called it.

Wilhelm Reich has written a great deal of rubbish, but his pamphlet *What is Class Consciousness?* brilliantly anatomised the Left's incompetence in countering National Socialism's psychological appeal. And that was a Left which included Brecht, Heartfield, Eisler, Piscator, Guttman and Munzenberger, no slouches when it comes to the imagination.

Given the enormous technical advances the means of mass

communication have made since the days when Lenin and Brecht were still talking with wonder about the political possibilities of valve radio, our ability to lay bare and to utilise the popular arts politically is immensely important. Yet it is in popular music – an area until recently either ignored or else patronised by Left-wing theorists, lacking in Arts Council grants and low on personnel with PhDs in Marxist Aesthetics – that there has been the most advanced fight to take hold of and politically shape a popular culture.

Pop music can be a force of either the most unmitigated idiocy or of extraordinary emancipation, but as a very young, highly exploitative and very fluid branch of modern capitalism, it offers unique chances. There is certainly delicious vulgarity, infuriating megalomania, desperate clamour for glamour and a bewildering obsession with style. But over the last five years since the punk explosion and the international recognition of reggae music, beneath all the crap a surprisingly high proportion of the music has aimed at educating rather than anaesthetising the senses – in illuminating rather than obscuring reality, in heightening awareness rather than promoting stupidity.

It is music that has, both in the subjective and the objective, recorded social life at a particular stage, indicated possibilities and been a part of the future it predicted. In this respect, it conforms far more to the classical Marxist definition of art than the self-enclosed and therefore self-defeating radicalism of conceptual art, agit-prop theatre and minimal film-making. To the orthodox Marxist, I ought to add the pietàs that lousy politics alone cannot be improved by flashy graphics alone.

To classical aesthetes, I would insist that in taking seriously post-electronic popular culture, I am not claiming that the Sex Pistols are a more lasting monument to human creativity than Edward Elgar, or that John Cooper Clarke surpasses Sir Walter Scott.

But those purists – and they are still plentiful – who regard punk rock and Rastafarian music or, for that matter, James Joyce or Luis Buñuel as symptoms of the decadence of capitalism, should simply have the courtesy to listen to Bob Marley's *Exodus* album or The Clash's *Sandinista*, or for that matter *The Majestic Dub of King Tubby* and reflect whether *The Blackleg Miner* or the original Count Basie Band is so relevant after all to us here in 1981. This ignorance and hostility is too often simple snobbery. For as Hobsbawm (significantly disguising himself under the pseudonym of Francis Newton) wrote in 1959 about jazz: 'It has not belonged.' Certainly it has not belonged in the intellectual milieu where 'it would be fatal not to have heard of

Wozzeck or Petrushka but no eyebrows would be raised if a citizen thought Art Tatum was a boxer or Charlie Parker somebody's old school pal.'

Although music is exceptionally hard to write about from a political point of view, it is a pity more socialists do not read 'Francis Newton' in his splendidly pedagogic *The Jazz Scene*, or the music theory of the Brooklyn Marxist Sidney Finkelstein, Frank Kofsky's *Black Nationalism and the Revolution in Music* or the able and authoritative reporting of Valerie Wilmer on contemporary jazz and Vivien Goldman on reggae. And it is a pity that many on the activist Left tend to regard modern music as the passionate but politically confused outpourings of noble savages who might make passable socialists if they were only given the right books to read.

Rock Against Racism (RAR) was founded in August 1976, a year before the Anti Nazi League, and still pops up all over the place. It was RAR's particular success that it recognised the music was in itself political. There was no real need for oratory on the need to fight racism after Steel Pulse had played *Ku Klux Klan* or an exposure of YOPs schemes after The Clash had just burnt through *Career Opportunities*.

The anti-racist theme was deep in the roots of the music, from Bessie Smith through John Coltrane to Dudu Pukawana, and in connecting music and politics at this point, neither side was ex ploiting the other: Bessie Smith performed for the Garveyites, Billie Holiday sang (in a front room) for the Algerian underground and Ray Charles and many other black musicians raised money for the civil rights movement.

But the musicians who came to the RAR wanted to do something more than traditional fund-raising, to show musical solidarity and express the political emotions of an audience which was not so very different from themselves.

There is, in this respect, a difference between the electricity and urgency of the RAR/ANL Carnivals of April and September 1978 and this year's moving Leeds Carnival, and, say, the slightly star-struck and rather passive mood of the People's March for Jobs concert in Brockwell Park with a self-indulgent Pete Townsend swigging Remy Martin brandy he said was from Len Murray and Aswad cut off after two (magnificent) numbers.

Still, the very welcome presence of a member of The Who at a political gig – unthinkable in 1976 when most rock musicians were talking like Tories about tax and the unions – shows how far the mood has drifted within popular music. Musicians are expected to express some sort of political attitude in their music and their interviews – even if it is anti-politics, neo-gothic gloom or a 'it's-all-out-of-control-anyway' dance stance. This is not only due to punk and music journalists; events themselves have played a role, plus Mrs Thatcher and Ronald Reagan's inadvertent politicisation of people.

But RAR's philosophy of militant entertainment did a lot to show that the funky politics mix – the appeal to head, hands and feet – could work. Music and political demonstrations of all sorts will never be quite the same again.

Although there was a lot of spontaneity, it is not the case that RAR was a Larry Lightbulb, Amateur Night effort; the core group was an effective mixture of older designers, photographers and theatre workers with nearly a decade and a half's experience on the cultural Left and who knew that Zhdanov and Breton were about as well as being keen on Lee Perry and Walt Disney.

Many of the punk managers were of the same hue, although, we used to maintain, of a more anarchistic and unscrupulous nature.

But the older RAR people were delighted to join up with people in their teens stamped with the exuberance and crazy confidence of the punk eruption. RAR's concern with image, presentation and graphic style at gigs and carnivals and with its stickers, badges and newspaper *Temporary Hoarding*, reflected a shared and longstanding dislike of self-imposed socialist cultural ineptness.

The instigators of the protest letter to the music press which founded RAR were the photographer Red Saunders and the graphic designer Roger Huddle.

Besides being long-standing socialists (of the revolutionary persuasion) they were both ex-Mods who were crazy and knowledgeable about black music and so communicated anti-racism in a passionate and positive idiom. Both seemed to have evaded the higher educational system entirely.

They were quietly joined by other designers at the *Socialist Worker* printshop, famine writers, street fighters, nail biters and miscellaneous socialist and feminist misfits who formed a genuinely collective ideas whirlpool. Very many of the people who made RAR and *Temporary Hoarding* work were art-workers whose sympathies were very far to the Left but who found it impossible to fit comfortably in conventional socialist organisations.

In its first three years, RAR went through an expansion process – from a letter in the music press to a national organisation able to put on major outdoor festivals – which was hard to keep up with. In the weeks before the last election, RAR took on a national anti-racist tour which mixed 30 bands, 100,000 leaflets, 30,000 posters, 10,000 issues of *Temporary Hoarding* and 4½ tons of PA and lighting right round the UK. While an unconvincingly avuncular James Callaghan was praising 'Family Life, National Pride and Moderation', RAR's message to the electorate (besides voting Labour) was 'Rock Hard, Life is Deaf' – a slogan pinched from the surrealist Mimi Parent which has proved only too appropriate to the Thatcher era.

Within weeks of the Alien Culture outburst came the murder of Blair Peach in Southall and RAR took out the seats of the Rainbow Theatre in London in concerts of defiant solidarity with the Southall defendants.

As Thatcherism ground on, meeting precious little effective resistance, RAR became rather less fashionable in the fickle world of rock. Many erstwhile RAR supporters, delighted with the electoral reverse of the organised fascists, did not anticipate quite how xenophobic the Thatcher cabinet would be on racial and law-and-order issues. RAR was also a victim of its own success in another way. There was now Rock Against Everything, from inner city ring roads to politics. And bands like the late lamented Specials, The Beat and UB40 with their on-stage racial and musical mayhem had taken the RAR idea to its logical conclusion: on stage, black and white and dynamite.

It was also clear that UK reggae, perhaps helped a little by RAR, was stepping forward unaided into its own British identity – no longer dwarfed by the Jamaican originals, but with its own hard, bad styling.

There have also been depressing bandwaggons of near-rapist heavy metal music, vogues for arty nihilism and the current phase of militant flippancy, elaborate hairdos and pseudo-Latin vocalists keener on getting down and boogying than standing up and fighting.

But, outside the cocktail bars of Covent Garden, the RAR punk spirit is, if older and wiser, still very much alive and now not simply anti-racist but anti-nuclear and anti-Tory too. And the young bands just keep on coming, about the only good consequence of youth unemployment.

What is required of the political Left is the imagination, the patience and the political clarity to relate to all that passion. And perhaps save it from getting wasted.

Otherwise we are waltzing with ourselves in a political hulk which may look imposing but which is sinking under the dead weight of its outmoded cultural and political forms. At least the *Titanic*, they say, had a good band.

19

C.L.R. JAMES*

Optimism is not a proper emotion for a dialectical materialist. But C.L.R. James justified it by his erudition, his political experience and the age he wore so gracefully, and I will always cherish this meeting.

'People are treating me with far greater concern than before,' C.L.R. James grimaces. 'It's very tiring.' James has his feet up in room 384 of the Mayfair Hotel. Beside him lies a John Berger paperback, a brown cardboard folder of manuscript, his wheelchair and a ham sandwich plastered with English mustard. 'My feet are tired but my tongue is not. I do not intend to give in.' He talks with a rare passion and erudition: of Bolshevism, of Caribbean politics, of calypso, Sartre, cricket and his beloved Uffizi gallery. His speech is as fresh and pungent as his sandwich.

To the best of my ability, I have attempted not to hero-worship this man who, if Marxists believed in such things, would be the greatest living Marxist. And failed. For my generation, James is the essence of political legend: organising the Africa Bureau with George Padmore, bearding Trotsky in Coyoacan, organising sharecroppers in Missouri, hailing Nkrumah as the black Lenin in Accra, wandering into a Havana revolutionary congress with a volume of Michelangelo plates. In his wiry, eight-decade-young frame is the historical eloquence of E.P. Thompson, the cricketing connoisseurship of John Arlott, the revolutionary ardour of Tony Cliff and the preciousness of John Berger, all mixed up with a wit and a way with paradox which is entirely West Indian.

The outlaw James had better be resigned to his eminence. The three volumes published this week by Allison & Busby bring together a body of work previously passed from hand to hand as mimeos, photostats and battered American paperbacks. One volume is a collection of 'notes' on Hegel, Marx and Lenin; two more bring together

* First published in *New Society*, 1980.

stories and essays. (A final selection of essays is promised, and the headstone, a volume of autobiography, is on the way.) But the centrepiece of the present triptych of publications is *The Black Jacobins*, an account of Toussaint L'Ouverture and the San Domingo revolution, which James wrote in Brighton in 1937. The extraordinary narrative power and analytic intensity of this well-known but widely unread book is famous. But James's motive for writing it is not. 'I decided,' he told me, 'that I was going to write the story of some blacks who were not persecuted and sat upon and oppressed, but who did something.' The book is not only a pioneering exposition of black pride but is also stamped with James's head-on collision with Marxism.

Cyril Lionel Robert James was born near Port of Spain in 1901. He was the son of a teacher, won a scholarship to Queen's Royal College school (thirty years later, V.S. Naipaul went there, too), and then became a schoolteacher himself. He also began playing club cricket and writing stories. It was Learie Constantine, the Trinidadian cricketer, then playing in the Lancashire League, who suggested James should come over to England.

He arrived from Trinidad in 1932, equipped with an exceptional grounding in the European classics. But at Constantine's home in the small Pennine town of Nelson, he was presented with volume one of Trotsky's *History of the Russian Revolution* and Spengler's Decline of the West. 'It was then necessary to read the relevant volumes of Stalin. And, of course, I had to read Lenin in order to trace back the quarrel. And thereby I reached volume one of *Das Kapital* and *The 18th Brumaire* of Marx himself.'

In a decade in which Stalinist mythology dominated the Left, James came to his own conclusion: 'I realised the Stalinists were the greatest liars and corruptors of history there ever were. No one convinced me of this. I convinced myself. But having come to this conclusion, I wanted to meet some Trotskyists.'

He eventually tracked down this endangered species in Golders Green, noting with some amusement that 'I was much more familiar with the political material than the people who ran the group.'

As disaster overwhelmed the German Left, and Stalin switched to the desperate alliance-mongering of the Popular Front, James – now editor of the Revolutionary Socialist League's paper, *Fight* – made regular clandestine visits to the Paris exile grouping of revolutionaries around Trotsky. 'They were very serious days,' James admonishes, inflecting the adjective 'serious' as only an old-time Trotskyist can.

'There was a German boy very active in our movement. One day we found him at the bottom of the Seine.'

Trotskyism Repressed

James was, with D.D. Harber, the British delegation to the founding conference of the Trotskyist Fourth International in 1938. This tiny body was established with the hope that, in the holocaust to come, a clearsighted International might find a way through the chaos. But Trotsky, and effectively Trotskyism, succumbed to the terrible repression.

In his last years, the Old Man blazed with political imagination, intrigue and epistles, as if beaming out his political SOS. James was duly summoned to Trotsky's fortress in Mexico City. I have read their transcribed discussions and they give a rare glimpse of the Great Exile debating with an intellectual equal. 'Although we disagreed, I was tremendously impressed,' James recalls. 'Trotsky started with the analysis – international, political, philosophical. But the action, the activity, always followed. I got a glimpse of what Bolshevism of the old school meant.' James had been lured to North America by the Trotskyist James P. Cannon – some way to remove a 'troublesome' element in British Trotskyist politics. And in America, James soon found himself at odds with the orthodoxy, in the same way that Cliff in London and Cardan in Paris were to break with official Trotskyism.

James faced another crossroads. He had friends and, by now, a good job as a cricket correspondent in London. To remain in America and work through his disagreements with Trotskyism was a commitment to ten years of intellectual work. But James accepted the commitment and once again kept his rendezvous with history.

He helped to develop a theory of global state-capitalism. He rejected the Bolshevik concept of a vanguard party and emphasised shopfloor organisation as the seed of the new society. This meant rediscovering the Young Marx. It is this necessary reshaping of the Marxist ingredients which is presented in *Notes on Dialectics*, one of the reprinted volumes. James reckons it is 'one of the most important pieces that I have done. I'm waiting to see what people are going to say about it.'

The book was 'written in Reno when I was seeing about a divorce.' It represents the condensation of one of the remarkable political collaborations of modern times: James's political and intellectual prowess, Raya Dunayevskaya's understanding of the Russian material, and Grace Lee's German studies. It is written with fearsome intensity, calling out names and ferociously bashing down the arguments. It is Marxist philosophy at red heat and ought to be read by those tepid academics who at present monopolise the science in Britain.

The making of C.L.R. James is also presented in the beautifully edited collection of essays which, with Edward Thompson's recent writings, will do a great deal to revive the fortune of the genre. They demonstrate the sweep, drive and attack of James's Marxism. They move from early fiction, through polemic against racism, to the critical essays he wrote under many Trotskyist pseudonyms on the literature of Shakespeare, Melville and Mailer. (In the early years of *New Society* he wrote on both West Indians and cricket: but those articles are not collected here.)

And James has as good an ear as his eye. He writes beautifully in these essays about the Mighty Sparrow, Trinidad's most famous calypsoan, whom he describes as 'the most intelligent and alert person I met in the Caribbean,' and with great feeling about the young Paul Robeson, with whose Moscow-line politics he so fundamentally differed (though he and Robeson appeared together in the 1930s at the Westminster Theatre, in a dramatised version of Toussaint's story). We agreed to disagree about reggae, but James pays tribute to the tremendous effectiveness of Rasta music: 'The Rastafari are leftists, with no particular programme. But their critique of everything the British left behind, and those blacks who follow it, is very sophisticated.'

James came back to England after the Second World War, and remarried. He now divides his time between London and the West Indies, with interludes as, for example, a visiting professor at United States universities or colleges.

When I saw him, he was just back from Kingston, Jamaica, where

> ... naturally, I had talks with Manley. But the crisis in the Caribbean is not the problem of the capacity of the individual leaders: it's the tremendous mess the imperialists left them in. What is happening in Kingston today is precisely what happened in Chile under Allende. The same procedures are being carried out: de-stabilisation, economic manipulation, sabotage, the strategy of tension. And Seaga [the Jamaican opposition leader] promises everything but will bring nothing.

James now plans to return to Trinidad as a guest of the oilfield workers' union. 'This organisation is the most powerful political creation of the people of Trinidad and Tobago since the abolition of slavery. It is not that some intellectuals have got hold of it. It has been made by the people themselves.' James, the black Cassandra, had sent a public telegram of warning to the young Left-winger, Walter Rodney, two months before his assassination in Guyana last month. There is pain, but not disbelief, in his face as he remembers his young friend. One is reminded just how many political deaths James has had to witness, grieve over and endure.

I retain important reservations about James's Leninist libertarianism. He has been insufficiently consistent in applying his own criteria for socialist self-emancipation to Nkrumah, Castro and other revolutionary nationalists. His devastating critique of 'vanguard' parties – those toy Bolsheviks who ape and misunderstand Lenin's politics – is in danger of writing off altogether the need for the sinews of socialist organisation. But this is very small beer beside one's respect, admiration and affection for a revolutionary intransigent who inhabits both classical and Marxist culture like a familiar home. He moves from ancient Greece to the Detroit auto plants, and then to Florence, in as many sentences.

Hitler, Stalin, Vietnam

Liberal reviewers of his earlier collections of essays, *The Future in the Present* (published in 1977), found it hard to conceal a certain surprise that such intelligence and such compassion could issue from such a committed Marxist. But this is not remarkable at all. James's excellence is because of his political vantage point, not despite it. 'I have seen nothing', James states firmly, 'to shift me from the Marxist view of the world I adopted in 1934. I have watched nothing but the decline of this capitalist society. I have seen the first war, Hitler, Stalin, the Gulag, Vietnam. And now do I think Carter and Ronald Reagan and Mrs Thatcher are going to fix anything?' He waves contempt softly about the bedroom. 'And it would seem to me that all this frantic manoeuvring in the Labour Party and the trade unions is once again to keep the workers in order.'

Then his voice lowers again, and hangs suspended, as if addressing an auditorium. 'More and more people, especially black people, are alert. They reject the political choices offered them and are looking for a new way out of the mess. They are the ones who are now turning to Marx and Lenin to see if they have something to say.'

They should also be turning to C.L.R. James, who has already answered some of the questions events have yet to pose.

PART II VICISSITUDES

20

The *OZ* Trial*

The OZ trial in 1971, although a lot of brave fun, was dwarfed politically by the severe deterrent sentences handed out at the Angry Brigade trial and the introduction of Internment in Northern Ireland. Still, as a piece of casual bigotry, the prosecution took some beating and was an ominous and accurate portent. I spent a lot of the early part of the trial as a McKenzie Lawyer, that is a lay legal advisor allowed into the well of the Old Bailey. We spent our time passing notes to the defendants and blowing kisses to members of the prosecution. My strongest memory is of the late Marty Feldman's gabbled anti-clerical diatribe, unfortunately delivered too fast to be comprehensible if you were more than eight feet away. I spent the second half of the trial on an elective in Community Medicine in Milton Keynes, from which I despatched to Richard Neville draft speeches evoking Spartacus, Sacco and Vanzetti, and the National Unemployed movement, which he wisely discarded. This is a more sober account for the rank and file magazine of the National Union of Teachers, stressing the essential innocence of the project which brought the prosecution.

Last summer's extended trial accused the three *OZ* editors of 'conspiring together with certain other young persons to produce a magazine containing diverse obscene, lewd, indecent and sexually perverted articles, cartoons, drawings and illustrations with the intent thereby to debauch and corrupt the morals of children and young persons within the realm and arouse and implant in their minds lustful and perverted desires.' The prosecution was made, the Court was told on the basis of complaints made to the Police by the NUT and members of the public against a magazine said by the chief police witness to be 'openly critical of society in the context of the family unit'.

The course of the trial, the verdict and the appeal in this modern

* First published in *Rank and File Teacher*, 1972.

morality play are well known and are now being re-enacted, with *OZ*'s characteristic and necessary eye for the market, as souvenir books, late night play readings and Broadway musical hits. Already the *OZ* trial has taken on the air of comic relief, offsetting the stark and sobering prosecution of the Mangrove 8, Jake Prescott and Ian Purdie and the next in the programme of intimidation, the show trial of the Stoke Newington 6. In a world where a virtual life sentence is the reward for addressing three envelopes and even a Tory MP in Notting Hill Gate has noticed that the jury verdict in the Mangrove case shows 'a very strong inference that a number of police officers were lying in concert and that with the connivance of senior police officers had been responsible for the persecution of particularly articulate black people', it's rather hard to still see the funny side of the *OZ* courtroom debates about the appropriate size for Rupert's foreskin. Those liberals still left can take comfort from the Appeal Court's reluctant modification of sentence; radicals are more likely to agree with Richard Neville's assessment that 'if Judge Argyle had been a little bit brighter, we'd all still be in jail'; and the revolutionaries will add it to the lengthening list of political prosecutions brought under the 'law and order' rubric, tighten their political belts and stoke up their anger. And somewhere in the Forest of Wyre, equipped with her Teasmade, bedside Bible and daily help ('a very nice woman, who seems to sense that I have a lot on my mind and gets on with the job') Mary Whitehouse is picking up her phone to make another complaint.

What seldom does get discussed are the issues the schoolkids who took over *OZ* for an issue wanted to talk about – their schools, their teachers and their lives and desires. Once again kids' interests have got trampled under the battle between adults in their name. But as someone expelled from grammar school for producing an unofficial magazine (called *Rupture* and containing the word 'contraceptive'), I found the trial weirdly echoing themes of my childhood attempts to erupt out of the situation of school, indeed of everyone who has experienced that bewildering state of frustration and cowardice, egotism and idealism which constitute adolescent revolt.

Viv Berger described in an episode the extent of the freedom of expression allowed in official school publications. He drew a cartoon for his school magazine of an ant dropping bombs on South Vietnam. What the *OZ* editors did was the reverse, to allow young people to take control of a national circulation magazine, not the kind of offer made frequently by *Socialist Worker* or *Marxism Today*. And what the kids wrote was a not specially brilliant or revolutionary issue, but one which reflected an articulate dislike for a violent, authoritarian and boring education and a passionate longing for a state of sexual joy and personal freedom which the Underground was expected to provide. It reflected a mood of innocence which is already history.

On its 'obscenity' Bernard Levin, scarcely a Trotskyist wrecker, put it refreshingly accurately: 'I had not seen the disputed issue of *OZ* before the case and when I finally read it, my first conclusion was that I must have got hold of an incomplete copy from which many pages had been removed; I was unable to believe that what was in it could have led to the court proceedings ... those who think such stuff pornography quite literally do not know what pornography is.' Sexual references were actually infrequent and consisted mainly of passionate but hopeless-sounding pleas for sexual honesty and frankness. The cartoon of a middle-aged school teacher, moustache, chalkdust, pipe and cane, brandishing his penis with one hand while groping at a schoolboy's buttocks with the other, was frequently cited by the prosecution as offensive. It was clearly meant to be and aimed to show authority as naked and sexually repressed and to connect corporal punishment with sexual sadism. The kids had not been obscene, they had deliberately confused those carefully drawn territories of private and public, or staffroom and class, of behind the bike shed and speech day. They had done what Jenny Muscutt did when she refused to be ashamed that she possessed genitals or what Martin Woodhams did in the essay which got him expelled for obscenity. They committed the crime of not being hypocritical.

Politics and drugs were in *OZ* 28 too. But not the strident clichés of Fleet Street, most of the Underground and some of the Left press. Politics was grappled with through the stages of doubt and organisation. A bitter account of an SAU organiser confessed her own inadequacy: 'We could talk, threaten all right, but we weren't really prepared to act on it'; a melancholy critic of street demonstrations asks, 'How many of us know our oppressed brother?' Despite the carefully blasé profiles, sex and drugs were approached as something difficult, inaccessible and probably the source of pain. The linguistic savagery of the New York high school militant ('Schools are either shitholes that are like used condoms which have been sitting around for years or so sterile they're like condoms straight out of the packet, sterile like hospitals') seemed scarcely real ... then.

Two years later, a Schoolkids *OZ* would be a lot different. The *OZ* schoolkids themselves have hardened and are much more political now, they've all experienced their own small impossible version of fame and punishment, they have watched the *OZ* 3's six-week trial and symbolic castration at the prison barbers for letting them do it ('we hope it reminded them of the sort of fun school can be and only too rarely is', wrote Jim Anderson, the main *OZ* editor, in the introduction to *OZ* 28). We are all, especially the schools movement, two years older now. Perhaps now Schoolkids *OZ* would write about girls' liberation and homosexual rights, free schools and truancy centres, Margaret Thatcher and Bernadette Devlin. But the *OZ* 28, which only stumbled into existence because of the *OZ* editors' determination to take themselves less seriously than the police did, still says more about the education system as kids experience it than a heap of Penguins. It speaks volumes about what the Communist Manifesto called 'the bourgeois claptrap about the family and education'. Beneath the articles and between its lines come bubbling new proofs of the old theorems of Marx and Reich, of Neill and Duane. A re-reading of the transcript is to witness the meeting of two entirely conflicting versions of children's rights and the meaning of education. And it is to be reminded again, as Marx said when accused of wanting to stop the exploitation of children, 'to this crime we plead guilty'.

21

OZ Obituary*

In a way* OZ'*s post-trial demise did mark the end of an era. It also highlighted the inability of that genre of radicalism to transform itself.

I first met *OZ* in early 1967. In those days he was square, upright, dressed mainly in black and white and told satirical stories out of the corner of his mouth. He had the confidence which comes of being utterly unknown and an innocence which he didn't hesitate to exploit. He was prone to rather unsuccessful parodies of his elders and fond of what he thought were brilliant attacks on the moralism and alcoholism of the British cultural Left. But, beneath the faux-naiveté and the inadequately disguised ambition, was an intuitive radicalism and a directness and a friendliness which was in violent contrast to the pomposity and straightforward lying of most of his contemporaries. With the exception of the young *International Times*, which even at that time was exhibiting a remorseless lack of taste, and the small, stout and ill-tempered *Black Dwarf*, which often shouted at him incomprehensibly, *OZ* was alone.

Everyone else was either patronising or hostile and united in a more or less critical admiration for the status quo. *OZ* had expected his distant grannies and great-uncles on Fleet Street to gloat over every set-back. But he hadn't anticipated the resentment of many people he had sneakingly, and later he felt misguidedly, admired. The intellectual weeklies, the new aged satirists, the media radicals and, above all, the socialist Left with its carefully achieved dowdyness and its organisational cunning, treated *OZ* with a curious disdain. Indeed, it was as much a reaction against this polite but icy disapproval that *OZ* first assumed the calculated visual excesses, the typographic flamboyance and acquired his considerable skill at insolence. At this early age, too, came the brief but intense affair with Swinging London and the beginning of *OZ*'s formidable intake of substances. And here too, to

* First published in *OZ*, 1972.

the discerning eye, was the early evidence of the hallucinations and the falling down in the street which were to herald *OZ*'s later tragic instability.

But the gloaters of Right and Left who viewed *OZ*'s 'depravity' with a barely concealed contempt were to see him, in his middle years, develop a remarkable following among young people. And for them, *OZ* was almost alone in fully expressing the energy and imagination with which they were reacting against the banality and restrictions of urban life: of home, work and school, of a future illuminated by moon launches, royal gymkhanas and the dole. Their chaotic kicking against a life-long career as an obedient producer and consumer was mirrored in *OZ*'s chaos.

At that time *OZ* was to provide, if not the first or the best, one of the fiercest and most compelling cries of rejection of the choice offered the young within welfare capitalism. He seldom said exactly what they thought but he did express how they felt. With a voice alternately cracked with passion and hoarse with laughter, *OZ* devoted himself to the destruction of those comfortable myths we had been brought up to cherish; the myths of the Cold War, of the disappearance of poverty, of the incorruptibility and virtue of the courts and police, of the worthiness of the schools and universities, of the existence of democracy. *OZ* took an early interest in the American war in Indo-china, the police regimes of our Nato Allies and the facts of an unendurable poverty and homelessness. And though *OZ* himself seldom attended the movements which grew to express a rejection of those myths, the May Events, the student sit-ins, the squatting and the demonstrations against the Vietnam War were increasingly part of his life.

It would of course be misleading to portray *OZ* as a stern political critic poring over maps of capitalism. He insisted on an almost annoying flexibility: one would meet him one month passionately enthusiastic about flying saucers and the next buried in Lenin. *OZ*'s personality was so contradictory that many feared a serious instability of character. But *OZ*'s own style expressed a desire to begin an alternative to the nightmare of the present now. *OZ* was attempting to promote a cultural uprising, his attack on society was not merely cerebral but displayed in the funk of its colour and music and the sheer delight of boogying along alive and free. Indeed, even at this stage of his life many of *OZ*'s enemies, their own lives a cage of postponed pleasures and suppressed desires, found *OZ*'s mere existence an outrage. *OZ* himself, on good days, still felt there was space and time to experiment with new ways of living and loving each other. But other mornings, when the attempt to both bring into being a new culture and then defend it politically was too much, *OZ* could be heard to moan that it was 70 per cent crap anyway and he would sit, in an insoluble gloom, complaining that he could hear nothing but cash registers in his ears.

OZ's insomnia and occasional depression was still concealed from all but close friends, and in the famous series of trials (soon to be reissued as a Commemorative Retrospective Tribute 22 Album Set) *OZ* was again to show his flamboyance, courage and organising ability. But although he bore the trial with stamina, and at times relish, the strain was considerable. *OZ* had finally stumbled rather than charged across those who control society. In his increasingly frequent serious moments, *OZ* regretted that his ideas about sex and education had not been more carefully thought out and his old desire to shock had not been linked to a movement which could actually organise. He was forced to accept what he had always known, that although the state depends on myths, it is not an illusion itself and that there must be a material basis for free minds. *OZ* was still prepared to look visionary but many of his old friends were more anxious to carp at his mistakes than develop his ideas. To survive *OZ* had been obliged to become notorious, to make use of a fame he actually despised and suffer the chorus of sell-out from a movement itself in a surly stagnation. And *OZ*'s long-standing romance with Karl Marx was increasingly causing both parties pain. The friendship had always been platonic but Marx became increasingly physically demanding and *OZ* found himself still incapable of surrendering to such a stern, even sadistic, lover.

It became increasingly obvious in his last years that many of his most deeply held ideas had rebounded. The movement *OZ* had tried to express had been towards, not an altered form of work and government, but the disappearance of both. But now that glimpse of the future was overshadowed by the instability of the present any longer to provide work, housing or a half-way decent standard of living. *OZ* was sympathetic but external to that fight. The Revolution which had meant to *OZ* the possibility of an altered and a freer relationship between man, woman and nature, had become a euphemism for the hounding of certain West London police officers. The music which had powered *OZ*'s wild dance was busy either parodying or consoling itself, half-buried under unreadable PhDs and unctuous DJs. *OZ* would be seen, half grumpy, half pitiful, at his old haunts being bought by a new generation of long hairs who had inherited the culture *OZ* had fought for but who were squandering it, wallowing in their own groovy passivity and doing what had been exciting five years ago as a reactionary routine now.

Almost an exile within the Underground and in the impossible situation of becoming a symbol for a generation, *OZ* was still snubbed by a Left who seemed to refuse to admit they had anything to learn. And *OZ*'s old and final source of power, the phallic self-confidence of his Australian youth, was, he realised painfully, finally counter-revolutionary. *OZ* could no longer wave his cock when in doubt. A sexual politics had come out, people were organising against the family, against the sexual training and sexual guilt that crushed women and hobbled men.

The last part of *OZ*'s life was spent in a wistful melancholy. *OZ* had been exhausted finally by demands which he could never begin to fulfil and he would talk bright-eyed of the irresponsibility of his youth. He was happiest among friends reminiscing and he would talk of the old days with a bewildered tenderness. *OZ* had grown hardened outside, but inside hurt by denunciations of movements he had helped to bring into being.

The circumstances of *OZ*'s tragically early death remain unclear. Whether *OZ* is dead, of suicide or sexual excess, or whether *OZ* is alive and operating under a series of new names is unclear at the moment. What is clear is that *OZ* bizarrely and for a short period expressed the energy of a lot of us. We regret his passing.

22

Death of a Hospital*

The impact of the cuts on the NHS, which were already apparent in East London in the 1970s, has become so marked in the Thatcher years that now none of the smaller East End hospitals exists, one having been converted to a luxury private hospital. But in 1974 the closure of Poplar Hospital was a momentous sign of things to come. My introduction to the Isle of Dogs, where I now practise, was by two of the women shop stewards campaigning against Poplar Hospital's closure. They took me into every workplace on the five-mile road which curves round the island: arguing with Sikh pattern checkers, making speeches in ship repair canteens plastered with pin ups, marching inside the fortifications of the West India Docks and round the back of the gas works. There were leaflets, flyposting and motions passed everywhere from the local darts team right up to the South East Region of the TUC. There were Saturday High Street marches with the kids and the paper carnations and the 'Save Our Hospital' signs, handwritten and heartrending. Finally, an audience with Barbara Castle herself. None of it worked. They closed Poplar for ever, knocked it down brick by brick and are now driving out the population it once served so well to build a shambolic mixture of post-industrial estates and yuppy ziggurats sans planning restrictions, sans planning, sans everything.

Among the many lights switched off by Edward Heath this week is one in the heart of East London's dockland which may never go on again. It belongs to the Casualty and Admissions Department of Poplar Hospital, a black, brick-built tower off the East India Dock Road.

It was never a very fancy hospital, no East London hospitals are. But for more than a hundred years it has served the dockers, factory workers and seamen and their wives and kids who live and work on the Isle of Dogs, in Poplar and down towards Newham.

* First published in *Socialist Worker*, 1974.

For a year now, the hospital administrators have been playing bureaucratic games with a strong local campaign to save the 81-bed hospital. The official local campaign, which consisted mainly of press statements by the local Labour MPs, was confident that their protests had registered and had in writing a promise that Poplar would stay open at least until April 1974.

Then, two days before Christmas, the bureaucrats struck. 'The staffing difficulties in Poplar Hospital have now reached a point where it is considered that the level of care that can be given to the patients is below that required for safety and in the best interests of the patients it has been decided that there is no alternative but to suspend admissions to Poplar from 31 December 1973 .... Arrangements will be made to divert ambulances .... As and when it is found that staff are no longer required at Poplar Hospital they will, if they wish, be transferred to other hospitals,' wrote L.C. Phipps, the Hospital Secretary, who had promised exactly the reverse only two months before.

The Labour MPs have issued another hurt statement, but the nurses, technicians, porters, telephonists and cleaners at the hospital, many of whom live themselves on the vast, isolated estates which surround the hospital, had no time for indignation.

Extreme

On the morning of 21 December, they were simply herded into a meeting, of which no warning was given, and told the hospital was to cease admitting patients. When nurses and doctors demanded to know who had decided 'the medical standards' had fallen, they were told there was 'a panel of impartial medical advisers'. When NUPE stewards wanted to know why management were suddenly concerned about 'staff shortages', the secretary could offer 'no details'.

And details of the promised alternative jobs in 'other hospitals' were vague in the extreme. As a NUPE steward at Poplar told me, 'At the rate the regional board is going, it doesn't look like there will be any hospitals left to transfer ourselves to. And after this shambles, I don't think any of us will ever believe another word from hospital management.'

For the people of the area, the news was broken still more brutally. Early on New Year's morning, a docker who arrived with a child with a badly scalded hand took a swing at the gate porter who had to tell him that the Casualty had been closed at midnight that night, for good.

Handful

When your kid is screaming with pain, you can't cope with 'shadow regional health authorities' and 'formal recommendations to the Secretary of State'. You just know that one more of the handful of amenities provided for East London workers has gone. And you lash out.

For anyone in a workshop accident, a pub fight or a late-night overdose on the Isle of Dogs, that vast floating housing estate circled by cranes, will now have another quarter of an hour added to their emergency journey. If they are on foot, and many casualties walk into hospital, the journey to the nearest, already overloaded Casualty Department at Bow could mean another half-hour.

And the loss of Poplar Hospital, which during the Blitz became something of a symbol in the East End and which has provided medical care for more than a hundred years to four generations of East Londoners, shows quite how severe the cuts in social spending are biting.

A man outside the closed Casualty with a hand dripping with blood who, surprisingly good-naturedly, offered to sign a protest petition in his own haemoglobin, said, 'Well, unless they start knocking down the estates and selling them for firewood, there's nothing much else down this way they can close, is there?'

For the implications of the Thames Group Management's apparent success in outmanoeuvring the protesters and disregarding one of the strongest Labour councils in Britain, MPs and all, are frightening. Plans to close the German Hospital, a fine old Lutheran charity hospital in Dalston, and the Metropolitan Hospital in Shoreditch have already been announced.

The London Jewish Hospital in Whitechapel is under the axe. Each East End hospital closure meets with a storm of local protest, packed town hall meetings, furious letters to the papers. People who have seen death and birth of those close to them in their local hospitals don't like them suddenly vanishing or being turned into old folks' homes.

Closure

On paper there are ambitious new plans to build regional super-hospitals, all piped music and waitress service. The Board of Governors of the London Hospital quietly announced last month they intend razing to the ground the East End's most famous hospital, with, of course, plans to replace it with a medical skyscraper some time early in 1980.

But given the overall economic situation, the continuously un-relenting cuts in health expenditure and the almost inevitable delays in all hospital building, East Enders are doubtful about the closure of existing facilities in the name of future medical promises.

A meeting of NUPE stewards in the Thames Group last Friday at St Clement's Hospital took a hard line against any loss in jobs or medical facilities until satisfactory alternatives are actually in existence. Hospital workers in the remaining open hospitals are learning the hard way quite how ruthless the new-style cost-conscious NHS administrators are.

Nobody, least of all the patients and staff of the threatened hospitals in East London, or the many other parts of Britain where the same battles are in the offing, are arguing that these old hospitals are the answer. However hard you try to overcome it, they are grim and still bear the stamp of the Poor Law.

If health care really was developing in Britain, these hospitals would probably be best developed as local community hospitals, run mainly by GPs, and housing day centres for the old, nurseries and antenatal and childcare centres which fitted what is needed for the continuous good health of the working class and not the emegencies of accidents and acute illness.

Until hospital workers and hospital patients can assert some control over the mysterious forces which govern the present health service and thwart their plans to dispose of existing medical services, this is so much pie in the sky. Ask the man with the scalded baby.

23

The Bangladesh Floods*

The flooding of Southern Bangladesh continues to be a regular but entirely preventable event. Despite the scale of the human loss, it is badly reported in Britain and I am kept better informed by Bangladeshi patients than the English newspapers (one of the advantages of being a doctor in an immigrant area). Browsing in the booksale in the Marx Memorial Museum recently, I found a late 1940s Communist Party pamphlet on the India Independence Movement, didactic in idiom, with test questions at the end of each chapter, about the destruction of the Indian textile industry, the parallels with Tsarism, and the role of Gandhi. The output of the present-day Left on the sub-continent does not compare well.

Nature has played the final cruel joke on mankind's most miserable nation.

Already in poverty-stricken Asia, Bangladesh is the pauper. But for the past month even the flat plains and rickety houses of the most waterlogged country in the world have been swept away in the worst summer monsoon in memory.

The rice fields and the towns are flooded, the earth dykes overwhelmed. Crowded rafts are moored to the roofs of submerged huts and in towns the sewers have been burst open by the sheer force of the rising water.

The sodden bodies of people or cattle who could not reach dry land are found caught in the branches of half-submerged trees. Cholera and starvation stalk behind the water.

Concrete and steel can survive the deluge, but 800,000 straw and bamboo homes have been simply swept away and more than 22,000 cattle drowned. Bridges, railways and roads have been engulfed and the Bangladesh Relief Minister estimates 2,000 people have died.

The summer rains are normally expected and welcomed by the peasant farmers. But this deluge has totally destroyed the summer rice

* First published in *Socialist Worker*, 1972.

crop, washed away rich soil and burst the few irrigation schemes built in an attempt to retain and control the monsoon rains.

Victim

Nearly a fifth of Bangladesh's rice crop is lost. In good years the country still has to buy food on the world market to feed its own people. This year, a year when the wheat harvest in North America is threatened by drought, the Bangladesh government will need to buy replacement grain costing more than £450 million. Bangladesh has just £16 million in foreign currency reserves to spend.

For centuries Bengal has been the victim of spring floods as the Himalayan snows melt, of cyclones crashing in from the Bay of Bengal and of summer monsoons. But its defencelessness against disaster is man-made.

Its rivers could be tamed, its rains could be used, the cyclones anticipated and prepared for. Most of all, the skills and the craft of its immense population could be allowed to go to work. In Australia, after the terrifying 1956 floods in New South Wales, a system of mountain dams and reservoirs were speedily built which could contain a flood of Old Testament proportions.

The cyclones that slash across Florida from the Gulf of Mexico are plotted by weather satellite and prepared for by coastguard, radio and civil authorities. Rescue relief is almost a formality by the time the whirlwind arrives.

Slump

But there are no precautions or warnings in Bangladesh. The country pillaged by Britain is instead experiencing the economic slump of Western capitalism in a terrifyingly extreme form.

Bangladesh was born in the Independence struggles of 1971 in the teeth of cyclones which killed 200,000, pillaging and mass rape by the Pakistani army and mass flight of refugees into India. But it had at least won its right to nationhood.

Since then it has experienced our inflation, unemployment and slump ... gigantically magnified. Basic prices have jumped between one and four times since 1970.

Starvation is now a fact of life. Children are literally born with malnutrition, starved of protein even in the womb.

Yet this picture of despair is the new reality for Asia in a world where Western capitalism has ceased to grow. In a rational, that is socialist, world the floods and the famine and the disease could be conquered. In a world dominated by a declining Western capitalism and the uninterested state capitalism of Russia, China, and Eastern Europe, the nations which possess the wealth and the knowledge to save the 8 million people of Bangladesh are instead pulling up the ladder.

For now that Western capitalism is scarcely bothered to exploit Bengal any longer, it has become an embarrassment on the international accounts sheet, a nation that is redundant.

In the stark words of the *Financial Times*: 'Bangladesh is too poor to be able to attract commercial funds.'

The chance of feeding the population is far off, of building dams non-existent. When the world is richer and more knowledgeable than ever in history, we are set for the starvation of an entire nation which we can watch on colour TV but not halt.

This kind of concern is well reflected in the Labour government's relief aid. After three weeks' warning, Aid and Development Minister Judith Hart spent most of last week trying to give the impression of activity by holding conferences about whether to panic or not. Eventually, a wretched £10,000 worth of cholera vaccine and a selection of army blankets were dispatched on a charter plane which proceeded to sit on a tarmac in Luxembourg for the next 48 hours.

Donors

In the circumstances, it is rather like contributing a seaside pail to the captain of the sinking *Titanic*. But it enabled Judith Hart to make several radio appearances gleaming with concern.

In fact, the voluntary organisations that provide the vast majority of disaster aid are a good deal more political about the problem than the Labour Left. Don Thompson, of War on Want, says,

> We say to our donors, 'Thank you very much. We'll endeavour to use your money reasonably. But have you ever thought about how our country has profited from Asian poverty?' It's all very well to profess concern about medical needs and to send cholera vaccine

> but Britain still has a typical exploitative relationship with Asian medicine. We take 2,000 of their doctors a year – that's a fifth of the registered practitioners. And household names like BP and Shell have squeezed the jute and textile industries out of existence with synthetics. We would be misusing public sympathy if we implied that a bit of intermittent compassion will alter the international structures which cause poverty.

The answer is not the compassion-on-the-cheap of Judith Hart or the more substantial but equally wrong-headed concern of the charity organisations. Both substitute the appearance of doing *something* for an explanation of why, in reality, nothing is being done. Both fail to understand the world capitalist system, to see how slow-down in the West means dead stop in Asia, that shortages here means starvation there.

But an answer does lie with the working-class movement, which must again take up the cause of the workers and peasants of Bengal. That means seeing the flood victims not as helpless objects of pity but as active allies.

24

The Rolling Stones' Tour of Europe*

Idiotically, I'd always fondly imagined that the Stones were really on the side of revolution. Their lack of overt socialist pronouncement was merely the work of their management and record companies, I presumed. It was a salutary shock to find them Tory dickheads after all. Still, the Tour of Europe at least took me to affluent Frankfurt and demoralised Glasgow in the mid-1970s, cities registering in different ways the shape of things to come. And gave a flavour of pre-punk disillusion with pop stars.

Frankfurt: big banks, big cars; money oozing quietly through the streets. A concrete paradise of consumption, it is the centre of commerce in the most successful bit of West European capitalism. Hard to find a car more than three years old or a cakeshop not crammed. 'Mit uns haben Sie in der Ganzen' and take the waiting out of wanting with the Stadt Kredit Bank's credit card. The advert shows stylish customers vanishing into old-fashioned shops to buy china, jewellery and cameras on tick. People bustle in the shops as if it's Christmas all year round. Prosperity rules, the Mercedes seem to be whispering in disdain as they whisk past the road-sweeping carts pushed by Yugoslavian 'guest-workers'. On the TV the commercials last longer than the programmes and half the channels show US Forces shows.

Sex is merely another greed to be satisfied and commodity to be supplied. Miles of respectable boulevards are lined with sex shops, sex bars and floor shows, opulent-looking establishments labelled in the Esperanto of eroticism, 'Sex Kino', 'Total Nudity', 'Sensation'. From their windows bleak pin-ups stare, their faces frozen in the masks and leers of the trade, pretending fascination with their own nipples or the corsets they are strapped into, pressing themselves against chains or bars. The props are on sale too, and already in late afternoon the first sullen and grey whores start to act out the acts in

* Shortened version first published in *Street Life*, 1976.

the doorways while rump-faced blokes stroll past, leering.

I was last in Frankfurt in 1968, the Year of the Street Fighting Man. It was the national conference of the German Student Socialist Movement. Danny Cohn-Bendit told jokes and Bernadine Dohrn said it was good to be a socialist in America because you lived in the heart of the monster. Helke Sanders, one of the founders of German Women's Liberation, threw protest oranges at the long-winded male orators and asked, 'Why do you speak here of the class struggle and at home about the difficulties of orgasm?' We men tittered smugly and didn't dare to look in each other's eyes.

Dohrn has been living underground in America since 1970, at one time the FBI's most wanted fugitive. Holger Meins, one of those exuberant orators, died on hunger strike in Stuttgart's Stammheim Jail in 1975 looking unrecognisably, inhumanly gaunt. Not very far away, Ulricke Meinhoff, systematically driven to despair in her noiseless, echoless prison cell, was edging to the end of the excruciating last year of her life. And the pathologists quarrel over her remains which suggest she died, not in defiant suicide, but after a sordid prison rape. Under new state security rules, over half a million German public employees have already been vetted politically. A Good German remains a politically adaptable one. Under the thin skin of liberal democracy, the re-militarised core of West Germany seems to find it only too easy to relapse into its old ways. A May Day poster tatters rather unconvincingly in the wind and a small hungry boy with a crew cut and big stary eyes presses his nose against the hotel where the greatest rock 'n' roll band in the world are waking up. The front porter hustles him away.

Onstage Jagger is fast as a whistle, fit as a PT instructor. The Frankfurt audience regard him gravely in a sort of trance. Sometimes you catch a man glancing at his girlfriend's rapt face and looking slightly worried about what he's going to do that night. They know they have come for the fantasia and Jagger knows it too and taunts them for it. 'You like it,' he tells the audience as he hoists his cock. 'You're starfuckers,' the band sings accusingly. 'What else can a poor boy do?' pouts Jagger, fondles his bum, then caresses his talc-coloured nipple.

One of the implacably bored attendants shoots a look of utter hatred, but the gleaming faces in the crowd are utterly absorbed with Jagger's series of sexual takes. It's not as simple as the fetishism of the sex shops, though the pouts and flaunts and poses are taken from the same stamp album. It's rather that he's adept at shuffling through the mannerisms of a sort of alienated fucking, bumping and grinding but never coming, all the forms of sex but without content or warmth. Grunts of submission, not cries of joy and release. By straining the stripper and the queen through the sieve of his own male arrogance, he alters both their meanings.

Men in the audience become fascinated by a man who can be completely camp, right down to his blacked-up voice, without relinquishing sexual power over women. Women can enjoy his narcissism and experience his mock sadism at a safe distance. But despite the rather cursory scenes of crowd abandon, the show's effect is curiously draining and people walk out rather numbed and exhausted, aroused but not released. On both sides of the lights, people are happy to stay trapped inside their fantasies.

Later Keith Richard and I have an utterly predictable row about politics. He seems to have a *Daily Telegraph* view of the world where the real problems are the tax laws and the trade unions. It ends with the usual get-out, 'I'm only a musician, man. Don't talk to me about politics. I hate politicians.' I try to work out a question about sexism that's not going to be boring, man, and realise abruptly what an incredibly male atmosphere saturates the Stones. A few bars of Emmylou Harris even got snatched off. But this pinnacle of male power is an emotional ice box. Suddenly get very depressed about the complicated nonsense everyone is laying on each other in the name of a Good Time and attempt to weep on Keith Richard's shoulder. Not a good idea. Charlie appears to be getting thrown out for upstaging Mick Jagger, which pleases CSM greatly. I appear to be behaving, in Keith Richard's words, like a 'neurotic provincial queen'. Big boys don't cry, at least not unless they are queer, come from out of town or have mental ailments.

The Stones' view of women has always been quite clear. In the *Angry OZ Magazine* produced immediately after the editors' jail sentence in 1970, there was a fine and fierce attack on Jaggerism:

> First let me explain why I write this article to Mick and all you men. I am the Stupid Girl who hit her head too many times against your heart of stone. I am the Factory Girl, the Honky Tonk Woman, Brown Sugar, the Parachute Woman and Ruby Tuesday. I am the girl who had to settle for your expectations, whose eyes were kept to myself while you could look for somebody else. I wanted your mind and was given your arm and leg. I had your knife stuck in my throat till it hurt. I am Yesterday's Girl. But then, SO ARE YOU.

And although nowadays Jagger sings more often of sweet angels than stoopid gerls, it's just another kind of condescension. 'Actually,' he told the readers of *Honey* later in the tour, 'I think women have had too many opportunities and they're not capable of using them properly. Men do most things better than women. They cook better. They make better secretaries. Generally, I think women are inconsistent. In Indonesia, I have seen women carrying bricks and building houses. It happens in China, too. That's real equality. But here, the women aren't ready for it.' The (few) women who are really into the Stones must know they are celebrating their own subordination. But the Stones have always been a boys' band, and what's upsetting is what the Stones seem to bring out in other men, not just the thousands of bands who imitate them or the jostling rock writers (male, as usual) or the sea of GIs. It's a scrappy, xeroxed sexual arrogance which has to do with pretending to be permanently in control, exterior, stylised and cold. It's probably very little to do with anything the Stones are like as people. But that idea of manhood driven by the need to dominate sexually and unable to surrender is very hard and lonely work sustaining.

Glasgow, the next stop, smells of sick and vinegar. On Saturday night the streets were more than usually full of revellers getting warmed up for the Stones and, more important, the European Cup Final for which the pubs were staying open until 3 a.m. 'Pernod Wilkommen' and 'Für Das Kommende Fussballspeil Viel Gluck Von'. Ladbrokes' posters have been plastered over the Glasgow Right to Work Committee's 'Wage Cut, Dole Figures Soar, We Won't Take It Any More' bills.

Glasgow is a town that's had its industrial guts kicked out over the past four years. There are now 32,000 workless. Once it was the leading engineering centre of the world. William Beardmore's factories designed and produced turbines, steam ships, taxi cabs, all-metal flying boats and armoured cars. The Parkhead Forge employed 40,000, mainly women workers, during the First World War. But now Marathon, the yard salvaged from the old UCS Combine in the 1972 work-in, is left making its last oil rig, for a drilling in Abu Dhabi. And when that's finished the yard will close and there is not much stomach for a fight.

Clydebank is literally dying. The barbed wire rolls on the fencing round John Browns and Marathon is crusty with dust. Only a few men in black boiler suits move over the grey rig and spark out the odd blue glint of acetylene. A Tunnel cement casting unit next to Marathon is under demolition but the equipment knocking it down had packed up. A couple of men with pneumatic drills nibble at the remaining huge up-ended towers, dented walls and reinforced rubble. I have never seen fresh bomb damage but it must look like this. Huge towers upended, walls dented, wires and cables hanging like creepers, concrete rubble, split open to show the rusty reinforcing steel which once held it together. A telephone box has been purposefully vandalised, its innards sag out and the telephone book is carefully shredded. Even the gulls have a look of despair. In front of this mess someone has propped up a 'Danger Asbestos Working' sign on a stone. Even in its death throes, Clydebank heavy industry is deadly.

The only new shop opposite the yards is a bright poster-red Army Recruiting Office. It has a photo of a British square at Waterloo, a cardboard model of a youth in denim saying, 'You want to learn to live, mate' and a hand-lettered poster which says simply, 'Leaving School: No job, No Career prospects, No pay? This could be you. The Army of the Seventies: Good jobs, Good money, Good times.' In a newsagent's box, 'The Strathclyde Police Community Involvement Branch invite you to their coffee mornings.' In a grassy field there is a big sign that says, 'This is the site of the new Hillingdon District Hospital.' It looks as if it has been there for some time.

Barrowland is Glasgow's Sunday market. There used to be a famous ballroom but, like most public places of entertainment, it got burnt down. Families wander round pinched and in permanent argument about money. You can buy second-hand trannies, hanging like radio fish on strings, socket tool sets ('ask Colin and Jeff for details of their "big tools" '), framed portraits of John Buchan, gents' undies with 'Watch Mae Willie' stamped on and vintage fridges. It's the tattiest tat I've ever seen, the bits and pieces of a society slipping from development into under-development, a jumble of pieces from the past. A grey, crew-cut man sells socialist newspapers with a haunting cry of 'Wages Held Down, Therefore Prices Will Rocket' and the air of a man who has seen it before.

From the second-hand TV stall, Margaret Thatcher's tiny eyes glint out, 'Prosperity and political freedom go hand in hand. We need to return to the old virtues of enterprise and self-reliance.' She is ignored as people sort through the tat. From a residual hippy store, 'You're a Fool to Cry' wafts out over the stalls. You don't have to be a neurotic provincial queen to feel like crying in this poor part of town. A crazy-looking man with a mouth organ starts rasping out and stamping his foot. His tune has no tune and sounds military. A lady with her ankles bagging over her shoes and bandages flapping from her leg ulcers puts her arms round him and comforts him.

Lois Hobbs works for Interval House, a battered wives' centre in about the last surviving bit of the old Gorbals.

> Well, it's got rats and it's filthy, and every now and then the kids upstairs smash all the windows with a brick on a string. But the women love it. It's their own. What's funny is how hard the men take it when the women go to a place that's women only. All these big hard men are just hollow inside. It's like these men who won't let their wives out of the house on their own. I think they must be very insecure or something. They find it awful hard to express their emotions. Unless they have had a bit to drink and then they can go mad. Some of those men, their mothers could be dying but they can't cry. Their jaws just lock. Hard men with hollow insides.

I clamber up to the top of the Necropolis thinking about the grimness of Lois's tales. It's the graveyard of Glasgow's bourgeoisie, black and cold and high in the city. Its tombs are ornate, pagan-looking: toadstools, chessmen, arrowheads, rockets. But they house the remains of the respectable Protestants who sternly built capitalism in Scotland, and took its power over the world. Calcutta, Ottawa, Sydney, Gallipoli, the death stones read. In the Necropolis hangs the presence of the religion with which the rising bourgeoisie terrified Scots workers into their factories and held them in their harsh, unbending families. On the skyline, the post-war tower blocks are like the tombstones of buried giants. Inside those flats are dead souls, too: marriages that have no meaning, feelings bottled up, people who have learnt to hurt each other as the only way to express themselves, nights of desperate, joyless boozing.

We live in an industrial system which is becoming a catacomb with the litter of its ideas blowing round our feet. Only the once-upstanding values, of Patriotism, of the Kirk and the Family are now as shrunk and seedy as the industrial system which gave birth to them. The Union Jack is a shopping bag or the badge for bullying blacks, religion has sunk to Songs of Praise and the family is rather a grand word for a group of people of different ages who overlap in an eighteenth-floor concrete bunker. When we make our socialism, our insurrection of the just, it will need to bring into being new ways of feeling, new sorts of values as well as different places to live and work inside.

In the meantime, all those slashing songs about being free end up leaving the audience more baffled and imprisoned than ever. Stuck inside a strange conservative ritual, a final turn in a Britain which is itself like a run-down variety hall.

25

Blood on the Lino: 24 Hours in Casualty*

During the 1970s, that political transition zone which delivered us to the mercies of Mrs Thatcher, I was working as a doctor in acute hospital medicine while attempting to write while on call or early in the morning. For over a year I was involved in a particularly gruelling Casualty rota at St Mary's Hospital, Paddington, which included one stretch of 24 hours without a break as the only Casualty officer in the hospital. This is an account of one such 24-hour stint, written up at 9.00 a.m. the following morning in the tea bar on Paddington Station.

8.00 a.m.
The morning starts slowly enough, sprains, twists and tears; lumps, spots and abscesses. The daily influx of patients returning to have their stitches cut out, their wounds dabbed and redressed, their tetanus jabs, their certificates and their reassurance.

Not that the mornings don't bring real emergencies. It is almost impossible to imagine quite the things that can fall upon, hit, crush and cut the human body. The world of Casualty is like a gravityless lunar capsule where limbs and surfaces are continually colliding and objects constantly tumble and drop. Heads are bombarded by falling saucepans, dropped cans, abandoned half-bricks and unexpected beams. Fingers are minced with an awful regularity on tin tops and chopping knives, scraped on potato knives and corkscrews – accidents of an awful banality and a great deal of blood and trouble.

Industrial work injuries are always on a bigger scale with flesh crushed instead of bruised, eyes bright red instead of pink and watery, fingers chopped clean off instead of sliced, hands burnt down to the wrist instead of scalded at their tips. A screwdriver falling from scaffolding unprotected by toeboards reaches a velocity lethal even to a helmeted building worker after 100 feet. What is chilling is not the wounds but the victims' stoicism. Manual workers still take damage

* First published in *Time Out*, 1976.

to their bodies at work as part of the deal and express an infuriating lack of anger over missing finger tips and sliced tendons.

And there are the morning regulars, those people mortgaged to illness and harnessed to pills, the dicky hearts continually dissolving tablets under their tongues to push away heart pain from hardening arteries, the diabetics for whom a single spot may grow to an infected boil and threaten life, the old with blocked and baffled circulation whose blood only just forces its way to toes and fingers continually threatened by gangrene. For them, Casualty is part of life and they will expound briskly on diagnosis and treatment, having overheard and memorised the seminars held for years over their faulty limbs. Regular, too, are certain medical emergencies, asthmatics who arrive panting on stretchers, blue and wrestling for breath, and epileptics raging with themselves.

It is a demanding kind of medicine and yet all the Casualty Officer is required to do with the urgent cases is to admit them to the care of another doctor as swiftly as possible. The job is therefore exhausting, bewildering and, since it places paramount importance on diagnosis and little on treatment, curiously unsatisfactory. Shift work, low pay and lower prestige, generally poor facilities and lack of career structure has made Casualty a dead end.

1.00 p.m.
Lunch time brings its small crop of violence. A warm morning in the pub which goes wrong by lunch time and ends with somebody's boyfriend bottling somebody on the next table in a fog of drunkenness; the first of the traffic accidents; falls and black eyes with unconvincing stories attached. Heads are strong but bleed a good deal. Casualty starts to look like Casualty. Much of the lunch time punching takes place inside the home, within the family. Frustration which ranges from a plate thrown accurately in anger to the systematic battering of a wife beyond unconsciousness. Those who uphold the sanctity of the family as a solution to all our problems might care to spend a few hours in a Casualty, to face the debris, when all the sugary ideals explode, when babies are bounced against the bedroom wall to make them stop crying and wives are loved and honoured and beaten up so thoroughly that they can't talk because their teeth are still chattering with terror. By afternoon there is already an hour-long queue to be seen and thirty pairs of eyes pierce any attempted emergency with the particular malice that the English reserve for queue jumpers.

4.00 p.m.
Just as the queue is thinning down and you think there may be time for a cup of tea, pandemonium arrives. An ambulance team pound through the doors with a corpse they have kept alive by thumping his chest and puffing and sucking into his lungs. A cardiac bleep summons anaesthetists clumping in theatre boots and surgical greens, a worried medical registrar who has to interpret the electronic squiggles of the ECG into decisions about drugs which must be shot straight into heart muscle, and other floating doctors and nurses who connect up leads and position electrodes, draw up syringes and slice off clothes. One anaesthetist threads a plastic airway through the bluish throat while another plunges the needle of a drip into a neck vein and pumps in replacement fluids. The cardiac man brandishes two electrodes the size of dinner plates and, dripping with salty grease, claps them on the chest and throws a 200 volt current through the patient, jerking him momentarily clean off the table. They banter all the while in measured tones about golf, their last cardiac arrest and hospital gossip. A nurse drops a bottle and everyone glares at her. Only the doctors are allowed to make mistakes. Someone is despatched to find out, in the nicest possible way, the patient's age from his wife, sobbing outside. Then, to everyone's surprise, the patient starts to revive, achieves a row of perfect cardiac complexes so that his pupils shrink, and goes a seedy pink again. 'Oh, God, I was hoping to go over to the boozer this evening,' says the registrar, glum at his success.

Another try at tea but you can't get away from the noise reverberating over the institutional surfaces: the groans of in-patients, the noisy sobbing, the over-loud conversations, the abandoned lung-bursting scream of kids in pain which echoes on long after it has actually stopped. But as night rises, a swath of drunkenness seems to sweep across the outside world, as single bemused and fallen creatures, couples propping each other up right, and the wounded dragged away from street-corner arguments and pub affrays by friends, lurch in.

With the booze comes violence. Between drinks and after closing time sober patrols of muggers round up the staggerers and relieve them of their valuables. The violence is bewildering, inexplicable, random.

1.00 a.m.
Fortunately, alcohol solves the problem of anaesthesia. Little lignocaine is used after closing time. The police breeze in and out,

squawking like upright birds. Their vital weapon is now their radio, not their truncheon. But it can order them away in the middle of trying to piece together a case against the person they end up arresting. Police vans shuttle drunks between the cells and the Casualty. The smell of stale alcohol and the tongue-tiedness of the drunk fill the rooms and the once prim and orderly department is reduced to a wash of plaster of paris footprints and bloody bandages. With the drunks come the suicides, midnight's other staple.

2.00 a.m.
The mentally ill who do come into Casualty are often curiously sane, just unacceptably honest about the lack of love in the heart of the city. A lab technician is lugged in screaming with terror, his whole appearance scatty, as if something inside has slipped sideways. He is terrified that he is dying from chest pain. In a quarter of an hour he has quietened down and desperately wants to talk, to show the family photos he sleeps with under his pillow. A young wife collapses, convinced she is unable to breathe, panting and screaming and shaking. When she pulls herself together she's worried that her husband will beat her up for breaking down. It's mental, all right: an acute anxiety state. But it's only just the other side of the Radio One phone-in and the Lonely Hearts ads and the sex shop.

4.00 a.m.
A tramp with magnificent eyebrows and a mane of silver hair describes the biblical proportions of his diarrhoea in language he has learnt to use to shut officials up. He says he is a shepherd by profession. Under the trolley his paper bag contains a large furry gorilla. 'Well, I am also a street entertainer,' he says with dignity. When he realises he is not going to get a bed for the night, he becomes wrathful. 'You're a Londoner, I suppose. Once London was a city. Now it is a mess.'

6.00 a.m.
It's almost morning. Still, unbelievably, people wander in with toothache and constipation exhausted by a night spent wrestling with pain. The night staff, alert but exhausted, having paced their weariness through the small hours with phone calls, fags and cups of coffee, are now anxious to stumble home to a morning bedtime. In comes a Belfast man shattered with drink but somehow totally in control. We sit in the corner of the waiting room while a Portuguese ancillary cleans the blood off the floor with an electric scrubber. 'I'm on these pills, you see, doc, Valium. I started taking them in Belfast and now I

have them sent over to me. Without them I just couldn't get myself across the front door. I take about 30 a day. You know I can only talk to you like this because I'm drunk.' He wants to go into a hospital where he can get off his tranquillisers. He wants a doctor to talk to about the terror in his head. The floor is almost finished now. 'Well, I can get you an urgent appointment with our psychiatric clinic?' I offer. He smiles without warmth. 'Well, I'm sorry to have wasted your time, doc. I just thought maybe you could help me.'

26

How Did Biko Die?*

The murder of Steve Biko made a tremendous impact in Britain. This article for Rock Against Racism's political fanzine Temporary Hoarding *aimed to let the facts speak for themselves. If the British establishment's complicity with Pretoria is a source of daily shame, one can draw comfort from Attenborough's skilful film* Cry Freedom *and Peter Gabriel's haunting song* Biko *which is becoming to the 1980s something like Adrian Mitchell's* Tell Me Lies About Vietnam *was in the 1960s.*

On Monday 17 May 1976, 1,600 children at Orlando West Junior School, Soweto, in South Africa, walked out of the gates of their school. They wanted to be taught, as before, in English rather than Afrikaans. They milled around the grounds uncertainly, some dancing and skipping. The teachers waited for them to change their minds. The Inspector of Education asked, 'Have you ever heard of 13-year-old children striking?'

It spread. One month later 15,000 black schoolchildren marched through Soweto carrying exercise book placards saying 'Afrikaans is oppressors' language' and 'Blacks are not dustbins'. The police tried to disperse the march with tear gas. Then a uniformed white policeman shot a 13-year-old boy called Hector Petersen with a revolver: in the back, stone dead.

In the subsequent eighteen months, the black townships rose: barely armed, poorly organised, desperately brave. Teenagers faced armoured cars with sticks, children threw stones back at police men who were firing sub-machine guns. On a blackboard in a school in Nyanga, someone drew a crude map and wrote 'Cape Town comrades, Mdantsane comrades, Soweto comrades, Maputo comrades... all these comrades must unite. NO RACIALISM. NO COLONIALISM. EQUALITY.' The rising was suppressed with systematic and merciless brutality. In the process the South African police have killed 456

* First published in *Temporary Hoarding*, 1977.

people and injured 2,160. Over half of those shot by police around Johannesburg were shot in the back. There are now 662 people held in detention without trial. More than 100 have been held for over a year. Twenty-three have died in prison.

One of the twenty-three, Steve Biko, a leader of the Black Consciousness grouping, and a believer in non-violent change, was detained in his home town of King Williamstown on 18 August 1976. He was alternately interrogated, beaten and then left naked in a police cell. During an all-night interrogation on the night of 6 September this year, he was attacked by his captors, suffering a brain haemorrhage from which he slowly and excruciatingly died as paralysis spread over his body in the next four days. On the final day of his life, now unable to speak, he was driven 750 miles tied up and bouncing in the back of a Land-Rover, stark naked.

The Minister of Justice, James Kruger, announced his death at the Transvaal National Party Congress, stating, 'It leaves me cold.' He stated officially that Biko had died as a result of a hunger strike. When *The World* and the *Rand Daily Mail* published evidence of his post mortem injuries, the Minister attempted to suppress their reports. 15,000 people mourned at Biko's funeral, although buses and trains were halted by police and passengers sjambokked. Fourteen road blocks were placed on the main road between Johannesburg and the funeral. On 19 October, Kruger announced the banning and house arrest of sixty individuals, the two newspapers that had told the truth about Biko and eighteen organisations including the Black People's Convention, the Soweto Student Representative Council, Black Parents' Association, the Medupe Writers' Association, the Zimele Clinic Trust Fund, the Black Women's Federation and the white-run Christian Institute of Southern Africa.

There is now no one left to arrest or ban. Liberalism is itself outlawed as the search for victims to jail and houses to raid proceeds. The repression feeds on itself. New captives are interrogated to find new victims.

The truth itself is illegal. Mass arrests are an everyday affair. On 18 November, during a house-to-house sweep near Pretoria, police arrested 626 blacks. The officer in charge described it as a 'perfectly normal raid'.

Since the 19 October crackdown, South Africa has made the final turn into a fully-fledged fascist state structure. Since 1948, over 300 pieces of separatist legislation have been passed to create the most repressive system of racial laws in the world. The black population,

70 per cent of the total, are either confined to the black homelands in the 13 per cent of the most barren of South African territory, or live without rights in the cities as migrant labourers. Television and radio are under complete state control. The army has 41,000 regulars with 130,000 reserves ready for call-up at 24 hours' notice. The National Party itself is controlled by the all-male Broederbond, a secret society with over 10,000 members including the Prime Minister.

Now even the facilities for white liberal opinion have been abolished. The Minister of Justice first lied publicly and then openly gloated over the prison cell murder of a non-violent opponent arrested without trial. A judge and ex-member of the National Party, Mr Justice Kowie Marais, has said, after the Biko death, that the electors who vote for Vorster in the 30 November elections will be responsible 'in the same way the Germans became responsible when they extended a mandate to Hitler'. And yet millions of white voters will give that mandate.

The British government voted in the United Nations, yet again, against business sanctions contra South Africa, which might do some small good, and for arms sanctions which are utterly worthless. The South African forces have already stockpiled and anyway are secretly provided for by the Israelis. The reason is twofold. First, Dr Owen relies on Mr Vorster to insist that Ian Smith co-operate in some plan to prevent military victory of the Black resistance in Zimbabwe. And second, Britain is still South Africa's largest trading partner and investor. Almost a quarter of South Africa's exports go to Britain and 4 per cent of British exports are destined for South Africa. Major British companies are deeply interlocked with subsidiaries in a South Africa they profess to disapprove of. Much of the material directly aids the police state. Plessey provides the expertise for electronic weapons guidance systems. Marconi are building an £8 million military communications system. ICI owns 40 per cent of a company that manufactured most of the tear gas used in Soweto. British Leyland in South Africa are expanding with British government funds in factories where black unions are illegal, making Land-Rovers for the police. The new head of British Leyland UK won his industrial spurs in Johannesburg.

The state that killed Steve Biko is, despite the diplomatic talk, deeply connected to Britain. To help black Africa to freedom, we will have to free ourselves.

27

The Winter of 1979*

Despite the rise (and fall) of the National Front and emergence of Margaret Thatcher as the spearhead of a new aggressive Toryism, things didn't seem so bad politically. Looking back, it is easy to chart a downturn gaining velocity much earlier. But, much enthused by Rock Against Racism and the young Right To Work marchers, I obviously felt the momentum was still with us.

Although the leading authorities assure us that the system is, once again, on the verge of collapse, the winter of 1979 is proving poignant as well as exhilarating for us lefties. The workers are out on the streets again, thank God, from Tehran to Tottenham Court Road, and the plump smile of the Stock Exchange has gone noticeably ashen. But are we really witnessing the birth of a new society, or merely a further instalment in the disintegration of the old? For even we, the benighted bootboys of the SWP, the rentamobsters, the mindless extremists, tertiary pickets and habitual Holders-of-the-Nation-to-Ransom, sometimes fall to pondering, 'Are we getting anywhere?'

It is a decade on from the Tet Offensive and the heady days when 100,000 marched in London in solidarity with the Viet Cong. Ten years since Danny Cohn-Bendit's infectious grin and Alexander Dubcek's wan smile seemed to be signalling, from Paris and Prague, new revolutionary possibilities. Only ten years since Bernadette Devlin and the young civil rights campaigners first raised their banners on the Bogside. And only five since a Tory government, hell-bent on high unemployment and stern wage restraint, was overthrown by wave after wave of industrial action – by builders, dockers, engineers and miners – on a scale which hadn't been seen since the days of the General Strike. Revolution did seem in the air, somewhere.

'Now what have we got?' inquires Sham 69's Jimmy Pursey of his motley followers. 'Fuck-all,' we roar in self-mocking delight. Tom Robinson's reply is more precise: 'Consternation in Mayfair/ Riots in

* First published in *Time Out*, 1979.

Notting Hill Gate/Fascists marching up the High Street/ Smashing up the Welfare State.' And don't write those lines off as rock and roll melodrama ... they could have come straight off the Telex tapes. One doesn't have to be punk or gay to feel that the UK in 1979 has turned out rather less appetising than the menu promised in 1974 of Social Contract flambéd in 'the red flame of socialist outrage'. Our new Jerusalem has turned out a harsher, meaner, poorer Britain.

This is Madness

Since 1974 the most radical post-war election manifesto and a Cabinet studded with Tribunite heavies has succeeded in bringing back mass unemployment as a permanent feature of the economy.

The only thing that changes is the length of the adjectives ministers use to deplore it. Whole regions of Britain are slipping quietly off the industrial map. Not just the Toy Town co-operatives so cynically set up by Citizen Benn but, over the last few months, household names like British Leyland, Dunlop, Triang, Massey Ferguson, Singers, British Shipbuilding, have announced major closures. Go to Liverpool or Wigan and Skelmersdale and see the bleakness in the streets and the despair on the faces. Jobs gone for good, skills made useless, redundancy pay that melts away. Town, community way of life crumpled like a card board cup. 'I've heard of homicide and suicide,' goes a current Liverpool joke about a girl in primary school, 'but can you tell me, Miss, what merseyside means?'

The only thing we can manufacture and sell is our past: Agatha Christie movies, stately homes and the cheapest tourism in Europe. In a weird double-take on nineteenth century imperialism, Arab sheiks shoplift C & As, black-locked prophets call hypnotically for the downfall of Babylon and the Tories demand we arm the Maoist millions for a Holy War against the Russian Bear.

The Welfare State and the 'Beveridge assumptions' of full employment and adequate social services were the political outcome of the Second World War and the high point of humane planning in Britain this century. Their inverse, the public expenditure cuts enforced so strictly over the last three years in everything from nursery schools to road repairs, are no longer just an exercise in budgeting within the Welfare State way of life. The cuts are a codeword for a social counter-revolution, the replacement of the very idea of public provision for those in social need with the philosophy of self-help, because I'm damned if anyone else will. The ideals of Attlee and Bevan are being replaced by those of Samuel Smiles and Mr Gradgrind.

It isn't just the closure of comprehensives and teachers' training colleges and art schools – the very character of education is being altered to fit the needs of industry more precisely. The nationalised industries, conceived as public utilities able to produce and distribute essential services efficiently and cheaply, are now run and judged on the same profit-ethic as Woolworths. Nursery closures are justified not just for the immediate cash saving but because, it is hinted, women shouldn't really be out at work in the first place. The National Health Service, the jewel in Labour's 1945 crown, is not just being neglected and starved of resources, it is being forced into mediocrity, often by administrators who talk of medical care but who have the mentality of asset strippers. David Ennals will be seen in relation to Britain's hospitals much as Henry VIII is seen in relation to Britain's monasteries.

The scale of the retreat is difficult to measure with the eye. It isn't socialism but a species of cost-benefit accountancy. As the late Anthony Crosland, theorist of the social-democratic consensus, is reported to have remarked at the end of the Cabinet meeting which accepted the full terms of the 1976 IMF loan, 'This is madness. But we must do it.' It is against this mentality, as well as their own meagre wages, that the public sector strikers protest.

Decline and Fall

Nor can any reasonably free-spirited person hold much confidence in the present Government's commitment to civil liberties. We have the most reactionary Home Secretary since Henry Brooke – a Methodist junta-man obsessed with official secrecy and deportations. Silkin is a standing joke and the Special Patrol Group grows in its audacity every year, an elite force apparently encouraged to regard itself above the normal limits of the law.

'No thanks darlin', that's not our style,' an SPGer told a friend when she offered him the key to a front door he was about to batter in first with a sledgehammer. Their performance at the Huntley Street squat and the Reclaim the Night Demo made *The Sweeney* look like *Dixon of Dock Green*. Oh yes, and in these radical days such old friends as Judge Michael Argyle, who starred in the fabulous freaky *OZ* trial, are still alive and well. Last July, four Asian brothers (the Virks) were given a total of 12 years, despite claiming self-defence against racist attack. The jails cram, Largactil doses go up, the police crack down and the Chief Constable of Greater Manchester who organised Martin Webster's £250,000 walkabout, confers on The Decline of Family Life (yes, it's declined so far they've had to send for the police). Of course Britain isn't a police state, but there are one or two police cities all right.

In some senses we've witnessed a 1931 in slow motion. Labour is the National Government and sod the Conference and the back-benchers. After all, the parliamentary alternative is indeed grim: Thatcher, the crazed prophet Joseph, and Paul Johnson as Poet Laureate. Watching the assemblage of hunt-ball drunks, High Street proprietors and bondage-freaks who seem to constitute the Tory Party Conference baying at John Davis, it seemed indeed enough to give one a brain tumour. And what of that last white-hope-turned-black-sheep, the Liberal Party, marching, as Jeremy Thorpe once rather unwisely put it, 'in the direction of the gunfire'? It is hard to see the Minehead cast of incompetent, unlikely millionaires and unstable company directors as the stuff of 'the New Politics'. The aroma is distinctly nineteenth century.

Apolitical

So life goes on. Those with money spend it; business is booming at Harrods and The White Tower and Jack Barclays. A slightly sinister apoliticism is fashionable, the reactionary chic of cocaine and art nouveau and surplus value games. No one, it must be said, has yet opened a boutique called 'Biko'. But one must view with some alarm a civilisation whose leading intellectuals combine vanity and reaction in quite such an overblown concoction as Messrs Levin, Johnson, Stoppard and Waugh. Left-wing Trendies were indeed rather distasteful, but Right-wing Trendies are a very great deal worse.

Meanwhile, the long-suffering general public attempt to get on with life if only the bus hadn't frozen up and the ambulances weren't on strike and a loaf of bread didn't cost 8/6 and *Any Questions* hadn't got lost on the dial. 'It's a disgrace' is offered up every so often, it's almost become a universal pietàs. Everything is a disgrace: the SWP and the NF, Labour and the Tories, Thorpe and Newton, unions and bosses. Punks think their parents are a disgrace and skins think teds are a disgrace. I think *Time Out* is a disgrace.

This is the real fruit of the three years of the Social Contract Somnambulence, a universal sense of resentful passivity, a nation of Fawlties, barely suppressing hysteria. We're doing what we're told, so it must be someone else's fault things still go wrong: the blacks, the Reds, the queers, the strikers. Those who stand out against the tide of national obedience; the Right to Work marchers with their valiant orange jackets and blistered feet, the fire-fighters in their strike-huts last Christmas, the Fight back Committee at the gutted Hounslow Hospital, they are blamed, held responsible for the very conditions they protest against.

Indeed, in the past few weeks we have endured a bourgeois version of the May Events, an enthusiastic pageant of Reaction, aimed at the honourable, dignified and reluctant strikers who seek to raise their appalling wages by withdrawing their labour and have the temerity to make their action effective. From all sides we are told National Salvation depends on an irreversible transfer of wealth and power to the wealthy and the powerful. Although it will require an explosive agent more potent than hot air to demolish the architecture of post-war working-class organisation, the experience has been so ugly.

One needs to be forcibly reminded that in 1975 and 1976 the level of strikes in Britain fell so low that it almost seemed that the great British institution The Striker was becoming an Endangered Species. Indeed, for three years we have been lectured so frequently on the virtues of self-sacrifice and moderation, it has been like living in a Calvinist seminary. Avuncularly by Callaghan, belligerently by Healey, worriedly by Ennals, hypnotically and hypocritically by the unfortunate Foot. The barefaced lie that wages rises are the main cause of price inflation was repeated so incessantly that it sunk in by sheer habit. The bosses took the hint dropped so heavily by Healey's pronouncements at City banquets. 'The employers united shall never be defeated' became their watchword and the tactics of George Ward of Willesden were soon taken up by Duke Hussey in Fleet Street.

There is, however, one problem about this great exercise in national belt-tightening. The cuts, the wage restraints and the government fiscal policy have been operated in the name of a transfer of resources to private manufacturing. But, despite the oil and one or two special exceptions, British industry has shown its customary reluctance to invest and expand, despite all the hospitals and schools being closed *pour encourager les autres*. There is nothing more galling than a pointless sacrifice. The exuberant rank and file industrial action of the last few weeks, seen by bourgeois commentators as unpredictable as an explosion, is the absolutely predictable fruit of three long years of severe wage control.

Contradiction

So what of the revolutionary Left, apparently so well-placed in 1974? And the Women's Movement's permanent revolution against patriarchy and capitalism? It would be betraying no great secret to admit that there has been a certain faltering of impetus here. The revolutionary Left in the 1974–7 period became very prone to purging and splitting and, as usual, quite a lot of people who couldn't see what it was all about anyway pushed off to have kids, or lick their wounds or do their horoscopes.

The SWP has now in fact nearly 4,400 members, roughly twice the figure of 1974. But their standing in the labour movement and their experience on the Left has probably declined in those years. The Communist Party was preoccupied for much of this period with a re-discussion of its own programme which has ejected formal Stalinism and replaced it with a species of chummy Left reformism which is masterfully ambiguous on several key matters. What strikes an outsider is that now that the Great Debate is over, the Party seems at a loss to know what to do and the level of its political initiative seems lower than for years. The small Trotskyist groups, and one should here say post-Trotskyist, neo-Trotskyist and in most cases sub-Trotskyist, divide and multiply, mostly in the fertile mould to be found in Constituency Labour Parties and Student Union Bars. The Libertarians seem unable to get beyond the status of a circle of friends, intellectually fertile but organisationally feeble.

One suspects that the great majority of ex-members of Left groups, monogamous feminists, browned-off trade unionists and retired avenging angels of the student barricades are biding their time rather than selling out their beliefs. One does not live by politics alone, especially in a period of pronounced rightward swing. Indeed, one is taunted daily by the apparent irrelevance of one's vision.

Revolutionaries in such times tend to elaborate their belief-systems ('theory') or opt for something, however reformist, which does at least group a few people together who will make a stand ('practice'). The two ends of the equation waltz away from each other like separated ballroom dancing partners. This bifurcation is all too obvious in the bookshops, which quake with unspeakable tomes of Marxist studies, alcoves of surplus value debate and corridors of Deviancy. I look with pity on the poor students stocking up on their pricey set-books of Althusser and Anderson. For them the red base turned out to be a grey rectangle.

But despite the hilarious contradictions presented by academic Marxism and careerist feminism, the growth of the independent socialist publishers and the collectives of sexual, philosophical and scientific radicals who meet and argue and publish in idioms and formats of such diversity is wholly healthy. The Publications Distribution Co-op busily parcel out journals, from *Gay Left* to *The Radical Ornithologist*, to a national network of radical bookshops whose audience must well exceed the 50,000 the Left Book Club had achieved by 1937. And the Left still does, however feebly, uphold the international solidarities incumbent on citizens of one of the oldest colonial powers.

For only when viewed internationally do we see the full starkness of the decade. Most disastrously, the military overthrow of Chile's Popular Unity Government was an upheaval as decisive as Franco's seizure of power in 1930s Spain. Then there were the massacres of JVP youth and students in Ceylon in 1971, the barbarous military coup in Thailand in 1976, the Lebanese Falange's murderous bombardment of the Beirut Palestinians.

Such acts of bizarrely efficient bloodletting inspire a certain dizziness. It is hard to retain a sense of moral perspective in a world where the strapping soldiers of the South African security police literally gun down schoolchildren who simply ask to be taught in English, not Afrikaans: week after week for nearly 18 months, until there are over 1,200 officially reported dead. And we march to Trafalgar Square one Sunday and think we've done something.

White Problem

As for Ireland, one sometimes despairingly wonders if there wouldn't be more response if it was happening in South East Asia instead of thirty miles over The Water. Leaving aside the issues of nationalism and self-determination, we are quite literally digging our own grave if we don't realise the technology of control being perfected in the streets of Belfast and Derry is intended, if and when required, for local application. 'The British Army are waiting out there,' wails Strummer in 'White Man in the Hammersmith Palais', the single of the decade. And he's dead right.

But it's when internationalism comes home to roost, in opposition to racism and fascism, that the far-Left can be proud of its success in turning what was becoming in the mid-1970s a very ugly tide. Remember when it was thought intellectually devastating to argue that the SWP was, in fact, identical to the National Front – a philosophical proposition which, as Orwell put it, 'is like saying rat poison is the same as rats'. The effort put into identifying the fascist cadres of the Front, the attempts to block their unwelcome passage with the ominous drum beat and the spiked Union Jacks through migrant communities, the public stance against any resurgence of Nazism made by the Anti Nazi League have met with an overwhelming response from people who felt too that it was time for a stand to be taken. The problem here is whether the Left can take the vehemence and passion of the initial anti-Nazi stand towards some deeper understanding of how respectable racism operates in the courts and the customs offices and how racism is a *white* problem at heart.

But here, and in the still more intimate field of sexual politics, battles, debates, squabbles, anger and misunderstanding still entangle, inflame and pain the Left's responses. Feminism's discoveries and questions can't just be 'fitted in' to an already existing, finished Marxism, and Lenin certainly doesn't tell you much about gay liberation. New forms, new definitions of socialism are needed which see resistance to sexual and racial oppression as part of the making of socialism. Such definitions are unlikely to be possessed in toto by any one party, group or creed. But the way in which sexual, racial and industrial issues are now intertwined in modern capitalism was exemplified by the Grunwick strike. Though the day was lost, it was about time British labour went on the line for a dispute led by black women. The performance of the TUC, Roy Grantham and Tom Jackson in snatching defeat from the jaws of victory will be recorded in another, less hallowed annal.

Still Infants

So this is the winter of 1979 – and what have we done? Well, I and I survive, like the badge says. The student visions of 1968, the working-class insurgency of 1972 and 1974, the socialist parties which tried to fuse them – all three hit an impasse in the late 1970s. We had to hang on for our very existence against a swing to the Right which was almost audible some nights.

Yet the system we oppose is itself in grave condition: its economics unstable, its products poisonous, its subjects rebellious. Perhaps the fascination with which the fate of the Shah is viewed, not least by our Foreign Secretary, is the evidence that events in Iran give of quite how dependent modern bureaucracies are on the loyalties of functionaries which can change overnight. And how the ideas of the extreme Left can suddenly become the property of the mainstream. Poor Mr Pahlavi – last year the most powerful man between Tel Aviv and Tokyo – now deserted even by his dog handlers and with the loyalty of his dogs in question, is truly an omen of our time.

As for our Left, bedraggled but alive, we are still infants. We have not yet come of age and are far from the height of our powers. But we survived and, in Tom Mann's words, intend to grow more dangerous as we grow old.

The New Left of 1956 vintage used to have a slogan – 'It moves' – meaning that there was at last a shift in the monolithic, frozen political structures of the Cold War. We can perhaps alter it to 'It grows'. In the grim faces of the striking ambulance drivers, in the amateur anti-cuts committees, grinding out another abortion petition against yet another attempt at restrictive legislation, in the heroism of Lewisham and the harmony of Victoria Park, in the hospitals and the mines, something is stirring again, coming out of the Social Contract anaesthesia. Orwell put it as bluntly as ever: 'The struggle of the working class is like the growth of a plant. The plant is blind and stupid, but it knows enough to keep pushing towards the light, and it will do this in the face of endless discouragements.'

28

I'm Not Going to Work on Maggie's Farm*

This was written for the 1979 election issue of Socialist Worker. *It was apparent before she entered office that Mrs Thatcher represented a more traditional and class-conscious Conservatism than the consensus Tories we had grown up with. It was also clear that she would provide severe problems for the ineffectual and ill-officered Labour Party. So don't say we didn't warn you.*

General Elections are not enjoyable times for socialists. Their purpose, said Nye Bevan – who should know – 'is to beguile democracy to voting wealth back into power'.

The Labour government's record in office has been so numbingly mediocre, and the lip service paid to socialism in the new Manifesto is perhaps the most feeble and grudging since the Labour Party became officially socialist in 1918.

But we should not draw the facile conclusion that it is indistinguishable from Toryism.

Because a Tory government, led by Mrs Thatcher, would be even worse than this government.

Mrs Thatcher is, even by Tory standards, lacking in human rapport. She seems to have an uncanny inability to appear relaxed, to 'fit in' or transmit the merest scrap of genuine compassion.

The fact is that Thatcher is out of place; the Tory Party are suffering badly from exclusion from the parliamentary power they once took for granted and both are desperate to fling Labour out, however they hide that desperation. The most coherent and stable capitalist party in Europe, born out of the most successful empire and expansive industry of the eighteenth century, finds its automatic right to govern gone.

The High Tory ring, bounded by Anglican piety, public school decency, Oxbridge loyalty, Stock Exchange insights and safe seats is disintegrating. The 1st Class carriages still pull into Paddington, but

* First published in *Socialist Worker*, 1979.

there's no *Times* crossword to hide behind and a season ticket costs a fortune.

The village green is dwarfed by a motorway, the chaps on the Rhine don't have enough spare parts for their second rate tanks, the vicar has put up a petition for Medical Aid to Zimbabwe and the Tory son and heir has gone off to be a punk rocker.

The British Medical Association (not unfairly known as the Tory Party at the bedside) still end their chapter on 'Ethics' with the advice that 'when all is said and done, a chap knows what's cricket'. But that was before Mr Packer's exercise in free enterprise.

The old school tie's gone to the jumble sale, the newsagent's been taken over by an Asian couple ('terribly nice people though') and the lovely little man at the garage is now a Toyota spares dealer.

The lights are going out all over the Home Counties: being a Tory is plain going out of fashion. There are complicated causes: stagnation in world trade, demographic movement into cities, secularisation, female integration into productive labour, the extending role of the state and most important, too many years in opposition. But that doesn't explain to the man on the *Brighton Belle* why 'Made in Britain' is a joke, or why his wife and children answer back and school doesn't seem to teach either good handwriting or good discipline any more and costs a fortune into the bargain. Or why that man Callaghan looks so damned smug all the damned time.

The Tory Party rank and file are a long-suffering body and this decade has been a particularly hard one. They have come to learn that when their leaders achieve office, they 'go pink'... make their peace with the multinationals and Home Office liberals and Yorkshire miners. They are numbed to their leaders' 'flexibility'.

But the rise of Mrs Thatcher and her Philosopher King Sir Keith Joseph, over the utter disarray of the humane wing of the party, marks a new course. We face a new Toryism, frankly elitist, not just making racialism respectable but Reaction itself fashion able.

By announcing an official end to Tory compassion towards the 'undeserving' and by her avowed intention of 'putting the unions in their proper place', Thatcher moves the Tory Party away from its traditional claim to mediate, rather like the Church of England, between all class interests.

Something called 'Freedom' is the battlecry. 'Freedom', it soon becomes apparent, is closely connected, if not identical with, money. Mrs T will grant us the freedom not to have any obligation towards fellow humans who are ill, out of work or incapable so that *we* can have the freedom to select whichever private ward, public school dorm, restaurant or town house we wish for ourselves.

Dazzling avenues of freedom will become apparent in the very same supermarket you naively thought you were doing the shopping in. With all the promised tax reductions, you might well be able to make a successful bid for the British National Oil Corporation, the British Aerospace and Shipbuilding Industry, or a slice of the local Casualty Department.

This morally squalid equation of freedom with the thickness of your wallet is still more horrible a formula when you consider that it can only be achieved by a deliberate campaign to make the poor poorer.

Mrs T's much-loved 'scroungers' who are at present hanging on to their dignity by their teeth and fingernails, will be formally and legally kicked over the edge. For their own good, of course, because Mrs Thatcher's new brand of Toryism knows that misfortune is but the evidence of vice, weakness or error, and that it is therefore kind to be cruel.

Ask Mrs Thatcher if there must not be 99 failures for every success and she will agree; the socialists, as she insists on calling them, only produce disappointment by asking for equality.

In this brave new barbarism, public spending cuts, which Callaghan and Co. at least pretend to regret, turn into positive virtues. The virtual halt on public housing is an emancipating act for the poor and overcrowded and unhoused since it will protect them from morally destructive dependence on the State. Further run-down of the National Health Service will be a tonic of great efficiency; those without money will no longer be able to afford to fall ill.

Strikers' children will learn about life, too. Going hungry alongside their parents will teach them a robust respect for their future employers. It will indeed be the Sale of the Century, and what remained of the Conservative Party's sense of social decency will be one of the items to get knocked down.

It is *The Archers* meets *Mrs Dale's Diary* with a touch of *Toytown*, introduced by David Jacobs. It is how The Queen might carry on if she lived at Crossroads Motel. It is not reality and never was.

Nor is the rapacious bustle of the Stock Exchange the peal of Liberty's Bell, and should not be so confused.

Hitting the poor may be expedient, but it is pushing it a bit to claim it as some kind of moral crusade to bring back the age of personal service. Mrs T reminds us that the gnawing of poverty is a better instrument of discipline than the policeman's truncheon. Not that truncheons are out of favour.

The proposals which will receive the hurrahs at Tory hustings will be for more corporal punishment, longer, harder gaol sentences, more police, bigger Borstals and prisons and the job-creation of a public hangman, that hooded creature of the barbaric days when torture was public sport.

And how do you get respect for law and order when respect for its agents does not exist? You teach people fear, that's how. You tell people that 'they are afraid of being swamped' or 'scared to go out at night' or go to Tesco without being captured by the Baader Meinhof Gang often enough and they start to believe it. You announce, as one prominent London Thatcherite did last week, that 'Lambeth has become the first Marxist state in the city of London.' You imply, in the pretend-shocked-but-suspected-it-all-along voice of the corner shop gossip, that crossing the average city street at night is only slightly less hazardous than the parachute drop on Arnhem. You garner your scared votes, you extend and improve state security and brutalise more effectively people who can, roughly speaking, be made to appear culprits.

'A short, sharp shock', promises the Tory Manifesto, licking its lips.

As for The Unions, one can say with conviction that there will be a great deal of dishonest verbiage in all possible directions until 3 May. Everyone claims to think that the unions have too much power but also knows most strikes this year have been isolated and defeated with precision and tactical skill by Mr Callaghan. The Thatcher philosophy is clearly to keep off the whole subject and leave Mr Prior to say unfrightening sensible-chap things.

But given her philosophy of Freedom as Obedience and her barely concealed distaste for the gentlemen of the General Council, it would seem likely a Thatcher government would seek to call the bluff of the TUC rather than indulging in the rather weary Old Pals Act that Jim, Len and David act out so gawkily.

While appearing to accept the Congress House end of the unions as something as essentially British as the Crown Jewels, she will simply dispense with the horse-trading, announce her plans and tell them to like it or lump it. There will be a sudden fall in the number of Len Murray TV interviews outside No. 10. As always in Thatcherland, you are free to be ineffective.

And with pickets licensed and labelled rather like pet dogs, solidarity action illegal and social security denied to strikers' families, industrial action which accepts those terms will actually be a declaration of weakness. This ground is already half conceded in the Concordat, that appropriate amalgam of Concorde and Dictat. Then watch unemployment take a quantum leap.

A maliciously minded person might almost think the TUC deserved such a deflation after its quite grotesque accommodation to every whim of the present Cabinet. But passage of a Thatcher Industrial Relations Act would be a serious blow.

Once again, Freedom would rule. Those who employ labour could then be gently relieved of all that tiresome red tape about safety and unfair dismissal and maternity leave. The present isn't much, but we have to hold on to it.

Over the last ten years, trade unionism has come to mean something more challenging than just bartering up the price of labour. Not the Gen Secs on *News At Ten* but the solid, unglamorous improvements in the condition and nature of work and the level of humanity between fellow workers. The muscle-bound thugs of the Tories' imagination are just that ... imagination.

Now Thatcher's trying to steal back our lines and our confidence:

'Say it loud, I'm capitalist and proud ...'
'Profit-makers come out – you have nothing to lose but your shame.'
'2, 4, 6, 8, We don't want a Marxist state.'

Her borrowed idiom is a curious tribute to us. Us, who are rendered invisible on the Swingometer but who have done more than we realise to shift the heavy pendulum of British politics over the past years.

We have clashed more and more openly with the powers that be, usually the police, about issues that are as real as our lives, not out in Hanoi or even Aldermaston.

We witness official Labour's shrinking of moral concern, the narrowing of its political eyes, the deadened reflexes. The unwillingness to really challenge the harsh new moral philosophy of Thatcher, except when it was convenient to drum LP members into activity they had otherwise long lost stomach for.

Yes, we will vote Labour this time too, and try to convince others to overcome their queasiness at the thought. Every working-class Tory vote is a tug of the political forelock.

But our business is to offer a perspective to workers, not an analysis about them. Our vision is becoming less and less far-fetched as the facts catch up with our predictions. 'Ours is no dream,' wrote

William Morris in 1883. 'Men and women have died for it, not in the ancient days, but in our own time; they lie in prisons for it, work in mines, are exiled, are ruined for it; believe me, when such things are suffered for dreams, the dreams come true at last.'

29

Gay was Good*

Gay News, *the national newspaper of the gay movement in Britain, collapsed in 1983. Its demise, partly self-inflicted, was another indication of the sexual-political Left's difficulties adapting to a new and harsher era. Had it survived, it could have been an invaluable defender of gay rights in the age of AIDS and Section 28.*

After *Gay News*'s unexpected demise last month, I traipsed out to the periodicals section of the British Library at Colindale to inspect the corpse. 'Oh, no, you won't find that here,' said the lady at the issue desk. 'It's a cupboard number, you see.' So back to the special section of the North Library in the British Museum, where readers of material deemed obscene have to sit under direct and constant observation – presumably to prevent them playing with themselves. Homosexuality out of the closet? After fourteen brave years of Gay Liberation, it hasn't even got out of the British Library's dirty books cupboard.

When Heaven is awash with amyl, leather and sweat, gay men can be glad to be gay. But as the Blunt-hunt and the vile hounding of Peter Tatchell have shown with a chilling clarity, while attitudes and amenities have improved no end, to be homosexual is still to be at constant risk. And there are a lot of people more powerful than the trustees of the BM or even the judge who in 1977 sentenced *Gay News*'s editor to a (suspended) six months' jail sentence for blasphemy who want it to stay that way.

Take just a handful of the letters *Gay News* staff received in the week of the closure. A young lesbian writes, 'I am a homosexual and have not been able to face up to this fact at all. I find the worry, secrecy and self-hate extremely crushing and destroying.' A married milkman writes of his persecution and probable sack when he was discovered to have a male lover. There is a letter of thanks from Wilfred Blunt over-underlined in crabbed courteous longhand: 'By far

* First published in *New Society*, 1983.

the best account of my brother I have read in any paper .... I don't know if I can re-xerox it?'

Indeed, given the obvious practical importance of *Gay News* (not to mention its political import and literary merit, which are both considerable), it is quite extraordinary that its liquidation has hardly been mentioned, let alone analysed, in the media which are otherwise obsessed with matters homosexual.

It is hard not to detect, in the deafening silence of the liberal establishment, a private relief that yet another of those damned hornets that escaped the Pandora's Box of 1968 has been eradicated. For the permanent loss of *Gay News* will be a grave loss not only to 200,000 regular readers for whom it was a unique source of information, communication and solidarity, but to everyone who wishes to resist the rolling back of the gains – and they were genuine, if often double-edged – of sexual-political movements of the 1970s.

The blow is all the more cruel in that it is, to some extent, self-inflicted. Denis Lemon, who emerged as the editor and then the owner of *Gay News* in the 1970s, is universally respected for his consistency, capabilities and energy. But it is hard not to see his secret sale, at a ridiculous sum, of the paper's assets to a not very gifted businessman, as smacking of avarice. And the GLC's much vaunted Enterprise Board appears to have given false hopes of a major loan to the staff, which deprived them of time which might otherwise have been used to muster funds to purchase the title and maintain the all-important continuity of publication.

Andrew Lumsden, who succeeded Lemon as editor and is otherwise surprisingly un-bitter about the situation, permits himself the single sardonic observation that 'a newspaper for men who like to make men, and women who like to make women, was destroyed by men who like to make money.'

A Trifle Sandy-and-Julian

The first issue, published in June 1972, had a front cover of Jimmy Saville – for some reason – in a bilious green. It was printed on the International Marxist Group's press, priced at 10p and boasted a simple editorial line: that Gay was Good. The initial tone is a trifle Sandy-and-Julian (the Biograph is 'that little haven by Victoria Station' and there are pieces on trolling in Capri) considering the gender-bending flamboyance of the Gay Liberation Front who at the time seemed to have discovered the epicentre of the world revolution wearing a frock outside the Colherne.

But backstage things were more raunchy. 'If I buy one, can I have you?' one street seller was asked. 'The answer was yes but the guy didn't wait!' And a later reminiscence describes the magazine 'germinating in a soil of male love, acid, red wine and poverty'. Yet the newspaper survived, consolidated and overcame the trials, the traumas and the people, like James Pope Hennessy, who 'did not see why homosexuals should have their own newspaper any more than people who like aubergines'. By its hundredth issue in 1976 it had 14 staff and 30 contributors – an extraordinary achievement for a paper which had originated in the margins of a counter-culture which was pretty marginal itself.

It was not just journalistic survival. *Gay News* contributed practically to many of the institutions and groups that make up the modern gay community. The Gay Switchboard, the pioneering 24-hours-a-day information exchange, much imitated but without peer, was initially founded to hive off the shoals of telephone inquiries the *Gay News* staff had to answer while trying to get their paper out. (It is said of the Switchboard that gays in Dallas ring to find out what's on ... in Dallas.) From Gay Sweatshop to Parents' Inquiry, there is hardly a gay grouping that *Gay News* hasn't at some time helped with national publicity, energy, resources and sometimes personnel.

If the endless editorials about the state of the newspaper's finances, or Peter Katin's benefit being banned in Harrogate, or whether Richmond Library will or will not stock *Gay News*, get a bit obsessional sometimes, well, being a bit obsessional is a necessary quality when trying to dent the sexual conservatism of the British establishment.

Above all, it existed. As the pop star Tom Robinson wrote, 'The great thing about your newspaper is the dignity it lends the whole gay movement by remaining just that – a newspaper, not a wank-rag.' And in the late 1970s, though there is clear evidence of growing strain between the post-blasphemy-trial Lemon and his staff, and a sometimes infuriatingly wilful and unwise apoliticism, there is also, in the writing of Keith Howes, Alison Hetegan and Jack Babuscio journalism of the highest calibre.

The tenth anniversary issue (No. 243 in June 1982) adopted a well-justified tone of celebration: 'Only 10, we should be 100 or 1,000. But as it is, it's a fantastic achievement. Some credit to us, but much more to the tens of thousands who in ten years have rejected all the misnomers that society has given gays and have accordingly bought us.'

Andrew Lumsden seemed to be bringing a new editorial impetus to the paper, widening its concerns and making a long overdue commitment to gay women readers in the autonomous 'Visible Lesbian' supplement. This was all the more important after the closure of *Sappho* in 1981; and the section earned the support of initially highly sceptical women. He may be a little large in his claim that '*Gay News* is the bravest publishing venture of the 20th century,' but it was certainly a paper of integrity, intelligence and not a little experience.

If the abruptness of the liquidation was a universal surprise, there are differing views on its impact on gay morale. There are those who are critical of *Gay News*'s involvement with the commercial scene which, among other things, gets expensive for UB40s. And some gay veterans argue that for isolated homosexuals and organisations, the loss of the paper for any length of time would be a devastating blow. Others see the movement getting going again and are less worried about Ferdinand Mount's ability to organise the sexual counter-revolution.

The new GLC-aided London Gay Centre, for example, though a quite common municipal venture in North America, would have been unthinkable only a few years ago. And there is no question of the generation of gay men and women who grew up post-GLF being made to take the shit and the shame again. Denis Lemon has announced the launch of a new fortnightly, *Gay Reporter*, and the majority of the *Gay News* staff and contributors are also committed to a re-launch of a paper. So, whatever the opinion of the trustees of the British Museum, gays are not about to be consigned to the closet once again.

30
Meeting Molly*

My first daughter died of Rhesus haemolytic disease in 1982 in the middle of the industrial action by nurses and ancillaries and the national stoppages which, although unsuccessful, were the biggest solidarity strikes since 1926.

I first met my daughter Molly in an operating theatre. She had been delivered by emergency Caesarian section, two months early, suffering from Rhesus haemolytic disease. She lay panting on the back of an anaesthetic machine: tiny, mahogany-jaundiced and with the gleaming, near-porous skin of the very premature.

I have worked enough in theatre to know from the air of controlled pandemonium, the litter of hurriedly discarded catheters and that particular scampering noise that theatre shoes make when things are going wrong, that it had been a close thing. She must have required immediate artificial ventilation to resuscitate her.

In the adjacent room, her mother Juliet was still unconscious and having a hasty blood transfusion. For a moment it looked as if I might be losing both of them. Molly and I were the only people in the crowded, harshly-lit room not wearing theatre greens, and I felt as naked and almost as helpless as she looked. I hardly noticed how beautiful she was or realised how brave she was going to be.

Doctors, and their kin, make notoriously bad patients; men are famous for finding that birth unlocks unexpectedly powerful emotions. As a doctor, I recognised the euphemisms consultants use in these circumstances: 'Long, uphill road'; 'sicker babies have survived'. I have used them myself. But as a father I just longed for them to say the one thing they couldn't guarantee: that Molly would make it.

As a doctor, I wanted the most intensive medical care possible and wanted to know about it down to the last platelet count and percentage of her conjugated bilirubin. But looking at her, hoist on the special baby unit operating table, grilled by overhead lamps, continuously

* First published in *New Society*, 1983.

exchange transfused, trussed by tubes and swaddled by machinery, it was impossible not to want to snatch her and hear human sounds instead of the electronic sighs and blips and flickers which came to signify her life.

Since Rhesus haemolytic disease had been diagnosed, I had been haunted by the drawing in the first available textbook of the stillborn 'hydrops' baby in the untreated cases, with its abdomen distended and ribs splayed by the enlarged liver and characteristically turgid skin. And those clinical signs and the problems of their neo-natal management were what my medical mind first registered. But my father's eyes simultaneously saw her long, delicate fingers and fathomless brown eyes. And felt that if only we hoped hard enough, her spirit would pull her through.

Rhesus disease is an essentially prosaic incompatibility between the blood group of the mother and her baby which leads the parent blood system to generate antibodies defensive to itself but potentially hostile to a developing child, like Molly, who had the misfortune to adopt her father's blood characteristics. Its consequences have been described, under various names, for centuries and its prevention is a major achievement of immunological theory and modern obstetric practice. I was examined on it for my obstetric viva in finals and have lectured medical students on its implications for perinatal mortality and health service policy.

Nonetheless, a mother can still acquire antibodies whose effect becomes more destructive with each pregnancy. And then an academic, diagrammatic matter becomes a harrowing drama with mother and unborn child doomed – thanks to the father's genetic contribution – to immunological war. Meanwhile, medical effort uses prodigious technology to protect the growing child from the maternal antibodies and the anaemia, jaundice and brain damage they will engender if not controlled.

So long before the drama of Molly's birth, Juliet's pregnancy had been turned into a high technology obstacle race which, without the thoughtfulness of the hospital staff, the solidarity of other mothers and her own courage, would have been an unendurable ordeal. Plasmaporesis, a transfusion technique which can separate out the destructive maternal antibodies, had to continue, twice weekly, through holidays, heartburn and heartache. When it went smoothly, it was an uncomfortable and exhausting procedure, but when veins collapsed or tubes blocked or the machine went wrong, it was agonising.

A Hair-raising Manoeuvre

Over the last two months, the plasma antibody levels need to be supplemented by examination of the optical characteristics of the amniotic fluid. So amniocentesis, which even as a one-off screening procedure can be traumatic and not without hazard, became a weekly ritual. And in the final weeks, when the haemolytic process can unpredictably accelerate, blood transfusion has to be made direct into the abdominal cavity of the baby as it bobs about in the womb.

This hair-raising manoeuvre, done under local anaesthetic, requires passing a fine catheter through the uterine wall and easing its tip into a safe position within the baby itself. Juliet and Molly had it and survived it three times while I sat on the end of the bed feeling the pregnant father's normal turbulent mixture of pride, passivity and irrelevance, magnified tenfold.

Outside, summer had turned into autumn and the banners of the hospital strikers smudged and misted outside the hospital front gates. Over syringes and biscuits, the nurses discussed how they would be voting in the ballot and whether the hospital would ever get the money to purchase the plasmaporesis machine now on loan. As Scargill toured the coalfields, Molly kicked and Juliet retched. The world shrank, against our will, to that little pattern of lines glimpsed on the ultrasound. Illness shrinks and birth privatises, and to experience both processes working against each other within someone you love is most confusing.

But, after such a dramatic birth, the first week of Molly's life was even more terrifying. Juliet chainsmoked two floors beneath the special baby unit awaiting the knock that meant another exchange transfusion and forcing herself upstairs to express breast milk and glimpse her daughter. I wept at home over the Polaroid photo the hospital provided and wondered if anything was real. Worry became a way of life: every advance had to be undercut with reservations, every hope guarded with doubt and clothed with caution.

Days of Hope

When the crises of the first weeks seemed over, I registered her birth but stuffed a leaflet about death grants into my pocket. Not that I thought it likely, but just to demonstrate that it was still a possibility.

Besides crying a lot, I did other uncharacteristic things like reading Lucretius and trying to assemble a 200-part cardboard model of the Tower of London which was the halfway point on the now numbingly familiar bus ride to the hospital. One day, I thought, I'll take Molly over the Tower Bridge gallery and we'll look down at the No. 47 buses and laugh about her turbulent transpontine birth and my clumsiness with cardboard models.

As the weeks passed and we grew to be on more equal terms, her mother and I peered through the plastic incubator and took turns to answer the phone and will each other up the stairs to the unit. Encouraged by the hospital to visit whenever possible, we watched her shape come back as the oedema eased, saw the jaundice fade and delighted as she took food into her stomach and began to put on weight.

Her 5-year-old brother visited: bemused and confused until through the porthole he had his finger squeezed by Molly's tiny hand. She grew strong enough to fight the nurses, tug at her drips and smile the most melting of smiles. After seven weeks she came off the respirator and at last breathed for herself. No celebration yet but we allowed ourselves to collect the baby bath the neighbours had been holding for us. It was the weekend of the big Greenham Common demonstration and, a little ashamed of our self-absorption, we thought quite seriously of making the first trip out of London for months.

We were right not to risk it. We were phoned unexpectedly by the registrar whose quizzical smile we had come to rely upon. Molly had had 'a setback' and needed to go back onto the ventilator. At first we were confident; she had survived the prematurity and the haemolysis as well as necrotising endocolitis and a septal heart defect. But Juliet caught Molly's eyes rolling. And by the third visit it was clear that something was badly wrong.

Molly seemed to have lost her way, her ability to concentrate on survival. We drove backwards and forwards through Blackwall Tunnel, unwilling to leave the unit but finding it unbearable to stay. By 3 a.m., it was clear that she had no more strength to resist an overwhelming infection. The doctors were taking it in shifts to 'bag' her but when manual resuscitation was stopped, the heart-rate on the monitor fell back remorselessly: 90, 70, 50.

'She's dying, isn't she?' we asked, unnecessarily. And once the ventilator and the other tubes were removed and the traces went flat and silent, Molly passed away in moments with one last gentle wave of her right hand. The nurse wrapped her body and put it into our arms. It was the first time we had been able to hold her properly. We had never heard her cry or laugh. And now we never would.

The shock of losing her after such effort and with success so near is overwhelming. The knowledge that the death of a baby is still a frequent experience in modern Britain and a commonplace in much of the world is no consolation. We tried to write letters of thanks to the staff but, as other parents agreed, there is no way words can express one's gratitude and admiration both for particular individuals and the system of health care which makes their work possible.

Words are not Enough

Nor is it easy to express the sadness. 'There aren't words really,' wrote one friend, rightly. Words are not enough and an attempt like this to externalise a private grief is infuriatingly unable to convey more than the surfaces of the experience. Nor is it possible to obtain the comfort of 'accepting' Molly's death as ordained or inevitable or after all for the best; she wanted to live too much. And I hope I will always feel about any such death like a close colleague who wrote, in condolence, but also defiance, 'Thirty years of practising medicine have still not reconciled me to these tragedies.' But within the misery there is something politically inspiring.

Molly was born and so nearly lived only because of a chain of organised and unselfish human beings which stretched from the unknown blood donors whose gift sustained her in the womb to the nurses who got Molly and us through so many nights and still spared a thought to tuck a white carnation in her death wraps. In the 1980s, politically dominated by the philosophy of pos sessive individualism, the NHS still allows a different set of values to flourish. And it makes manifest the spirit of human solidarity which is at the core of socialism, and which our present rulers are so concerned to eradicate. While Molly's death is a tragedy, her life was something brave and marvellous.

31

Doctoring*

I spent most of the 1980s working full-time in general practice in East London, which does not allow much time for reflection. But as well as being emotionally and physically draining, it can be inspiring. The courage and generosity of working-class people, even under extreme pressure, is sometimes stunning. And I am fortunate to work with a group of medical colleagues who share an unsentimental appreciation of the ideals of the 1960s. But one does often wonder if the palliatives we often have to offer aren't a substitute for lasting social change. This piece, written during the Falklands farrago, was predictably depressed.

It is 7.45 in the evening and I have been doctoring all day. Forty-three consultations, 430 decisions, 4,000 or 5,000 nuances, eye muscle alterations and mutual misunderstandings have left me emotionally drained and so exhausted that it is a considerable mental effort to remember quite how to double-lock the surgery door. But don't pity me. I get paid – quite well by my patients' standards. Pity the patients instead.

There was the batty woman who 'has always suffered with her legs'. A forklift truck driver with asthmatic attacks to whom I explained three times the action of sodium chromoglycate in stabilising mast cells – until we both agreed I should give up the effort and he should keep taking the pills. There was Mrs J, making light of the fact that her devoted husband, as well as herself, now has cancer, asking with genuine feeling about my family, and insisting on giving me £2 'for the holidays' which she could ill afford but I could ill refuse. A man with a brain tumour who hasn't told his wife and who keeps this agonising secret with me and his hospital doctors. An ex-services amputee who clanks his tin leg against the chair, and a widow still in tears ('we'd been together since the General Strike').

And so it goes on: wax in the security guard's left ear; a nasty

* First published in *New Internationalist*, 1983.

childhood eczema; several sore throats and coughs, two of which are selected for the five-star anti-smoking tirade, one of whom tellingly replies that he will give up his cigarettes the moment someone stops the pollution from lorry exhaust fumes that blackens the air of the local streets.

Why haven't I got the time or energy to refuse an old dear the sleeping pills which one of my colleagues commenced, on a strictly temporary basis, fifteen years ago? Am I really making anyone happier, except perhaps the drug companies whose over-priced, crudely advertised ('Narcoxyn 500 Has the Power') – and occasionally unsafe – products I have been prescribing all day?

I once heard a consultant colleague, who meant it as a compliment, describe general practitioners as 'specialists in highly skilled reassurance'. I would much prefer to be a highly skilled specialist in making patients angry: because these so-called medical symptoms have causes – and cures – far beyond my sphere of medicine. We're not trained in the installation of hand rails or the delivery of meals on wheels. That's somebody else's business – despite the fact that any major improvements in health have been because of political and social reform rather than 'medical breakthrough'.

Today – against my better judgment – I referred for specialist investigation a bus conductress with a run of 'funny tummys'. I wrote her a comprehensive referral letter and she was carefully and competently examined by a specialist physician who, in turn, wrote a comprehensive and illuminating letter back to me explaining he too could find nothing specific and suggesting she might wish to try bran on her breakfast cereal. Were we maintaining a show of professionalism to mystify our patient or simply justifying the existence of the technology at the specialist's teaching hospital? Or did the bus conductress simply want a little time off to postpone facing yet another new brain-bending fares scheme?

Probably my time was better spent visiting a recently bereaved wife whose husband's ghastly death is still vivid in both our minds. And I would certainly do better if I were to bully the housing authorities to forbid a neighbour breeding pigeons next door to a diabetic man with life-threatening asthma, than I would by increasing his bronchodilator dosages still further.

But then again, just as one has almost talked one's own profession out of existence, along comes a good, old-fashioned emergency, calling for high-tech hospital medicine and some very fancy clinical management ... but fast.

It came this morning with the unpredictability which is so typical of general practice. It should have been an easy visit: just another case of chickenpox. Some common-sense advice, a bottle of calamine, maybe a squint in the ears, and you can usually be out of the door again in a couple of minutes. This time I was greeted by two kids running barefoot down the length of the council house corridor – naked but for grubby towels, and covered from the soles of their feet to the roots of their mouths with weeping scabs. Inside, their baby sister lay face down on the carpet like a discarded doll, with a burning fever, rigid neck stiffness, swollen eyelids shut tight over her eyes and with skin almost obliterated with pox craters.

Trying, whilst on the phone, to make light conversation, I asked where Dad was. He was, his wife explained, on remand in Brixton Prison on a charge of attempted murder. Oh, and since he had suffered brain damage in a road accident he was now so deranged that he literally tore his cell apart if not visited every day by his wife. So would I be able to arrange for her to speak calmingly to him over the phone before she accompanied her daughter in the ambulance?

A bad day; we all have them.

It only becomes a futile day when I get home and try to unwind in front of the TV set which is celebrating, yet again, that profitless and very expensive adventure in the South Atlantic.

I doubt if I have 'saved' more than half a dozen lives in my life or, to be perfectly honest, prolonged or greatly improved the quality of more than a very few. Yet instead of tackling housing and working conditions, our society has perfected weapons which can blow a cruiser full of teenage conscripts out of the water, which publicly gloats over those boys' deaths and which boasts its ability to blow the entire world into a desert of radioactive dust. What price then the stabilising effect of sodium chromoglycate on mast cells?

Perhaps I should have the courage of a colleague who recently – and with a certain icy logic – gave up her medical career to work full-time for nuclear disarmament: perhaps the single most fruitful measure of preventative medicine that modern society could take?

Obviously this is not my conclusion. I remain more convinced now than I was ten years ago, as a rather naive young hospital doctor, that if we are to have a society genuinely enjoying good health – rather than a medical sector snuffling after the causes of sickness like a baffled bloodhound – we need fundamental changes in the way our society is owned, ordered and organised.

Health care according to need rather than wealth is not just a good moral principle. It has been shown to work. And to be more efficient and effective than the commercial medical sector in North America. This is ground which must be held against governments who make no secret of their wish to return to the old two-tier medical care of charity and minimal medicine for the majority with a lucrative private sector providing VIP care to those who can foot the bills.

But if I ever get complacent about what can be achieved by medical measures alone, I need only go as far as I did this lunch time: to the local supermarket. There I will almost certainly know half a dozen shoppers and will be able to see the trolleys quaking with pop and sugar, cheap cosmetics and ciggies: not because my patients are bad people. But because those products are cheap and filling and quick and keep the kiddies quiet. And it's then, not in the consulting room, that I renew my practical and intellectual commitment to social change.

In this respect, it is conventional to think of doctors like Ernesto 'Che' Guevara, Norman Bethune and Joshua Horne. But I have more affection for those flaming words of Sylvia Pankhurst (whose mother and baby clinic – a converted pub called The Mothers Arms – was only a stone's throw away from where I practise today) to the judge sentencing her, once again, to jail for sedition: 'I have sat up with the babies all night and tried to make them better. But this is the wrong system and it cannot be made better. And I would give my life to see it overthrown.'

32

Yippies to Yuppies: New York in the 1980s*

New York in the 1980s was no longer a town of pop art, poetry and dissent but a playground for developers like Donald Trump and Co. Even the art galleries had yuppy appartments installed and the deregulation of rent controls had successfully expelled those radicals left (although artists of an apolitical sort were in fact the leading edge of the lower East Side's redevelopment). The sheer banality of Reaganism in its triumphal phase was chilling. This disenchanted piece served as an introduction to a British travel guide to New York, countered by an encomium from Quentin Crisp, a successful celibate who then made the inexcusable mistake of falling in love with Manhattan.

I first went to Manhattan nearly twenty years ago; a terrified teenager clutching a '99 Day, $99' coach ticket. America seemed to be curling open like an old tin can before my eyes, the civil rights movement was spilling into the northern city ghettos, the Berkeley students were discovering pot and 'organising within the knowledge factory' and a huge plume of smoke hung above Los Angeles from the gleeful riot in Watts. 1960s New York was fast, belligerent and scared. My strongest memories were the poster over the Students for a Democratic Society's HQ saying 'No Vietnamese ever called me Nigger'; the smell of hot oil and rubber inside Greyhound Stations and queues of poor people with their parcels wrapped up with infinite patience and newly achieved dignity.

Back again in 1974, New York still felt, to a European, a radical city, a place of imminence, a mix of the older 1960s possibilities and the new spirit of the women's and gay movement which still meant change. The Watergate Tapes were on sale in the supermarket check-outs, Vietnam was in every other sentence, and the Movement was still moving. Political optimism was only temporarily stalled, the Empire was uneasy.

* First published in *City Limits*, 1986.

So the first shock of New York deep into the Reign of Reagan is its platitudinous self-confidence, its intellectual conformism and a social conservatism so profound it has ceased to be a cosmetic and has been absorbed into the very civic skin. Never mind the homeless sleeping out in the public parks, subways unfit for cattle, the poor hawking second-hand goods on the street corners and the plummeting Stock Exchange; there is a tennis clip on every mountain bike, a new restaurant in every intersection, and if you don't *enjoy* it's your own damn fault.

Typical is what's happened to the poor old Statue of Liberty, spruced up for its Centennial as the new brand image of capitalism, another product from the people who gave you freedom. The statue was a democratic gesture, its catchline was written by the socialist poet Emma Lazarus and the French fundraising effort was an act of defiance against absolutism. But its incessantly produced image now beams benignly over the aerial bombardment of Tripoli and the tooling up of the Contras or whatever wheeze comes next from the patriots who now direct US foreign policy.

Inside Liberty's tower, a Museum of Immigration is now housed (rather tough on black Americans, who mostly arrived in shackles at the plantation ports) which even includes Samuel Gompers, George Grosz and Helen Keller. But the Museum is deserted while thousands stand in a queue to photograph themselves looking out from Liberty's flame. While I read a panel on the rise of the No-Nothing-Party before the First World War and its campaign against dope fiends and alien gunmen, someone strides past in a 'Don't Mess with the US' T-shirt shouting, 'All this history bores me.' Indeed.

History is now New York's enemy and if you inquire about Watergate, let alone Stonewall, people brought up on TV and leisure magazines look back with alarm. Being a European sentimentalist, I trot off to the usual shrines, eating a cold turkey sandwich on the spot John Lennon got shot; gawping at the Apollo and the Cedar Bar and visiting Trotsky's old print shop in St Mark's Place. While wading through throngs of New Yorkers queueing for 'Vienna 1900' (a kind of Habitat catalogue for the Franz-Josef era) at the Museum of Modern Art to see the Pollocks and the De Koonings, I hear the gallery guide announcing that 'the Post-Impressionists were like the European romantics. That is, they were alcoholics and committed suicide.' Ahem. But the real New York is another time-space continuum. Now.

As a city it has lost none of its architectural exuberance and manic energy. The taxis still swerve rather than drive, the sign language is still imperative and muscular ('Don't block the box', 'Touchbank Here', 'Stop Cheap Steaks') and people throw frisbees as if their life depended on it. There is less English spoken, more babies with bald fathers and a lot more purple prose in the delis which now stick reviews over their midget vegetables and lake sturgeons and offer varietal grape juices. Enjoy is the supreme injunction.

If you think gentrification is people sticking brass door knockers on their Stoke Newington front doors, you should see the gentry in operation in New York. There a neighbourhood can be razed, and replaced by yuppie lego in a matter of months and gourmetified and art-galleried in the process.

Which is not to say all the cultural landmarks have been built over by sushi bars and designer bike shops. Despite AIDS, people still strip for charity, organise telephone sex-linkups which are shown on your telephone bill as long-distance phone calls, and queue to see *My Beautiful Laundrette* which, along with Laura Ashley, muffins and antique clocks, was one of the few signs that the United Kingdom exists.

The US labour movement, once mighty but now organising only 17 per cent of the workforce, soldiers on, thank God, and the best day I spent in New York was being shown round the back of a power plant, Mafia-disposed toxic waste and all, by a rank and file organiser. And there is a Left, although in comparison with the movements of the 1960s and 1970s it is microscopic.

So I was delighted to meet Victor Navasky, the editor of the Nation, an organ of sensible liberalism which, in the current circumstances, seems crypto-Bolshevik; to come across writers for the post-Murdoch *Village Voice* who are as appalled by Reaganism as most Europeans and to meet people who are, ahem, Marxists.

What is surprising is the degree of self-delusion among those tyros of empiricism, the bankers themselves. Banker availability is a New York speciality; they are young, they are noisy and they are everywhere: restaurants, gallery openings, nightclubs, and all younger than oneself. I interrupt one who is discussing the investment potential of a Jamie Reid Sex Pistols daub at the Reid's New York opening at the Josh Bauer Gallery.

'Does it matter to you that since Reaganomics, the USA is not only a net debtor, but the biggest debtor in the world? And why are all the farms going bust?'

He isn't worried, his art collection will see him through; if the Exchange busts, he has a Schnabel under the table.

Steve Mass, founder of the Mudd Club, is also delighted by the ironies of yuppies shelling out for Situationist off-cuts, but equally off-beam. 'What we really needed in New York was someone like Dick Hebdige to tell us what it all meant.' Ahem. Was it like this in 1928, I wonder?

At the Palladium, which has less style than Stoke Newington's Three Crowns on Friday night, more bankers are waiting to meet the Eurythmics, whose co-leader's birthday we are celebrating. 'Do you know any good bands in Britain? Up and coming and with investment potential?' asks one. I take a deep breath. 'Well, there's this group called the Redskins. You seem to have plenty of statues that need kicking down.'

33

The Underground Press in Perspective*

Perspective was something that the underground press didn't have and didn't want. Still, it did have a messy but effective system of direct input by writers and, in Richard Neville, one of the most charming and valiant editors I was ever cut by. But it was only one moment in a history of dissident British culture which stretches from Wycliffe's sermons to pirate radio and warehouse parties in London in the late 1980s.

In the beginning was the IBM golf ball. Twirling and dancing above an electric typewriter, it enabled anyone with keyboard skills to produce justified typesetting which could be gummed on to card, embellished with Letraset, bootlegged illustrations and tea stains and be despatched to cheap offset litho printers. Back came newspapers, off went street sellers, and when the bills came in you changed printers or importuned a rock star. It was something as silly and as simple as that which made possible the underground publications of the late 1960s and early 1970s: the unstamped press of the late twentieth century. But by 1972 it was clearly not a joke to the Establishment. The combined monthly sales of the underground, community and far Left press in Britain probably exceeded 200,000 and was increasingly making common cause with the upsurge of rank-and-file trade unionism. Police action, most famously and fatuously against *OZ*, was meeting determined and flamboyant resistance. And the underground press's ad hoc mode of production was creating a new kind of highly graphic literacy among its readership: non-glossy, subversive, excitable, the polar opposite of the design styles of the 1980s so high on white space and low on ideas.

What had stamped the press as political was also simple but a great deal more important: the Vietnam War. John Wilcock, the Yorkshire-

* First published as a review of Nigel Fountain's *Underground: The London Alternative Press 1966–74*.

man who invented the underground press, always insists the war was the constant backdrop. It was not just that it was unjust, unequal or imperialist, but that it was prosecuted with such a bizarre combination of the ideology of Disneyland and the technology of Cape Canaveral, that it seemed to require an equally surreal response (classical Dadaism was the model). If an alliance – even at the emotional level – between the cadres of the NLF and the offset lithos sans culottes, especially in view of both parties' subsequent evolution, seems implausible, one must forcibly remind oneself quite how successful official American propaganda was for most of the 1960s. Until the Tet Offensive, the view that the NLF had no indigenous support in the South was widely accepted and a kind of liberal Atlanticism which regarded post-war American foreign policy as essentially benign was almost universal on the Labour Left. Wilson was doing his level best to get British troops implicated and opposition, despite the efforts of Russell, Sartre and Mailer, was small and worse still respectable and neo-Stalinist. Quite a considerable mental break was required. The underground's collective rejection of lies about Vietnam and the economic system and political mentality which produced it, was more courageous than it now seems and the bedrock of its other dissents.

The American war in Vietnam contributed in another important way to the London underground by providing a cadre of politically creative American emigrés. A high proportion of the journalists of the underground press originated geographically as well as psychologically outside the boundaries of what Tom Nairn, perhaps surprisingly a regular *OZ* contributor, calls Ukania. This is not simply true of the Sydney grouping around *OZ* (themselves influenced by the Big Push movement of New South Wales anarchism) and the North American beards-bored-with-Marxism influential in the early *International Times*, but the South African political refugee (now rug dealer) Alan Marcuson who edited and financed *Freindz*. A similar tendency is to be found on the far Left in Britain whose most influential figures have been Tony Cliff from Palestine, C.L.R. James from Trinidad, Ted Grant from South Africa and Gerry Healey from Eire. This is exactly the opposite of the exiles-as-vectors-of-reaction advanced by Perry Anderson in *Origins of National Culture*.

The point here is not that we native Ukanians lack cultural get up and go (we managed to re-invent rock and roll) or that the underground was an import but that exile-immigrants found it easier to see through and to break through the protective rituals with which the realities of power are veiled in Britain. We thought we had no illusions but they had even fewer and were rightly impatient with the cosiness and apolitical etiquette of London cultural life. The North Americans in particular brought with them a more developed dissident culture. *IT* was a fairly single-minded vehicle for Beat poetry and attitudes, by the presence of William Burroughs and the 1967 visit of Ginsberg and Ferlingetti. Cue mad polemics! And explosive punctuation!!

However, it would be wrong therefore to regard Britain as a backwater of radical culture. The 1956 crisis and the original New Left had antedated the formation of an independent Left in other European countries by several years and the networks of folk clubs, poetry magazines, R and B and art colleges had created an indigenous bohemian network of some importance. It was an era not just of rock and roll but of cheap books, expansive state education and limited TV. And despite the electoral dominance of the Labour Party, the labour movement, much of it unofficial and shop steward-led, had its own networks of co-operation and dissent. Some of the cultural exiles were specifically drawn to Ukania because of our theatrical and artistic traditions: Blake, after all, perhaps the first and the fiercest rebel against the urban capital, was the central figure in Ginsberg's new cosmology.

But to attempt to define the politics of these children of Attlee and LSD is to become unstuck. It was potluck and depended who got at the boards last. During my mercifully brief editorship of *OZ*, for example, a board game designed to pillory the class nature of British justice got transmogrified into a duotone of a 1940s pseudo-lesbian pin-up and this was fairly par for the course of a magazine which moved editorial position from Leninism to Flying Saucerism in a matter of weeks. Vietnam continues to provide a common cause and an organisational focus (radical newspapers are a waste of time if they don't organise). It was Vietnam, almost Vietnam-as-metaphor, which impelled psychiatrists to discuss imperialism and hippies to encounter Marxism. But there were a lot of other factors underlying the psychedelic samizdat which lay somewhere between electric typewriters and imperialist wars.

To some extent it was demographic, the point at which the ideas and products of the cultural radicals of the 1950s and early 1960s first found large young audiences. The rise of the rock and roll industry and the mass popularity of original artists (the reverse of today) was of critical importance and, through advertising and the open-air concerts, had a direct impact on the press. So while fiercely declaiming against the consumer culture of the Cold War era, the underground press was itself involved in some brisk merchandising, of new travel destinations (Wilcock was a staff writer for Arthur Frommer's $5 a day guides), of clothes, music and leisure facilities. One of *IT*'s initial campaigns was the distinctly unrevolutionary demand that the tube trains should run later. The implications of this process, which has now given us the Thatcherite leisure conglomerates headed by ex-hippies Elliott, Branson and Dennis, hot on de-regulation and enterprise, were bitterly contested at the time, inconclusively and in highly moralistic idiom. But the truth is that the magazines most closely tied to marketing – the leisure press – survived best, notably *Time Out* which recently celebrated its twentiety birthday with a kind of Ideal Home exhibition for aspirant yuppies.

Another part of the underground press's role, especially in the Australian and pre-psychedelic English *OZ*, was the satirical bit, what Richard Neville used to call intellectual slum clearance, the very necessary work of lampooning judges, insulting the monarchy, casting aspersions on big business and tilting at the other Aunt Sallies of Ukanian life, perhaps with a little more force than English public school boys who imagined themselves as devastating social critics. In this debunking sense, the underground was in a direct lineage with a long tradition of free-thinking, dissident press. Neville at his best has a Carlisle-like ring to him and was equally effective in kicking disbelief into the vernacular. And this insolent iconoclasm is sorely missed, with the possible exception of the work of Steve Bell, now that we really need it. Certainly the exuberance of the underground's anti-censorship, anti-Grundyish hedonism did some thing to heave Britain finally out of the monochrome doze of the 1950s with its fearful snobberies of class and sex, if only by rather flippantly proselytising battles others had won.

Drugs certainly played an important role and a very different one to their contemporary use as hard currency for arms and Right-wing crime and as a bolster of possessive individualism. LSD's profoundly disinhibitory effect on the sensory nervous system was expressed in the synaesthetic subjectivity of much of the best design and a kind of political pantheism which was both idiotic and divine. And if the staple diet of cannabis sometimes produced fatuous thought, it did not produce the anergia of heroin. The bohemian communism *worked*: it was self-supporting, unsubsidised and you didn't just get involved for the sake of your CV.

There was also an element in the underground press who saw themselves consciously as revolutionaries deriving inspiration from an

Anglicised and ill-understood Situationism, a Blakean anti-urban pantheism or one of the various Trotsky- or Mao-derived, worker-based groups which, after a long sojourn in the wilderness were being replenished by new recruits from Vietnam and the student movement. Present, too, was classical anarchism and concern for free love and the rights of women which almost inevitably came to the fore in any revolutionary upsurge. It is hard to evaluate the extent of their influence outside London: the odd *OZ* got passed around in factories, maybe the people who read *IT* also bought the *Socialist Worker*; certainly I can remember a couple of hundred young workers swamping Barking Town Hall at a hastily arranged meeting in protest against the jailing of the *OZ* editors. But to ask if the underground was truly revolutionary is to ask the wrong question. Only a fool or a yippy expects the revolution to be led by the producers of multi-coloured broadsheets who think socialism consists of themselves and their friends being beautiful in an endless series of geodesic domes.

It was anti-bourgeois, lacking in the emphasis on personal self-aggrandisement so universal in the 1980s and, surprisingly against one's own memories, intellectual.

It is argued that the underground press collapsed under the impact of the women writers' and producers' growing awareness that the general freedoms advanced in the publications they slaved over did not seem to apply to them. Perhaps the high point of this revolution within the revolution is when, after Sheila Rowbotham's resignation from the *Black Dwarf*, her ex-colleagues at her request spent five minutes silently imagining that 'you are black, not white, imagine you have cunts, and not cocks' (that is, until one cracked and blurted, heroically, 'I think that's absolutely preposterous').

But that is a little too simple. The women's movement was not homogeneous, contained virtuosos of self-regard and often adopted 'pro-women' positions which, bereft of class analysis, became openly Right wing. Had the underground press been run by the most perceptive of genuine sexual radicals (which it certainly was not), there would still have been a political crisis as the 1970s ground on. The problems were more general, the crisis of a cultural radicalism attempting to transform itself into a political force. The underground press was the journalistic expression of a social sea change which had been welling up since the 1950s. It was interested in altering attitudes but put a lot of the emphasis on being just that bit more hip than the masses, a chic elitism. But in the 1970s attitudes were taking social forms, not just the women's liberation movement but republicanism in Ireland, rank and file trade unionism, factory occupations and prolonged national strikes which in 1974 were to lead to the fall of the Heath government. A dissenting journalism which reflected and expressed that much bigger social movement would have to alter its own attitudes, to overcome its habitual metropolitan bias, its disdain for the ordinary Alfs (as *OZ* called them) and its reverence for the insights of stoned pop stars. The best of the underground press took up the challenge: in the spirit of psychedelic Bolshevism, *Freindz* frontpaged a luminous NUM banner and *OZ* sent its reporters to the UCS occupation. *Time Out*'s newsroom remained a beacon within an increasingly consumerist magazine. But the underground press pioneers lacked the experience or the skill to make the turn or the many others which might have meant their survival into the Thatcher era. Indeed, far from storming the reality studios, some of the writers were having increasing difficulty in opening the toilet door. The sexual and artistic rebels against the First World War had Soviet Russia and the Communist Parties to orientate them. And while the subsequent artistic consequences of Stalinism were quite disastrous, so was the underground's political disorientation as Dadas without Bolshies.

Revolution by underground press was bound to be a self-defeating attempt at totalisation. The libertarian Left were exhausted if they fought on every front and cop-outs if they didn't: the moralism which had been so potent was now presenting its bill.

In some ways the crisis of the London underground press prefigured a rollercoaster which was to disorientate and destroy much of the European Left, most spectacularly in Italy. And in the upsurge which will follow the end of the Thatcher era, there will no doubt be echoes of the movements of the 1960s, perhaps with South Africa playing the international role that Vietnam did, with pop music still putting its unscrupulous oar in, with sexual politics of a type we cannot yet define and a renewal of the endless disputation between the political Left, the artistic avant guard and the bohemian communists. But now the press, viewed from our much darkened age, remains more dazzling than it really was.

34

Enter Stage Left*

Much of the theatrical radicalism of the 1960s and 1970s has compromised or just vanished. But some hasn't and theatre remains a vital source of political insight and inspiration. Indeed I think one should support live entertainment in itself against the deluge of video pap, style mags and bland pop. I'm afraid I prefer Ken Dodd on stage to Sammy and Rosie in the front room.

It started with the domes, the bulbous, terracotta knobs with which the architect Frank Matcham crowned his thousand-seat, three-tier, cantilever-balconied Hackney Empire whose construction was one of the last great architectural acts of nineteenth-century London. The Empire, which opened on 9 December 1901, is a place which sets theatre historians atremble. A 'Number One' Stoll Theatre, it put on everyone, from Lily Langtry, Stan Laurel and Little Titch through Max Miller and the Fields (WC and Gracie) to Tony Hancock and Gerry and the Pacemakers. But it was theatre history. In the somnambulent, TV-sated 1950s when *Sunday Night at the London Palladium* killed live entertainment, Mecca bought the carcass, hung a huge Housey Housey board over the stage and sealed the proscenium. Until in 1979 when, almost by magic, terracotta tiles started to fly loose, the domes looked dangerous and Mecca, injudiciously but Mecca-like, removed them.

Hackney council, whose own mausoleum-like town hall is 50 feet up Mare Street, managed to notice. And so did English Heritage who confirmed, to everyone's amazement, that in the heart of Hackney, wedged between the doner-kebab takeaway and the plastic training-shoe retailers of the borough's main shopping street, was a building of international significance. Listed, inside and out, Grade Two. Even Pevsner had missed it (while he noted a 'not bad' 1930s Odeon up the road). Repair of the domes alone (they are being recast in specialist kilns in Lancashire) would have set back Mecca £250,000. The other

* First published in *New Society*, 1987.

potential fines and penalties for neglect or destruction, which can be exerted retrospectively, gave Mecca's accountant paroxysmal nocturnal dyspnoeia. So, 'Theatre For Sale: Excellent location, Period Features, Needs Some Work.'

Enter Stage Extreme Left, Roland Muldoon, accompanied by Claire Muldoon ('My partner in life, in theatre, in everything') in search of ... a theatre. For twenty years, first with CAST (The Cartoon Archetypical Slogan Theatre), then with New Variety, they had been performing, producing and promoting radical live entertainment in the upstairs rooms of pubs, trade union halls and, once in a blue moon, on a stage: the Ziegfelds of alternative cabaret. Muldoon's ginger-nut beard, demented beanie and demotic-psychedelic-Cockney diction is not unknown on the theatrical Left (an Arts Council official has called him 'a combative, dogged, awkward cuss'). Brought up on an overspill council estate in Weybridge, he did the theatre management course in the Bristol Old Vic and gravitated to the old Unity Theatre in King's Cross from where he and Claire were said to have been expelled in 1965 by Stalinists on the bar committee for 'Freudian-Trotskyism'.

In revenge they set up CAST, the independent theatre group famous for its acrobatic style, fast pace and roll-neck black sweaters. They started in folk-club intervals with cartoon Marxism: hitting the audience before it could get to the bar, scaring them, making them laugh, pointing out the contradictions and pissing off before anyone could think up the answers.

After the ferment of 1968 and the proliferation of agitational theatre, CAST eventually entered the era of subsidised theatre. Mercedes vans and Equity rates – not without a good deal of vituperative debate in the style of the Soviet artists of the twenties; that is, ferociously extolling their own virtues and denouncing everyone else in sight. But Arts Council money was, in the Thatcher era, bound to come to an end. And CAST was never a very grateful recipient. 'The grants were bound to stop,' remembers Muldoon. 'So we did everything possible to insult them and be as horrible as possible. We thought it was our duty.' In *Sedition 81* they handed out large joints to the audience, telling them it was a government rebate, cut the Queen's head off, shot Prince Charles, threw the chairman of Turner and Newells into a vat of boiling asbestos and sent all the Left-wing playwrights to the House of Lords. Their grant was not renewed.

The GLC came to the rescue. 'We were looking for new angles,' says Muldoon, 'and this man called Tony Banks came along with some bumptious plan to bring culture to London. So we said we had some experience in this field.' Instead of compulsory Acker Bilk and Arnold Wesker in draughty town halls, New Variety set up pub and community centre venues across London, putting on not just the stand-up comedians the Comedy Store were breaking in Soho but live acts: socialist magicians, radical ventriloquists, interminable mime duos with funny names and general mayhem. New Variety was the New Line and launched the Joeys, Benjamin Zephaniah, Happy End and, literally, hundreds of others. In the process, the Muldoons became, themselves, a mini-Arts Council. It was classic cheer-ups for the New Depression but bubbling with angry, extreme talent and, for once, paying the union rate. And it was still political, if less explicit: in the year of the miners' strike the groups performed non-stop and, against the stereotype of the north–south divide, were part of the great fund-raising movement by London workers which did so much to feed the strikers and their families.

But the GLC was also doomed. And most of the money was ending up in the brewers' pockets anyway (bar takings are a key element in the finances of live shows). And when the acts got big, the venues were far too small and they had to crawl back to the West End managements. The GLC was interested in the purchase of a large theatre and so the Muldoons found themselves auditioning auditoriums in Kilburn, Tottenham and, eventually, trying to sneak a look past Harry the Doorman of the Hackney Empire. It was love at first sight. Or perhaps *folie a deux* between the ragamuffin hustlers of New Variety and Matcham's glorious, imperial theatre.

The Lyceum is majestic but seldom a theatre nowadays; in Wyndhams you need oxygen to get to the upper circle, the view is lousy and the gin and tonics expensive. The Theatre Royal at Stratford is exquisite but quite small. The Empire is as beautiful architecturally and underneath Mecca's decorative efforts has a real proletarian grandeur. Empty it is formidable, with a full house it exudes warmth, majesty and sheer size. Matcham (creator of the Coliseum and son-in-law of the then Lord Chamberlain, which helped with planning permission) managed to arrange the pillar-less balconies, circles and nook-like boxes so that every seat has a good sight line.

The New Variety coup was executed with precision. A provisional deal was hammered out with Mecca with the incumbents taking responsibility for renovation of the domes and, in October 1986, the new management were let in the back door by Harry Godding, newly employed as live theatre custodian. They raced past the bewildered

Bingo-persons to start dismantling the stage to see if the fire curtain was intact. The following weeks became an E8 version of *42nd Street* with frenetic preparation to reopen on the theatre's eighty-sixth birthday, 9 December 1986. It was a dream come true. The old theatre alive again with a capacity crowd, the best of the alternative performers queueing up to give their all.

'It was like a wedding day,' remembers the greasepaint gamin side of Muldoon. 'Everyone was special that night. The acts went down a storm. The audience just wouldn't stop clapping.'

But as even the surly estate agents' weekly *The Hackney Gazette* was moved to remark, 'It was an occasion as joyous and historic as any gala West End premiere ... this is one show that must go on.'

What happened was rather more complex. The Hackney Empire Preservation Trust (chairman Benjamin Zephaniah) is the charitable (and therefore 'non-political') body which will own the theatre. New Variety (Hackney) which is funded, although not by Hackney council, arranges the day-to-day running of the venue which is leased to independent producers as well as putting on its own shows and running the bar. So in the first months when the theatre was inundated by acts who thought bonanza time was here, the Empire's first advice was, get yourself a producer. It's not like putting on mates in a pub room; it's the biggest light entertainment venue this side of Wimbledon.

This also explains the use of the theatre by the local police for a pensioners' benefit and the appearance of Frankie Vaughan, Ken Dodd and David Essex over the last year which has raised some eyebrows on the purist Left. It was, in fact, the phone call from Dodd's agent in April 1987 which proved that the Empire was in the big league. (Backstage Dodd to Muldoon, impressed: 'This is all paid for by the loony Left?' Muldoon, justifiably sore about lack of support from Hackney council: 'I wish it was.') And Vaughan, who works the stage superbly, was in fact an early show-biz sponsor of the Anti-Nazi League, even if he does play *God Save the Queen* at the end of his act (to the bafflement of most of the staff). Essex is said to have insisted to his promoter, Mel Bush, that he played the Empire, being something of a sentimentalist about old theatres.

But the first lesson of the first year is that the Empire is not some sort of theatrical Red Base. What it is, is the biggest theatre in London controlled by a non-commercial management with sympathies to the Left. And that management takes the view that if Dodd and Essex hiring the theatre can enable them to put on things like the South African workers' play *The Long March* then so be it.

The Empire would obviously not stage, or allow back, anything offensive to a modern Hackney audience, which would certainly rule out the acts the Empire used to house like *The Chocolate Coloured Coon*. But someone like Alf Garnett is more problematical. Muldoon, but not all the theatre's board, was for staging Garnett: 'I think he is passing comment on something that exists and which white liberals find very hard to admit exists.' But Warren Mitchell won't be asked back. The act was repetitive and fairly unfunny.

Harry Enfield's character Stavros the Greek has also troubled the dinner parties of Mr and Ms Hackney-Fluorescent-Bicycle-Clips who see it as 'offensive to Greek men'. In fact, Enfield's creation, based on a kebab house philosopher in a local take-away, is one of the best things the theatre has put on, selling out by word of mouth and much applauded by the chef on whom it is modelled. The act is classic Chaplin.

In fact it was a considerable achievement to keep the theatre open, let alone to stage such a wide variety of acts.

The audiences have been equally varied: white East End Cortina-boys worship Lenny Henry, Hackney Muslims use the Empire as their most important auditorium west of Frankfurt, there is a strong lesbian following for women comedians and musicians, notably Sweet Honey on the Rock, the acappella virtuosi. Vaughan brings in the older, often Jewish, Hackney residents who remember the Empire in the old days, the Rocky Horror Show still has a big troupe of transvestites in its entourage. In audience terms the most remarkable was *Black Heroes in the Hall of Fame*, a virtually amateur show which puts Huey Newton alongside Toussaint L'Ouverture, and Soujourner Truth which had a word of mouth sell-out to a 90 per cent black working class audience packing Hackney with Brixton BMWs.

It's too early yet for the audiences to cross over and the old ladies to enjoy the Joan Collins Fan Club (another darling of the Empire) and for the Turks to get into the Wolftones, but the presence of the building and the management's enlightened booking policy is doing more against racism and for working-class unity than mounds of windy declaration. Roland's old sparring partners are certainly impressed. Pam Brighton, ex-CAST and the co-founder of the Half Moon Theatre in neighbouring Tower Hamlets, now retired wounded from live theatre and qualified as a solicitor, simply says: 'He's done it at last. What we all dreamed of.' And Chris Rawlence of Red

Ladder, CAST's old adversaries and now a TV producer and writer, thinks simply: 'It's marvellous.'

Hackney itself is the same inner-urban mess of desolation, poverty, rowdiness and HGVs and the Empire won't change that. But it has given a new pride, élan and a sense of possibility to the borough. At the first annual general meeting last month there was much anguishing about the mistakes and the scale of the fund-raising challenge (the first £50,000 is now needed in four months). But a commercial management would have been patting itself on the back if it had achieved a tenth of what the Empire's team have done in just a year. Harry the Doorman seemed to think it was all very simple. A great theatre is lit again. And the volunteer who operates the follow-spot thought the same sort of thing. 'All I know is that I see a lot of heads. There's grey and bald and dreadlocks. But they all love being here.'

35

Too Much Monkey Business*

Chuck Berry, well what more can you say?

'If you tried to give Rock 'n' Roll another name, you might call it "Chuck Berry",' said John Lennon. It is a truism which contains a good deal of truth. Berry was the poet of commodities, the man who did most to take black musical forms into the fast lane of Cadillacs and TVs and to what he calls 'transistor-radio teenagers'.

Not only could he rhyme 'windowsill' with 'dream De Ville', but, over the airways, his precisely enunciated voice could pass as white (arriving at a Knoxville gig, the promoter told him, 'It's a country dance and we had no idea that 'Maybellene' was recorded by a niggra man'). Although not an outstanding guitarist, his sound is the most imitated in music. And he brought to his stage act the vaudeville traditions still strong in 1950s black music: the salacious lyric variations, sharp stage moves, sheer boogie and humour. So if anyone embodied what were to become the 1960s rock values, it was him.

It is no surprise that he had such an influence in Britain as the most potentially commercial of the Chess Records artists (Jagger and Richards are said to have met on the Dartford suburban BR train by clocking each other's Chuck Berry albums and the Stones' first single, 'Come On', was a Berry cover). Even the Sex Pistols owe a good deal to Uncle Chuck. And in a dozen pubs tonight, bands will be blasting through the wonderful chord sequences of 'Johnny B. Goode' and the joint will come alive.

The arrival of a coffee-table autobiography does not, however, establish Berry as a seditionary. There are some lovely details: the verse about Venus de Milo in 'Brown Eyed Handsome Man' is derived from Leopold Von Sacher-Masoch's 'Venus in Furs' and Berry's Baptist father denounced his son's early amorous activities with the injunction, 'Never turn this garage into a bordello,' which describes exactly what most Berry songs do.

* First published in *New Society*, February 1988.

Berry notes Charlie Christian as an important early influence on his guitar phrasing, which fills a missing musicological link; he adores John Lennon and is cheerfully iconoclastic about sex and his 'excessive desire to continue melting the ice of American hypocrisy regarding behaviour and beliefs that are now "in the closet" and only surface in court, crime or comical conversation.' But, perhaps understandably, he cannot see quite why R and B, the music of the black American urban working class, made such a stir in the rest of the world.

For what we tend to forget is that, even by the early 1960s, black music was segregated in the United States and hard to obtain in Britain. Keith Richards had to write off to the Chicago offices of Chess Records to get his supplies and the Beatles were getting their Ronettes and Orielles albums from seamen in dockside pubs. And the long struggle of the civil rights movement was far from won: when I travelled on a 99-day $99 Greyhound bus trip through the deep south in the mid-1960s, it was as segregated as South Africa is now. And Britain was still a much more dozy, dreary male-dominated place. Only if one makes the effort to think oneself back into that greyness is it possible to understand why just hearing 'Route 66', 'Nadine' and 'No Particular Place to Go' was so exotic and exciting.

I have spent a deplorably large part of my life listening to music in dives. But I will never, ever, forget the impact of seeing Cyril Davies and his Allstars steaming into 'Smoke Stack Lighting' in the Ricky Tick Club in Windsor, the first R and B I'd ever heard live. Davies was a panel beater from Walthamstow who, alongside the sorely missed Alexis Korner, was a founder of British R and B and a Chicago purist. He humped over his mouth-harp, spat his lyrics and drove his band like a galley master. The noise was phenomenal, a humping, thundering blast.

Davies, who died tragically young of leukaemia, was a true fanatic. And we loved him for it. Behind him sat various apprentices juddering along in his wake, doing respectful imitations of Chicago Southside-as-glimpsed-at-Croydon. These hopefuls were mainly Thames Valley art students who have subsequently become rock millionaires or OD'd. But then they were people just like us with spots and girl trouble (we didn't know any). Long John Baldry sat in the front row of tubular steel chairs with a bowler hat reading *The Times* and, to our bafflement, eyeing up the boys.

It seemed at the time unbearably exciting, even though the hall would be used by the scouts the following night. Looking back it was unbearably male. Not in the sweaty-jockstraps or scouting-forever sense, rather in an utterly rebellious delinquent footloose, sexually boastful way. Really, we were spotty virgins skipping homework, but the music made us 150 Hootchie Cootchie Men.

For it is no accident that the wave of male rebelliousness, which started in the 1960s, identified with the music of Chicago in the 1930s, an equally male-dominated musical era. If a woman had got up and sung 'Careless Love' to a piano, we would have sent her along to the *Gang Show*. Blues was men. Women blues singers were contemptibly respectable and English, permed creatures like Beryl Marsden and Ottilie Patterson.

It was not even fashionable to take an interest in the all-women singing groups that the markedly less musically chauvinist Beatles were absorbing. And, as Simon Frith and Howard Horne have so astutely documented in their recent book, *Art into Pop*, this was going on in a hundred other such clubs. And out of it came the British pop and rock music of the 1960s and 1970s which was to conquer the world (including the white American world who had found the R and B originals too raw for their well-manicured ears). Bob Brunning's underestimated study, *Blues: the British Connection*, will stagger even the most knowledgeable music lover in documenting quite the scale of influence that a handful of bands and musicians had on a whole generation.

Part of the intensity of the identification was about adolescence, simply the train-spotting syndrome: young men's passion for inventing areas of ritualised expertise suitable for complicated, pointless conflict. The classroom expert with his underarm LP sleeves turned outward, topping off conversations with musical facts carefully learnt and casually imparted, the fax-and info-kid who has mastered personnel lists, the bitter musical debates about sell-outs, has-beens and curios, all these collectors of the rare are senior lecturers in a self-created faculty.

So, being interested in something rigorous and esoteric fitted quite well with the intensely meritocratic ambiance of secondary education in the 1960s.

The school I attended was one of that dying breed, the grammar-school-with-pretensions. It was the last Grammar School Show, an educational version of *Hancock's Half-Hour* where a rather seedy group of teachers, who clearly felt themselves destined for higher things, attempted to bully some culture into a group of roughs who were much more interested in motor bikes and the *Bert Weedon*

Guitar Tutor and 'getting off with birds' – as we described our largely imaginary sexual efforts.

The staff attempted to provide airs for their graceless pupils and had inherited an honours board in oak and gilt (although only a handful ever made it to university), a school song in cod-Latin (which had a couplet about the school's lofty position over the railway sidings) and a panelled headmaster's study (where the head would beat you with a strap and show you his holiday slides of the Parthenon on successive days).

The masters had bicycles and wore mysterious gowns on speech day, but for all the imitation-public schoolery it was still run on exams, intimidation and competition, while we remained dumb and as insolent as was possible. The rising spirits of suburban beatnikery engaged with the philosophy of sadism-as-character-building. Apart from engraving CND signs on our desklids and hurling a can of *The Seventh Seal*, which the film society had borrowed from Contemporary Films, down the said railway siding, our most effective mode of resistance was to become the ultimate pariah-boffin, the Sixth Form Jazz Fan.

Our form of schoolboy one-upmanship took the form of erudite conversations about Miles Davis's mutes, the *Loverman* sessions and who exactly played fourth trumpet in the various Ellington sections. And listening, mesmerised, to *Just Jazz* and *Jazz Club*'s eerie, invisible clapping and effortlessly witty introduction with the same absolute attention afforded to *Hancock's Half-Hour*, the other main alternative to homework. The BBC deliberately cancelled and rearranged its meagre jazz ration in order to confound schoolboy listeners who were forced to track down some of the obscurer US Forces wavelengths advertised in *Melody Maker*'s radio jazz column.

Jazz was a euphemism for adultness and the excuse for sorties in London to gain entry to Ronnie Scott's Club (then a tatty basement in Gerrard Street) or gawp at the great Duke Ellington Band as it surged through the Hammersmith Odeon. There he was, the real Paul Gonsalves, asleep as was promised, and Johnny Hodges just like on the record. The afternoon the late Tubby Hayes sat in at five minutes' notice and read his way through the entire Ellington book produced raptures of musical patriotism.

Under protest, we would even go to the soul and blues packages at the Fairfield Halls, Croydon. The bluesman used to sit down with heavy spectacles not present in the photos in our jazz and blues *textbooks. But jazz became a somewhat unrewarding passion, always* just out of tune on the radio, or on a new record you could not afford or in expensive clubs full of older men knowing what to do and doormen asking your age. Worst of all, there was no dancing (except to 'Trad' which we despised like the musical Savanarolas we were). So you could neither take nor find girls.

Which is why we ended up skipping our A-level Tudor constitutional history and going in a battered blue van to an R and B club in Windsor called the Ricky Tick and run by John Mayall, who used to live in a tree until it was declared unsanitary by Windsor rural district council. And where I fell for a music which, a quarter of a century later, I am still entirely happy to listen to John's son Gaz playing in a dive in Soho. I now also love the minor operas of Verdi, Orlando Gibbons and Irish traditional music. But R and B remains the root: passionate, sexy and highly political. So thank you, Chuck. And roll over Beethoven.

Index